No Money, No Beer, No Pennants

NO MONEY, NO BEER, NO PENNANTS

The Cleveland Indians
and Baseball in
the Great Depression

Scott H. Longert

Ohio University Press   Athens

Ohio University Press, Athens, Ohio 45701
ohioswallow.com
© 2016 by Scott H. Longert
All rights reserved

Printed in the United States of America
Ohio University Press books are printed on acid-free paper ⊚ ™

26 25 24 23 22 21 20 19 18 17 16   5 4 3 2 1

Library of Congress Cataloging-in-Publication Data
Names: Longert, Scott, author.
Title: No money, no beer, no pennants : the Cleveland Indians and baseball in
  the great depression / Scott H. Longert.
Description: Athens, Ohio : Ohio University Press, 2016. | Includes
  bibliographical references and index.
Identifiers: LCCN 2016026044| ISBN 9780821422434 (hardback) | ISBN
  9780821422441 (pb) | ISBN 9780821445853 (pdf)
Subjects: LCSH: Cleveland Indians (Baseball team)—History—20th century. |
  Depressions—1929—United States. | BISAC: SPORTS & RECREATION / History.
  | SPORTS & RECREATION / Baseball / History.
Classification: LCC GV875.C7 L685 2016 | DDC 796.357/640977132
LC record available at https://lccn.loc.gov/2016026044

CONTENTS

ILLUSTRATIONS

PROLOGUE

It was a brilliant afternoon, just made for baseball. Sure, there had been a small chance of rain, but the temperature stood at a comfortable seventy-nine degrees. The thousands of fans who walked down the new concrete ramps were filled with anticipation of what was going to take place. The long-awaited debut of Cleveland Municipal Stadium was just moments away. Since 1928, city officials and fans had been patiently waiting for the gigantic new facility to become a reality. Now, on Sunday July 31, 1932, it was about to happen.

League Park had been the home of Cleveland baseball dating all the way back to 1891. The seating capacity at that time was nine thousand, quite adequate for the up-and-down Cleveland Spiders. Nearly twenty years later, owner Charlie Somers put a brick-and-steel second deck on the park that doubled the original number of seats. Jim Dunn, who acquired the team in 1916, found a way to push the seating capacity even higher, carving out another seven thousand seats. When the Cleveland Indians made their first World Series appearance in 1920 (and won, 5–2 over the Brooklyn Robins), temporary seats and standing room squeezed another thousand or two fans inside the grounds. Just one more row of seats and the park might have exploded.

With a much-deserved World Championship, the bar had been raised for Cleveland baseball. In spite of its friendly confines and neighborhood appeal, League Park could no longer deal with the crowds that wanted to see the hometown boys play ball. American League stars like Babe Ruth, Lou Gehrig, Jimmy Foxx, Charlie Gehringer, and a host of others generated more ticket requests than could be handled. An alternative to the historic park at 66th and Lexington had to be found.

A combined effort from civic boosters and the city manager's office built the huge stadium downtown, right off the Lake Erie shore. It was their belief that a stadium located a bit north of the business district would be an economic boon for the city. They had no way of knowing in 1928 that the Great Depression was about to paralyze the entire country.

Now, though, the Philadelphia Athletics were in town to christen the new stadium. An incredible crowd of 79,000 was on hand to see Robert "Lefty" Grove match pitches with Cleveland's curveball wizard, Mel Harder. Special trains brought several thousand fans from as far away as Pittsburgh. Athletics owner Connie Mack had put together a champion club with players including center fielder George "Mule" Haas, catcher Mickey Cochrane, left fielder Al Simmons, right fielder Bing Miller, and slugger Jimmy Foxx at first base. This would be a formidable test for the Indians and their new home.

The pregame ceremonies were well planned. The invited guests included the rarely smiling commissioner of baseball Judge Kenesaw Mountain Landis, American League president Will Harridge, Ohio governor George White, and Athletics owner Tom Shibe. Governor White threw the first pitch to Cleveland mayor Ray T. Miller. A large number of former Spiders, Naps, and Indians were in attendance. They were introduced by another ex-ballplayer, Jack Graney, now the Indians' radio play-by-play man. Graney had a long career in Cleveland baseball, starting with the Naps and lasting long enough to retire as an Indian. He became the first ballplayer to climb into the radio booth and describe the action on a full-time basis. He introduced the old favorites one at a time. There was Cy Young, the great pitching star of the 1890s. Young had been a major factor in bringing home the Temple Cup in 1895. He had won a phenomenal 511 games during his long career. His catcher, Charles "Chief" Zimmer, came out, pleased to be recognized some thirty years later. In his day, Zimmer wore the thinnest of gloves on his catching hand, nothing like the mitts worn by the current Indians catchers. One could only imagine how he held on to Young's fastballs.

Graney then called out members of the Cleveland Naps. They were led by Napoleon "Larry" Lajoie, the game's finest second baseman. A huge roar came from the crowd when Larry jogged onto the field. From 1902 through 1914 he had been the face of Cleveland baseball; hence the team name, "Naps." Next were Lajoie's outstanding teammates, third baseman Bill Bradley and right fielder Elmer Flick. Both were local products, still making their homes in the Cleveland area.

Graney finished the introductions by calling out three heroes of the 1920 World Series, Elmer Smith, Bill Wamby, and player-manager Tris Speaker. In the pivotal fifth game at League Park, Smith walloped the first bases-loaded home run in World Series history. During that same game Wamby executed a spectacular unassisted triple play, a feat that has never been duplicated in post-season play. Speaker had been the catalyst throughout the entire World Series, making one tremendous play after another. The ovation for the three stars was deafening.

The ceremonies came to an upbeat conclusion and all that was left was to play a baseball game. What a game it was! At this point in the season, the two clubs were fighting hard for second place.

Grove and Harder were untouchable inning after inning. Reporters noted that the center-field bleachers were filled with several thousand men wearing white short-sleeve shirts. They claimed the batters were distracted by the white background and could not see the ball leaving the pitchers' hands. Another factor in the lack of hitting might have been the sizzling fastballs thrown by Grove and the razor sharp curves of Mel Harder.

The Indians lineup did not quite match up to the hard-hitting Athletics. On the other hand, the outfield—local hero Joe Vosmik, Earl Averill, and Dick Porter—could more than hold its own. First baseman Eddie Morgan could hit fairly well, along with shortstop Johnny Burnett. Luke Sewell, the younger brother of former Indians shortstop Joe Sewell, was catching.

With both pitchers on top of their game, the innings piled up with neither team able to score. At one point Harder struck out the side, setting down the A's sluggers Cochrane, Simmons, and Foxx in order. The game would go seven full innings before the Athletics put a run on the brand new center-field scoreboard. In the top of the eighth, Max Bishop led off with a walk. Mule Haas sacrificed him to second. Then Mickey Cochrane hit a shot up the middle that just got by Harder's outstretched glove and Bishop raced home for the only run of the game. In the bottom of the ninth Eddie Morgan launched a drive to deep right field, but Bing Miller glided back and made the play to end the game. The newspapers would mention that Morgan's drive would have easily cleared the short right-field wall at old League Park.

That was another time, though. A new era in Cleveland Indians baseball had begun.

Chapter 1

CHANGE OF THE GUARD

Cleveland baseball in the 1920s turned out to be a brief stop in the penthouse followed by a quick trip to the ground floor. The 1920 Indians captured a pennant and went on to whip the Brooklyn Robins in a thrilling World Series. Owner James C. Dunn had built a championship team with the likes of Tris Speaker, Stan Coveleski, Jim Bagby, Elmer Smith, and Joe Wood. The World Series champs seemed poised to dominate the American League for at least the next few years.

In 1921 the club performed well enough but fell victim to the New York Yankees and their superstar in the making, Babe Ruth. For the season the twenty-six-year-old Ruth hit an inconceivable fifty-nine home runs and notched 170 RBIs. The entire Cleveland team hit fewer than forty homers. The Indians won ninety-four ball games, good only for second place. Speaker had a terrific year, though, batting .362 and leading the Major Leagues with fifty-two doubles.

Jim Dunn knew quite well that changes needed to be made to compete with the Yankees. In 1916, when he purchased the Cleveland franchise, Dunn overhauled the roster. A total housecleaning was not in order; nevertheless, some new talent had to be acquired. His initial move was a disaster. He traded first baseman George Burns and right fielder Elmer Smith to the Boston Red Sox for light-hitting first baseman John "Stuffy" McInnis. In 537 at bats, McInnis walloped a total of one home run and seventy-eight RBIs.

To go along with astoundingly bad trades, Dunn had serious issues with his health. A bout with the flu sidelined him for several weeks. The Cleveland owner was fifty-six, somewhat overweight, a cigar smoker, and a faithful visitor to the speakeasies in greater Cleveland. In May 1922 he became ill with heart problems, having to return to his home in Chicago for treatment. On June 9, 1922, Jim Dunn passed away in his sleep. His death was a terrible blow to the Cleveland franchise that had flourished under his leadership. The club was inherited by Edith Dunn, his widow. Her first decision was to install Ernest Barnard as team president, responsible for all operations. "Barny" had been with Cleveland for many years and was a competent executive. Then again, he lacked the flair and nose for talent that his former boss possessed. The Indians dropped to fourth place, barely staying above the .500 mark.

Despite the outstanding play of Speaker, the Indians continued to deteriorate. The 1924 season saw the ball club fall to sixth place with a record of sixty-seven wins and eighty-six losses. Attendance at League Park dropped off significantly: the Indians drew 481,905 fans, for an average of 6,425 per game. In 1923 attendance had equaled 558,856, or 7,165 each game. The difference between the two years was an alarming 76,951, a reduction of nearly 14 percent. The Yankees and Tigers drew over one million fans each, while Cleveland was near the bottom in attendance figures.

The steady profits racked up by Jim Dunn were beginning to erode. Mrs. Dunn, although a fan of the game, was reluctant to put more funds into the franchise. It remained for Ernest Bernard to bring the club back to a suitably profitable level. If that did not occur, the sale of the team seemed to be the other alternative. Surely Mrs. Dunn, a full-time resident of Chicago, had to be thinking in those terms.

The 1925 Indians failed on the field and at the box office. On the positive side, Tris Speaker just missed winning the batting title, losing to Harry Heilmann, while Joe Sewell hit .336 and knocked in ninety-eight runs. The pitching turned out to be abysmal, with George Uhle the leader at thirteen wins. Attendance continued to plummet, with only 419,005 for the season. The economy rolled along, jobs were plentiful, but Cleveland fans had given up on the ball club, spending their money on other diversions. The Cleveland front office knew the only thing keeping fans away from League Park was a below-average team.

They had reached a familiar juncture for Major League teams. The owner had circled the wagons, reluctant to put any additional money into the team. Without funds to spend, Barnard had nowhere to go to bring the Indians back into contention. Another issue arose when the possibility of Ban Johnson's retirement began to gather steam. Johnson had been president of the American League since its inception in 1901. His combative personality had worn on the owners for a number of years. The smart money was on none other than Ernest Barnard to become his successor. If this was the case, Barnard would be obligated to sever his ties with the Cleveland organization. That scenario would leave Mrs. Dunn completely on her own to run the ball club. Barnard, being an honest and loyal executive, would not let that happen. Barring a miracle comeback, it became more apparent that the sale of the team was imminent.

As if ordained by the heavens, the dream nearly occurred. The 1926 edition of the Indians fought tooth and nail for the pennant. The Yankees, with Ruth, Gehrig, Tony Lazzeri, and the rest of the wrecking crew figured to run away with the pennant. Still, the Indians caught fire in midseason and made it interesting until the very end of September. In May they fell off the map, losing seventeen of twenty-nine games. Heading into June it looked like the season was over. Yet, the Indians were far from done. For the remainder of the year, they reeled off sixty-six wins against forty-four losses.

In mid-September the Yankees came to town to begin a six-game series at League Park. The Indians dropped the opener but then won four straight games to pull within two of the leaders. The final game drew an enthusiastic sellout crowd to League Park. The nearly 30,000 attending cheered like it was 1920. In spite of the home-field advantage, Babe Ruth and Lou Gehrig blasted home runs for an easy Yankee victory. The Indians still had a chance for the pennant but dropped three out of four games to Philadelphia to end their most improbable run.

The unexpected pennant chase lifted attendance by more than 200,000 fans. The huge spike upwards gave the team operating money and perhaps funds to throw around for the acquisition of key players in the off-season. Unfortunately, events were about to be revealed that would cast a shadow over all the accomplishments of the past season. The Indians were about to suffer a national embarrassment of epic proportions.

Tris Speaker had been a fixture in the Indians lineup for eleven years. As player-manager he had led the franchise to many successful seasons. For the 1926 season Tris had batted .304 with seven home runs and eighty-six RBIs. That was subpar for Spoke, but for most players a quite acceptable campaign. When Speaker announced his retirement in early December 1926, the Cleveland fans were rightfully shocked. He was no longer a young man but still quite capable of playing good baseball. Tris told his fans he was entering the steel business to work with his good friend, Dave Jones. The business was great and Tris had the opportunity to make a lot of money. In spite of the reason given, both fans and sportswriters were not quite buying the explanation. Their suspicions were confirmed when Commissioner Landis announced an investigation into an alleged game-fixing incident involving Speaker, Ty Cobb, Joe Wood, and former Detroit pitcher Hubert "Dutch" Leonard. The game in question was played in 1919 near the end of the regular season. The Tigers had a chance to finish in third place and Leonard claimed the four players met before the game and agreed to let the Tigers win. According to Leonard, the accused players bet money on the outcome as well. The fact that Leonard waited seven years to bring this to Judge Landis is strange indeed. He did have a letter from Joe Wood that on the surface was rather incriminating. It read in part, "The only bet West [the Tigers clubhouse man] could get up was $600 against $420. . . . We won the $420. I gave West $30, leaving $390, or $130 for each of us." This evidence was fairly solid, but made no mention of Speaker at all.

Judge Landis summoned Leonard to Chicago for testimony on the affair. For some unknown reason Leonard declined to appear. Without his testimony the allegations against Speaker were unproven. In January 1927 Landis dismissed the charges against Cobb and Speaker. They could resume their baseball careers, but not with Cleveland or Detroit.

When Speaker first announced his retirement, Mrs. Dunn and team president Barnard remained silent. On the first day of the new year, Mrs. Dunn released a statement to the newspapers.

She mentioned that, back in November, Speaker had visited her in Chicago to tell his side of the story. According to Mrs. Dunn, Speaker expressed a great concern that the allegations against him would injure the Cleveland baseball club. For that reason alone, he decided to retire quietly. Mrs. Dunn telegraphed Henry Edwards at the *Cleveland Plain Dealer* to let the fans know she did not ask Spoke to resign. She said, "When I left Chicago on November 26th, I did not know whether Mr. Speaker would go through with his idea of retiring or would change his mind and fight for vindication. I am sure that he would have had the support of the Cleveland club in his efforts to vindicate himself." Mrs. Dunn added, "Since Mr. Speaker was not asked to retire by the Cleveland club, I feel sure that he must have had what he considered very good personal reasons for taking such action."

It is interesting to reflect on whether Mrs. Dunn was giving the company line to the press or was truly supportive of Speaker. She could not know how the proceedings in Chicago would turn out. A guilty verdict might do the franchise some irreparable damage, particularly with the stockholders. What about the player in question? Did he truly retire to save the Cleveland organization some real embarrassment or was he simply trying to save his own reputation? The assumption can be made that all this negative attention may have been too much for Jim Dunn's widow to deal with. For many years she had had great faith in Speaker, in his ability both as a player and as leader of her team. The allegations no doubt shook her belief and may have led her to a pivotal decision. Within a year she would sell the team.

Besides the Speaker-Cobb investigation there were other matters being dealt with by the Cleveland front office. Ban Johnson's lengthy reign as American League president was indeed about to come to an end. For various reasons at least half of the American League owners now wanted him out. Commissioner Landis had never seen eye to eye with Johnson and completely welcomed the uprising. The two men had had hard feelings ever since the Black Sox scandal of 1919. Johnson's recent handling of Speaker and Cobb infuriated Landis to the point of no return. The judge had spent too many years presiding over cases of ballplayers gambling and fixing games. Just when he thought all that had passed,

Johnson brought forth the 1926 allegations, forcing Landis to convene hearings again.

When the anti-Johnson owners were ready to make a change, Johnson became seriously ill, causing the militants to put him on indefinite leave. Rumors started circulating on who could possibly replace the only president the American League had ever had. Among the names floated was in fact Cleveland Indians president Ernest Barnard. The only thing holding him back was his commitment to Mrs. Dunn. But he could also presume that, for Mrs. Dunn, selling the team was the only prudent thing to do. She could bow out of the picture with a large return on her late husband's investment. She would not have to go through the difficult process of hiring a new team president and support staff. It was reasonable to assume that Mrs. Dunn would not stand in the way of Barnard's rise to power. The time to walk away had arrived.

In May 1927, a possible sale of the Cleveland Indians was reported throughout the country. The man stepping forward was, surprisingly, former player-manager and current Washington Senator Tris Speaker. It had been four months since he had been cleared of any wrongdoing by Commissioner Landis. Apparently, Tris felt it was time to step back into the spotlight once again. He revealed his plans at a fancy banquet dinner in Cleveland. He told curious reporters that, if necessary, he could raise $500,000 within twenty-four hours. Speaker's partner would be his close friend Dave Jones, the president of Geometric Stamping. There might be a third party ready to invest, but the name was kept out of the story. Speaker believed Mrs. Dunn had no objections to selling him the team. Even if that was so, the majority of American League owners had to approve the transfer. He had more than a few hurdles to overcome.

A short time later an article appeared in the *Plain Dealer* claiming that Speaker's syndicate included Alva Bradley, a local man with vast real estate holdings in the downtown area. Almost immediately, Bradley denied any intention to buy the Indians, stating that his other interests would prevent him from getting involved in purchasing the team. He told the newspaper, "Last night Speaker mentioned to me that Mrs. Dunn was willing to sell but he, Speaker, could not swing the deal alone. He did not ask me to go in with him and I did not volunteer." There was not any fire yet, but the smoke was beginning to gather.

In less than a month another group surfaced via a secret conference in Cleveland. As is usually the case, local reporters quickly found out the details. Some very big names were mentioned in the proposed syndicate. Harry Frazee, the former owner of the Boston Red Sox, was supposedly involved. Phil Ball, the current president of the St. Louis Browns, had an interest in the group, along with Tom Walsh, the Indians vice president. Walsh had been a close friend of Jim Dunn and an original stockholder of the Cleveland team since 1916. Evidently, Walsh was acting under orders from Mrs. Dunn to find a suitable buyer for the team. The papers speculated that the deal would take place in July. Another story had Ed Barrow, the general manager of the New York Yankees, as an interested party. He led a syndicate of men ready to make Mrs. Dunn an offer the following day. There were denials from all the men involved, but the likelihood of a sale became greater every day.

Throughout the summer, interested parties waited for an announcement of a change in ownership. Speaker's group appeared to have fizzled out, but the others seemed to still be in play. On September 8, word came through that Alva Bradley, contrary to earlier statements, was ready to buy the Indians. Sportswriter Henry Edwards, still digging up scoops for the *Plain Dealer* after twenty-seven years on the beat, was all over this story. His source was Chuck Bradley, the brother of Alva. Chuck told Edwards, "Alva has changed his mind. He has decided that in order to boost Cleveland, a Cleveland man should buy the ball club instead of having it owned by residents of other cities." Edwards asked Bradley if he intended to be a partner but could only get a maybe in reply.

The Bradley brothers may have planned to boost Cleveland, but in reality they had numerous interests of their own to advance. Alva had a large block of real estate downtown that could be turned into restaurants, hotels, and new offices for the Cleveland team. The only thing missing was a new stadium to cash in on. Edwards mentioned that other individuals had been talking about a new lakefront stadium that could seat over eighty thousand fans. Perhaps the Bradley brothers would lead the charge to make the talk reality. It made sense that downtown businessmen would see the huge investment opportunity in a state-of-the-art facility just a few blocks away from their real estate. The time had come for Cleveland men to take back the team.

Mrs. Dunn continued to make things exciting by acknowledging the Bradleys' interest as well as that of two other mysterious syndicates. She cautioned that no other names would be mentioned, but that she preferred to sell the club to Cleveland buyers. It did not hurt that the Indians were playing good-quality baseball in September and showed some faint promise for the future.

On September 15, news broke that Alva Bradley was in serious negotiations to buy the Cleveland Indians. A price had been agreed upon, but the one sticking point was that Bradley wanted to buy out all the shareholders. He told Edwards, "We will not buy a share unless we can buy every dollar's worth. We want no minority stockholders." When Bradley made the statement, he already had an agreement with the three original partners of Jim Dunn: Pat McCarthy, Richard Lane, and vice president Tom Walsh. With the trio on board, the remaining minority holders would likely give up their shares.

Bradley mentioned in his interview that he wanted to give Cleveland a representative ball club and a modern stadium to go with it. Fans had heard the whispers about a huge new downtown stadium for several years. This was the first time the rumor had some real weight to it. Bradley mentioned a seating capacity of seventy-five thousand, more than two-and-one-half times the size of old League Park. Fans had to be excited by the news, realizing they would have a sporting chance to get tickets on weekends and when the Yankees came to town. When Ruth, Gehrig, and company were playing at League Park, tickets were extremely hard to come by.

Edwards asked Bradley why he wanted to buy the team. In a revealing answer, Bradley replied, "We are not going into this because we are such great baseball fans and are eager to get mixed up in the national game. But we feel that a winning baseball team is a splendid asset to any city and we are for Cleveland first, last and all the time." This was a novel approach for a prospective Major League owner. In 1901, Charlie Somers started the Cleveland franchise mainly because he loved baseball. Certainly, he saw the opportunity to earn a fortune, but his heart and soul belonged to the game. The late Jim Dunn had seen the Indians as a money-making proposition. He learned to orchestrate trades to his advantage and within five years brought home a world title. "Sunny" Jim had great affinity for his players and the fans, but managed the bottom line extremely well. So here, in Bradley, we have a new man, one who wanted to enhance the city by owning the team.

Just who in fact was Alva Bradley? He was a leap year baby, born in Cleveland on February 29, 1884. His father was Morris A. Bradley, one of the top men in the Great Lakes shipping industry. Alva's paternal grandfather, Alva, Sr., was the first Bradley to sail the open seas. He began as an ordinary deckhand but showed enough skills to later become a captain. With his expert knowledge of ships he took on a partner and by the 1860s made a mark in the shipbuilding trade. Their warehouses were located in Vermillion, Ohio, where the partners concentrated on building the largest wooden ships in the Great Lakes region. The business later moved to Cleveland, where he added to his already large fleet. The Captain piloted many of those ships and never lost one during his time at sea.

After the Captain's death, Morris Bradley shifted the family interests to real estate. He accumulated nearly ten million dollars' worth of real estate, most of it in downtown Cleveland. Property was held in the Wholesale District, a series of buildings from Superior Avenue north to the lakefront. Other holdings were from West Ninth Street going southeast to Ontario Street and Public Square. In sum, the Bradleys owned much of the property over a three-block area in the heart of downtown. Just about everybody who did business off Public Square paid rent to the Bradley family.

Morris Bradley had a home at 1375 Euclid Avenue, right in the heart of Millionaire's Row. This was an area of land that stretched from Public Square and extended east several miles. The richest folks in Cleveland built spectacular mansions on the available land. Among the residents were John D. Rockefeller, one of the wealthiest men in America, and Marcus Hanna, the political boss of Ohio and future United States senator. The Bradleys were right at home.

In the late 1890s Alva began attending University School, an elite private school east of Cleveland. He was a good student, often scoring As and Bs in his classes. He was quarterback of the football team while his younger brother Chuck played tackle. They had a tremendous team, with many of the players later starring at Case Tech, Yale, and Minnesota. In a game against Kiski Prep, a boy's school in Pittsburgh, fists were flying from the opening kickoff. Chuck Bradley in particular was taking a pounding from the Kiski defensive tackle. Nobody had helmets or much padding in those days, which led to many a bloodletting. During a pileup at the line of scrimmage, Chuck suddenly rose to his feet and began throwing punches at the defensive tackle. He had to be restrained by the officials and dragged off the field. When asked what happened, Chuck would later say, "I didn't care how much he hit me, but when he landed on Alva that was different. Anyone that picks a fight with Alva has got to fight me first!"

After graduation Alva enrolled at Cornell University, where he studied engineering. He drew up a series of designs for ornamental lights to be installed in front of all the Bradley properties. Morris Bradley politely reviewed the plans but thought them too flamboyant for the Bradley reputation. Alva still had a few things to learn.

While Morris presided over the family holdings, the younger Bradley spent his time learning all aspects of the family business. In his spare time he played golf and tennis and sailed the family yacht. For years, Alva kept a season pass and a private box at League Park. He usually gave the seats away to friends and his employees. One afternoon he decided to watch the Indians take on the Yankees. He entered the park and realized he had forgotten his box seat ticket. He checked his wallet and to his relief there was his season pass. He walked to the pass gate and showed his card, but the man at the gate had never seen Alva before and believed him to be an imposter. There was a stalemate at the turnstile. Bradley looked around and spotted another ticket taker whom he knew personally. The man came over and verified that there was no fraud, and Alva was allowed in to see the game. Later he would tell *Baseball Magazine*, "Guess I will have to keep the pass gate man on the roster. If he will try to keep out the president of the club I guess he may be depended upon to keep out those who really have no right to pass."

Morris Bradley passed away in 1926, leaving Alva to run the Bradley empire. Overnight, Alva became chairman of the board of the Cleveland & Buffalo Transit Company, president of the United States Coal Company, and the sole head of Bradley Real Estate. As was the family custom, he became involved in civic affairs, serving on multiple boards of local charities. He had numerous friends, including, significantly, Ernest Barnard, the Indians executive. The connection here cannot be overstated. When Barnard attempted to sell the team for Mrs. Dunn, knowing her preference was to sell to a Cleveland man, the obvious choice was Alva Bradley.

In later years, Bradley enjoyed telling the story of how he bought the Cleveland team. In September 1927, Tom Walsh stopped by the Hotel Cleveland and met Alva and Chuck Bradley in the steam room. Barnard was also likely in the room, as was John Sherwin, a wealthy banker who wanted a piece of the team. While everybody dripped with sweat, a deal was put together. Bradley and partners to be named later would buy the Indians for a million dollars, double what Jim Dunn paid in 1916. All the stockholders in the Dunn group had to give up their shares before any documents were signed. Everybody shook hands, and unofficially, as Bradley would say, it was the only time a baseball team had been sold in a steam bath.

By October, almost all the stockholders had agreed in principle to sell their shares. Nevertheless, a select few dragged their feet. Despite the best of efforts, the sale of the team remained in limbo. Alva Bradley kept busy assembling a team of investors. John Sherwin, the president of Union Trust Bank, came officially on board, along with Percy Morgan, the owner of Morgan Lithograph. These men were giants of Cleveland, capable of pumping hundreds of thousands of dollars into the ownership group. They were sportsmen as well. John Sherwin raced horses as a member of the exclusive Gentleman's Riding Club. Percy Morgan was a skilled golfer, often shooting in the low eighties. When he was not on the golf course Morgan produced billboard advertisements and movie posters for the local theaters. The new Cleveland ownership group represented some of the most prominent men in town, if not the most wealthy.

By early November the remaining stockholders from the Dunn era had been whittled down to one. The lone holdout was W. J. Garvey from Chicago. Mr. Garvey wanted double the price of the Bradley group offer. The men went back and forth with the obstinate Garvey, who refused to budge on his 156 shares. Ernest Barnard, now the president of the American League, kept in touch with the old stockholder, trying to dissuade him from blocking the sale. On

November 15, 1927, Barnard telephoned Bradley to let him know the final roadblock had been removed: Garvey had agreed to part with his stock. The next day, newspapers from Seattle to Boston reported that the Cleveland Indians had been sold.

When the details of the sale were released it came as a surprise that Alva and Chuck Bradley only controlled 18 percent of the total stock. There was ample money in the Bradley fortune to purchase a considerably larger share of the club. For reasons not mentioned, the brothers chose to keep their investment a conservative one. Alva was the driving force behind the sale, yet he would be only a minority shareholder. Percy Morgan bought 20 percent of the stock while John Sherwin acquired 30. Other Clevelanders, including attorney Joseph Hostetler and former secretary of war Newton Baker, bought up the remaining shares in varied amounts. When officers were named, Alva Bradley became president and treasurer of the Cleveland baseball club. Percy Morgan would be the vice president. The new owners all agreed that Bradley was the decision maker and spokesperson for the group. The job of rebuilding the Cleveland Indians rested on his shoulders.

The Cleveland papers began to speculate on what the first moves of the Bradley regime would be. Within days, the Cleveland club began to hunt for a general manager, a relatively new position in baseball. This person would be responsible for acquiring and developing talent, player trades, and salary negotiations. The new hire had to be a baseball man, fully knowledgeable about the intricacies of the game. It seemed plausible that the new general manager would be an ex-ballplayer or manager. Surely, a reasonably intelligent man who had played the game most of his life had the qualifications. Or a manager, skilled at analyzing talent and keeping his players in line, might be ideal for the job. Yet, Alva Bradley went a different route for his choice. On November 29, he named umpire Billy Evans as the new general manager.

What were the credentials of Billy Evans that led to his hiring? Certainly, in his twenty-two years as an American League umpire he had seen every aspect of the game. Evans was born in Chicago on February 10, 1884. The family moved to Youngstown, Ohio, when Billy was a small child. He spent two years at Cornell University, where he played freshman baseball. The death of his father caused

Evans to leave college and return to Youngstown. He took a job as a sportswriter for the *Youngstown Vindicator*, covering local baseball and other sports. It was there that fate intervened for young Mr. Evans. On a whim, he was asked to umpire a local baseball game. He was astounded to learn his pay was fifteen dollars for the game, which equaled his weekly salary at the *Vindicator*. Soon he was umpiring Class C baseball in addition to his reporter's job. While working a game between local rivals Niles and Youngstown, Evans made a late strike-three call against a Niles hitter. The partisan crowd stormed the field, prepared to give the young umpire a complete thrashing. Evans kept his cool and managed to survive the game without a scratch. In the stands was former Cleveland Spider star Jimmy McAleer, who admired the young man for his courage. Now the manager of the St. Louis Browns, McAleer convinced American League president Ban Johnson to hire Evans. At age twenty-two, Billy Evans became the youngest umpire in the Major Leagues.

Evans became a trusted arbiter, rarely blowing his top. He withstood the heated tirades of American League managers, often using diplomacy to get his points across, but every once in a while there were exceptions to the rule. In September 1921, Evans challenged Ty Cobb to a fight after the conclusion of a ball game. Reports were varied, but Evans seemed to have gotten the worst of it, wearing bandages on his face for the next several days. There was nothing to be ashamed of. More than a few ballplayers had come up short in their efforts to teach the widely disliked Cobb a lesson.

Evans traded on his popularity as an umpire to write syndicated baseball columns throughout his career. The articles covered a wide variety of topics related to the baseball world. One of his readers was quite likely Alva Bradley, who apparently saw Evans as much more than an umpire and writer. Another factor in Bradley's decision was that Evans had made Cleveland his home for the past twenty years. All the Indians stockholders were from Cleveland and Bradley wanted no outsiders associated with his club. That was the clinching argument as Billy Evans accepted the general manager position.

As the new man in the front office, Evans agreed with Bradley that current manager Jim McAllister had no chance of being re-hired. Speculation centered on big names from the Major Leagues, including Eddie Collins of the Philadelphia Athletics, Bucky Harris of Washington, and Art Fletcher, manager of the New York Giants. Collins was near the end of a brilliant playing career, but had stated that he wanted to pilot a ball club when he retired. Harris was player-manager of the Senators, but he was not thrilled with the fans, who had been riding him for the past two seasons. They had somehow forgotten that Harris had brought home two pennants and a World Series win in 1924. Fletcher, the manager of the New York Giants, had not indicated he was looking to change jobs, but the Cleveland sportswriters believed he could be had for the right price. Bradley and Evans told the writers a new manager would be in place in time for the minor-league meetings scheduled for the first week of December. Cleveland fans were quite eager to see what kind of manager the new ownership had in mind. The process went on longer than expected. On December 11, the front office surprised a number of folks by hiring former Cleveland Naps shortstop Roger Peckinpaugh.

Once again, Alva Bradley was following the Cleveland-only rule. The Peckinpaugh family had once lived in Wooster, Ohio, just a short train ride south of the big city. There, on February 5, 1891, Roger was born. The family moved to Cleveland when Roger was a small boy, settling in the Hough neighborhood. By coincidence, League Park, the home of the 1890s Cleveland Spiders, was only a few blocks away. In the early 1900s the neighborhood was honored to have a certain gentleman from Philadelphia move in: Napoleon "Larry" Lajoie became a full-time resident.

Roger's father John had played semipro baseball in the 1880s, eventually getting a tryout with the Cincinnati Reds. A shortstop by trade, the elder Peckinpaugh failed in his opportunity, causing him to leave the game behind and become a salesman. Roger attended East High School, where he played football, basketball, and baseball. A legend on the sandlots, "Peck," as his friends now called him, was the best young shortstop in northeast Ohio. He joined the Collinwoods, a semipro team where he apparently accepted some cash for his services. Later, during Peck's senior season, an anonymous letter surfaced, claiming he had been paid for play and was a professional. The East Senate League suspended Peck from further play.

After graduation Roger continued his dazzling play on the sandlots. The Cleveland Naps paid close attention, signing him to a contract in February 1910. Stories circulated that it was Lajoie himself who urged the Naps to acquire the nineteen-year-old infielder. The contract offered $125 a month, yet John Peckinpaugh still had deep misgivings about his son becoming a ballplayer. This may seem odd, that a former player would be strongly against his son pursuing a professional baseball career, but John Peckinpaugh enlightened his son that ballplayers were drunkards who did not want to work. Regardless of the stern warning, Roger signed the contract, joining the Naps for spring training in Alexandria, Louisiana. Henry Edwards recalled his first impression of the young shortstop, writing, "I never will forget how Roger did swat the ball that spring. There was a river back of the left field fence and Peck became a very expensive asset because of the baseballs he hit into the water." Pitchers soon figured out that Peck had trouble hitting the curve, though, which stopped the baseballs from landing in the river. The Naps decided to send Roger to New Haven, Connecticut, where he worked on making contact with the breaking ball.

In August, the Naps brought Roger to Cleveland. He appeared in only fifteen games, but had to be thrilled to play next to the great Lajoie. They may have walked home together after ball games, stopping at Hough Bakery, where Lajoie enjoyed flirting with a young redheaded girl behind the counter. At any rate, Roger was now moving with the fast company.

The 1911 season found Peck in Portland, Oregon, playing in the Pacific Coast League. It must have been quite a jolt for him to depart Cleveland and travel all the way to the West Coast. There were few cowboys and Indians left on the way, but a trip of this magnitude was a lot to handle for a twenty-year-old.

Despite the odds against him, Roger blossomed in Portland. He hit a decent .258, stole thirty-five bases, and made all the plays at shortstop. The newspapers admired his ability, labeling him as an up-and-comer. The Naps were quite impressed with his progress, and for the 1912 season Cleveland would be his home. All he had to do was walk the few blocks from Hough Avenue to League Park. There would be no more trips to the minor leagues.

For most of the season Roger split time at the shortstop position with Ivy Olson. He still had problems with American League hurlers, batting a measly .212. Despite the problems with the bat, Roger had a good opportunity to be the regular Cleveland shortstop. Just when things appeared to be falling his way, though, a major obstacle blocked his path. His name was Ray Chapman. The new infielder had rocketed through the minor leagues, hitting and fielding like no other shortstop in the organization. He would take the job away from Peck, causing the Indians to trade the local boy to the New York Yankees.

Roger played nine seasons in New York. There he became the consummate shortstop. He had enough quickness to go deep in the hole and gun the ball to first base. Roger could dash behind second base, spear a ground ball, and fire across his body to get the runner. While batting he held his hands slightly apart and generally slashed the baseball to left field.

Near the end of the 1914 season, manager Frank Chance resigned. The Yankee ownership did not hesitate to make Peck the interim manager. It was only a handful of games, but valuable experience for a twenty-three-year-old. He showed a lot of maturity for a young man, which would later result in him becoming a Yankee captain. A few years later, Babe Ruth joined the Yankees and became fast friends with Peck. In fact, the two became close enough that Babe asked for a thousand-dollar loan. That was a considerable amount of money, but Roger wrote the check. To this day, Peckinpaugh family members assert that Babe eventually paid back the loan.

In 1921, the Yankees overtook the Indians to win the American League pennant. They lost the World Series to the New York Giants, but the Yankee dynasty was taking root. Stories remain that Ruth and several other players were feuding with manager Miller Huggins and insisting that Peck be named player-manager, but before the start of the 1922 season Peck was traded to the Boston Red Sox. The timing of the trade was quite curious, since Roger had an excellent previous season for the Yankees. He batted .288, hit seven home runs, and scored 128 runs, a career high. Newspapers mentioned a time during the season when manager Huggins was ill and Peck took over the team: almost immediately the Yankees went on a winning streak. This may have been a case of Peck becoming more popular than the manager and as a result being shipped off to the lowly Red Sox. Norman E. Brown, in his syndicated column for the Central Press Association, wrote, "The recent trading of Roger Peckinpaugh, Yankee shortstop and captain, to the Boston Red Sox is the most coldblooded deal ever put over in baseball. . . . As far as Peck is concerned it is the dirtiest piece of business ever put over in the big show."

The trade brought Sam Jones and Leslie "Bullet Joe" Bush plus shortstop Everett Scott to the Yankees. The Red Sox got Peck, Harry "Rip" Collins, Bill Piercy, Jack Quinn, and $100,000. Harry Frazee, the Boston owner, always had a blatant need for cash to support his theatrical ventures. He was a ceaseless trade partner with the Yankees. It seemed whenever the Yankees had issues, Frazee was more than willing to help. In 1919 he recklessly sold Babe Ruth to New York for $100,000. Boston fans watched glumly while their owner undid his team, squandering his money on Broadway plays.

Less than a month later, Frazee sent Peck to the Washington Senators as part of a three-way deal with the Philadelphia Athletics. Frazee insisted that there was no cash in this trade. In spite of this, Joe Dugan, who went from Philadelphia to Boston, somehow wound up in New York during the 1922 season. The Yankees, with all the newly acquired talent, would win another pennant while the Boston Red Sox finished last with a ridiculous total of fifty-three wins. The word "collusion" comes to mind here.

In Washington, Peck played alongside Bucky Harris. The two would become one of the most formidable double-play combinations in the game. Roger played in two more World Series, bringing home a championship in 1924. In game two of that series, against the New York Giants, the score was tied going into the bottom of the ninth inning. With a runner on base, Roger laced a double to win the game. The Senators took the series four games to three. The winners' share totaled a handsome $6,000 per man.

The Senators repeated in 1925, but lost the series to the Pittsburgh Pirates. A number of the games were played in poor field conditions, leaving the diamond a sea of mud. Roger had a fielding nightmare, charged with eight errors for the seven games. Despite the awful time at shortstop he was voted Most Valuable Player in the American League. He beat out players including Al Simmons, Harry Heilmann, and Mickey Cochrane. The vote was handled by the senior sportswriters in each American League city. The writers had a complicated point system where the maximum points a player could get was sixty-five. Peck totaled forty-five, just slightly ahead of Simmons.

In 1927, Peck was off to the Chicago White Sox, where aching knees reduced his playing time. When Billy Evans became the general manager of the Cleveland Indians he believed the veteran shortstop would be a strong candidate to lead his ball club. In December, Roger gladly accepted the job and the chance to come back to his old stomping grounds. There was much work to be done.

Chapter 2

STARTING TO BUILD

In 1928, Cleveland, Ohio, was one of the leading cities in the nation. The population of the greater Cleveland area was over one million, making it the sixth largest city in the United States. The downtown area was thriving with first-class restaurants, hotels, and a popular theater district. Playhouse Square had multiple theaters including the Allen, the Hanna, the State, and the Ohio. The new phenomenon of talking motion pictures attracted thousands of viewers.

Just one year earlier, the Terminal Tower opened for business, the second-largest building in the country. The massive structure had fifty-two floors and stood over seven hundred feet tall. The project was the brainchild of the reclusive railroad barons, brothers Oris and Mantis Van Sweringen. Described as having "innate modesty," the two men proposed building the gigantic structure on Public Square. Incorporated in the plans was the construction of a huge railroad terminal directly underneath. The 3.5-acre complex included major retail space, a sleek hotel, a medical building, and a post office. The cost of the project totaled a whopping $179 million. To encourage all the thrill seekers in town, there was an open observation deck built on the forty-second floor. Statistics were not kept on how many crazed individuals rode the elevators up the dizzying heights.

Since 1924, Cleveland government had been run by a city manager system. The person in charge was supposed to be nonpartisan, able to work with either Democrats or Republicans. William Hopkins, a successful businessman, ran the city. He reported to the city council but usually succeeded in getting his plans approved. In 1925, he got the authorization to build a municipal airport, one of the first in the United States. It would be a few years before regular passenger service, but mail planes began to make daily flights to and from the airport. Hopkins had big ideas to develop downtown Cleveland, among them a new place for the Indians to play baseball.

Though Prohibition still ruled the land, savvy Clevelanders knew where to find a good bottle of scotch. Bootleggers sneaked boats across Lake Erie to Canada, where a vast supply of gin, whiskey, and vodka could be purchased. Government agents patrolled the shipping lanes, but many boats were able to reach the Cleveland lakefront and get the alcohol to any number of clandestine warehouses. In the winter, men would drive their cars and trucks over the frozen lake and bring back all the booze they could carry. This was one industry that Cleveland officials did not openly boast about.

By 1928 there were three major radio stations in town, WHK, WTAM, and WJAY. The stations offered a wide variety of programming including music, news, comedy shows, and a small amount of sports reporting. The sports programming at WTAM was handled by Tom "Red" Manning, the former public-address announcer at League Park. Manning used a four-foot megaphone at the ballpark to announce the lineups to the reporters in the press box. He had to tone down his voice a few decibels when behind the radio microphone.

Recreation and leisure time were important components of the 1920s lifestyle. The economy steamed ahead, with good jobs that were easy to locate. Both men and women had disposable incomes which allowed for the purchase of cars, radios, refrigerators, and a robust nightlife. Nightclubs were everywhere downtown, and dinner, dancing, and a bit of romance were there for the asking. Young people, many of them college educated, spent their money freely, which made Cleveland a genuine hot spot. Now it was time for baseball to return to the forefront.

General manager Billy Evans had a difficult job awaiting him. The 1927 Indians won a grand total of sixty-six games, which got them sixth place in the American League. Remaining from the

1920 World Champions were shortstop Joe Sewell, outfielder Charlie Jamieson, pitcher George Uhle, and first baseman George Burns. Luke Sewell, the younger brother of Joe, had been with the club since 1921. The veterans were still going strong, leading the club in most of the offensive statistics. The elder Sewell could be counted on to hit over .300 while striking out less than ten times per five hundred at bats. Joe always claimed he could see the ball hit the bat. Based on his strikeout ratio, he was probably telling the truth.

Charlie Jamieson was one of the most consistent players in the game. He usually hit around .300, scored plenty of runs, and played excellent defense. Charlie had a lot of range in left field, always among the league leaders in assists. He was a fan favorite at League Park, a fixture on the ball club.

George Burns fit the category of an aging veteran, but still had his moments on the field. Burns was the American League's Most Valuable Player in 1926. His statistics that year were amazing, batting .358, with 216 hits, a league leading sixty-four doubles, and 115 RBIs. As the reigning MVP, Burns received a salary boost to $12,000 a year, but the following season his numbers dropped considerably. At age thirty-four, Burns could still hit, but he was on the inevitable decline. Billy Evans had a decision to ponder at first base.

George Uhle, born and raised in Cleveland, was the ace of the Indians pitching staff. He had won over twenty games three times, the most recent being twenty-seven wins in 1926. Uhle was one of the few pitchers in the American League that Babe Ruth did not terrorize. Though Ruth hit over .300 against George, his home runs were few and far between. That in itself was quite an accomplishment.

Luke Sewell was a fine complement to his older brother Joe. Though he generally hit around .250, he always got his bat on the ball. The Sewell brother just did not strike out. Luke was an exceptional defensive catcher, several times leading the American League in assists. His percentage in throwing out base runners was well above average. For some years he sat on the bench behind Steve O'Neill and Glenn Myatt, but he grabbed playing time when the Indians traded O'Neill to Boston. Luke was a durable catcher, playing over 120 games a year. This was one position manager Peckinpaugh did not have to concern himself with.

The remaining part of the Cleveland roster was somewhat unsettled. Billy Evans did not have the time needed to implement the immediate changes he felt necessary. Alva Bradley and his partners were willing to spend a small fortune to acquire some top-shelf talent. They believed that if enough money was waved around, great players were sure to follow. Bradley reasoned, if he offered the Yankees George Burns and $100,000, they might part with Lou Gehrig. The team president would learn quickly that players of Gehrig's ability were not available even for a yacht filled with cash.

With spring training just around the corner, Billy Evans thoroughly studied his roster. The infield was decent enough with Burns at first base, the veteran Lew Fonseca at second, Joe Sewell at short, and a young Johnny Hodapp at third. Fonseca, primarily a singles hitter, could bat well over .300 but had difficulty staying healthy. The Indians acquired Hodapp in August 1925 from the minor-league Indianapolis Indians. He was a big kid, six feet tall and weighing 185 pounds. He came from a family of undertakers, an always steady profession, although slightly on the morbid side. The club shelled out between forty and fifty thousand dollars to bring Hodapp to Cleveland. There was a two-week delay, during which the twenty-one-year-old refused to report until he got part of the purchase price for himself. Manager Tris Speaker was probably not too angry with the holdout, as Spoke had done the same thing in 1916 when Cleveland purchased him from the Red Sox. Hodapp did eventually arrive and showed some potential in the last two months of the season.

The outfield was solid on the corners, with Jamieson in left field and the reliable Homer Summa in right. Still, since 1926 center field had posed a substantial problem for the team. Tris Speaker, after his eleven outstanding seasons, had abruptly departed the franchise. The Indians had nobody waiting to pick up the slack. Billy Evans and his scouts would search the United States but it would take another year before they could find a long-term replacement for the magnificent Speaker.

The most difficult problem for Billy Evans was the pitching staff. After his great 1926 season, George Uhle had been plagued with arm trouble. In 1927 he only appeared in twenty-five games, winning just eight. Along with Uhle's troubles, Joe Shaute had a record of nine wins and sixteen losses. Garland "Gob" Buckeye, a lefty, had a great name but his record was abysmal, a total of ten wins and seventeen losses. Buckeye had the distinction of weighing over 260 pounds while standing six feet tall. No, it was not all muscle. There was Emil "Dutch" Levsen, a three-game winner that season with seven losses.

Cleveland's leading pitcher in 1927 was Willis Hudlin. Born in 1906, Hudlin was a high school sensation from the small town of Wagoner, Oklahoma, in the northeast part of the state. The small community was created as a railroad town in the late nineteenth century. At the time Willis was born, the local population stood at approximately four thousand. During his high school years, Hudlin was an All-State football and basketball player, track star, and the best baseball pitcher for miles around. His spectacular play brought college football recruiters from Texas, but Hudlin only wanted to play baseball. In the spring of 1926 he signed a contract to play for the Class A Waco Cubs in the Texas League. Hudlin departed for Waco without finishing high school. The Cubs manager was Del Pratt, a former St. Louis Brown and American League RBI champ in 1916. Pratt knew a ballplayer when he saw one, and Hudlin turned out to be the real deal. Willis pitched against some seasoned competition but showed he was their match or better. He had a blistering fastball which he threw both overhand and sidearm. The pitch had a pronounced sink to it that baffled the minor-league hitters.

Scouts rapidly descended on Waco to get a close look at the star pitcher. Despite the Cubs lounging in the cellar, Hudlin managed to win sixteen games. The New York Yankees emissary believed Hudlin had a major-league arm that was nearly ready for the big time. Pratt sensed the opportunity to make a big score and announced that the price for Hudlin would be $25,000 plus three players. The Yankees put down an option to buy, good until June 7. They were reluctant to part with three players but did not want to pass on the hot prospect. The Cincinnati Reds badgered Pratt to accept a $5,000 payment up front with the balance due sixty days later. They wanted time to determine if Willis could help their club.

During all the high-level bargaining, Cleveland scout Cy Slapnicka waited quietly for an opportunity to move in and steal the prize. He was everything you wanted in a scout: aggressive, resourceful, slightly devious, and willing to bend the rules. Along with these qualities, Slapnicka had a great eye for talent. One way or another he was going to bring Hudlin to Cleveland.

On the morning of June 7, Slapnicka walked into Del Pratt's office and asked if the Yankees had picked up their option. Pratt answered no, but they had until 1:00 p.m. to do so. The Indians scout eyed the clock for another two hours, then visited Pratt again. Time was now up for the Yankees. Slapnicka reached into his suit pocket and pulled out a check for $25,000. He negotiated with Pratt on the additional three players for Waco and the deal was done. The value of the transaction including the three players was $40,000, a remarkable amount of money for a nineteen-year-old not quite finished with high school.

The Cleveland fans were quite eager to get a look at the best pitcher from the Texas League. On August 16, 1926, Willis Hudlin started the opening game of a doubleheader against the St. Louis Browns. The fans packed League Park to the tune of 25, 000 spectators, an overflow crowd. Willis made it through two innings but completely lost control in the third. He walked the first three batters, then gave up a base hit. Speaker pulled Hudlin from the game but the relief pitchers did not help, the Browns winning, 11–7.

On August 31, Hudlin made another appearance against St. Louis, this time in relief. With the game tied he pitched seven scoreless innings to record his first major-league win. The Indians stole the game in the bottom of the twelfth when Homer Summa scored on an error by the Browns shortstop. Cleveland fans were delighted in what they saw from the young pitcher.

The second-place Indians still had a chance to catch the Yankees, which meant Hudlin would ride the bench for the remainder of September. He trekked back to Wagoner to compete his high school education, but had a rough time paying attention in class and ultimately gave up all thought of finishing school. He would later tell reporters, "It is pretty tough work trying to study geometry when you are thinking of how to throw a curveball past Babe Ruth." That winter he did a different type of studying. He built a wooden ballplayer and put canvas behind the dummy to stop the baseballs. Hudlin added a wooden strike zone from the knees to the chest, then practiced throwing strikes throughout the winter. If nothing else he would get an A for effort.

In the 1927 campaign Hudlin would win eighteen games, leading the Cleveland pitching staff. He might have won twenty, but a bad-hop grounder hit him right between the eyes, resulting in a concussion. For too many days he was light-headed and frequently bled from the nose. Regardless of the accident, Hudlin still had an exceptional season. He was one of the bright spots in a vastly disappointing year.

Team president Bradley and general manager Evans certainly wanted to improve their ball club for the 1928 season. This posed quite a challenge for the Indians as well as the other American League teams trying to unseat the World Champion Yankees. The New York club was an absolute powerhouse with no hint of slowing down. In 1927, Babe Ruth broke his own home run record with sixty, while Lou Gehrig trailed with a paltry forty-seven. Next in line was Tony Lazzeri with eighteen. The Ruth-Gehrig combination knocked in an amazing total of 339 runs. If that was not enough, Bob Meusel had 103 RBIs while Lazzeri finished with 102. The Yankees won 111 games against forty-four defeats. One has to go back to 1906 to find a club with a better record, that being the Chicago Cubs of 1906, led by first baseman/manager Frank Chance. If for some reason the big bats were silent, the Yankee pitching staff could easily take up the slack. Waite Hoyt led all American League pitchers with twenty-two wins, followed closely by Herb Pennock with nineteen.

Truly the Yankees were a dynasty, with few teams that could throw down with them. One was Philadelphia. After more than a decade of being hopelessly inept, Connie Mack had his Athletics competitive again. Young players, including pitcher Robert "Lefty" Grove and outfielder Al Simmons, were leading Philadelphia back to the upper division. A new third baseman named Jimmy Foxx was about to pay big dividends for Mr. Mack. The Washington Senators were a solid club and St. Louis usually played above .500. The Indians had to improve tremendously to jump over any of these ball clubs.

With a number of obstacles to overcome, the 1928 Indians prepared for spring training. The new ownership determined to move camp to New Orleans, a familiar location for Cleveland teams past. A few weeks before they left, City Manager William Hopkins addressed the city council. He advised them that a meeting had taken place on January 25 with Alva Bradley, Chuck Bradley, and team secretary Joseph Hostetler. A new stadium was on the table and Hopkins wanted to test how much the Indians might pay for an exclusive lease. He had in mind an enormous facility on the lakefront that could seat approximately eighty thousand fans. Osborne Engineering, the firm that had built League Park, gave Hopkins some tentative plans that included a price tag of two million dollars.

For the stadium to be built, a bond issue had to be submitted to Cleveland voters in the November general election. Hopkins estimated the bond interest and carrying charges would amount to $155,000 for the first year. He wanted Bradley and the other Indians owners to pay for the bulk of it with additional money coming from football games and world-class boxing events. Hopkins explained to the *Cleveland Plain Dealer*, "When we go to the people for a bond issue we want to be able to say this won't cost you a cent. We want to know in advance that the income from the stadium will pay the carrying charges on the bonds."

It is likely the opening of the Terminal Tower gave the city politicians plenty of optimism about a new project. If that massive structure could be built, why not a new stadium? Civic pride was taking hold in Cleveland. It stood to reason that the time was now to take on another large-scale project. Perhaps the momentum had indeed swung in the city manager's favor.

Though public support seemed to be within reach, Hopkins had some major obstacles to overcome. The largest was the right-of-way the railroad companies enjoyed at the lakefront. At present, the rail people could build track on much of the land needed for the new stadium. He required their approval to set aside the area for construction. All things considered, it was an ambitious plan. Even if the bond issue passed and the railroad barons gave their okay, Hopkins still had other battles to fight. Most importantly, Alva Bradley needed to be on board for the lease agreement. Full support from the city council had to be achieved. If Hopkins was successful on all these counts, the voters in Cuyahoga County were still a big question mark. Was a new stadium really necessary? League Park had been doing fine for thirty-seven years. The park at 66th and Lexington had good views, was easy to get to, and brought in revenue to the businesses located in and around the field. For years, the neighborhood kids prowled Lexington Avenue in hopes of snagging baseballs that sailed over the towering right field wall. They would be out of luck if the Indians moved to the lakefront. City Manager Hopkins had let the genie out of the bottle. He needed to be exceedingly shrewd in getting his wishes granted.

On February 19, 1928, the Indians pitchers and coaches boarded their train for the trip to New Orleans. Everybody in the group was eager to once again play ball. No doubt they all were motivated to show their best stuff to the new management. The reporters and photographers for the city's three daily newspapers were falling all over themselves to board the train and escape the frigid Cleveland winter. The sportswriters and the camera guys for the *Plain Dealer*, *News*, and *Press* had been going south with the team for many years. This was a chance to get some exclusive interviews and talk baseball in a relaxed setting. It had to be one of the great perks of the job.

Upon arrival the squad headed for the Hotel Roosevelt, one of the finest places to stay in New Orleans. Unfortunately, the boys had arrived at the conclusion of Mardi Gras and the celebrants were still in their suites sleeping off all the fun. Everybody gathered in the lobby, waiting for rooms to open up. Local reporters sat down with manager Peckinpaugh to see what he thought about the Indians' chances for the season. Peck told the writers, "I'm not going to make any predictions because we can't estimate our strength until Uhle and Levsen show whether they have come back. We are certainly stronger than we were last year if only because the team's spirit is bound to be better." Peck would go on to say the Yankees and Philadelphia were the class of the league with Washington right behind. Possibly Cleveland could move up to fourth place. The new manager was being conservative, but he knew the American League as well as anyone else if not better. He wanted fans to be hopeful but not expect a contending team right out of the gate.

A week later the infielders and outfielders arrived in camp. Full workouts were under way. There was the practice of leapfrog, where the players took turns jumping over one another across the field. The Indians had been doing this going back to 1916 when Lee Fohl was manager. It is difficult to determine the benefits of leapfrog, but the players seemed to really enjoy the drill. They ran a brisk lap around Heinemann Park and got in their share of calisthenics. Peck did not drive his players to exhaustion, but he made certain the entire squad got in a good day's work. He even allowed them to play golf after the workouts.

Billy Evans had sent a large number of ballplayers to New Orleans to give his manager a chance to find some raw talent. There were three or four extra each of shortstops, catchers, and outfielders. One of the shortstops was a football and baseball All-Star from Syracuse University who impressed Peck immediately with some good fielding and timely hitting. His name was Jonah Goldman.

The new prospect was born in 1906 in New York City. He was by far the best athlete at Erasmus High School in Brooklyn, excelling at football, soccer, basketball, and track. With all the time devoted to sports, Goldman fell behind in his studies, causing him to spend a year at prep school. Many colleges were interested but Goldman decided to attend Syracuse University. There he immediately played halfback on the freshman football team and shortstop on the baseball squad. He quickly drew attention for spectacular long runs on the football field and belting doubles and triples on the diamond. The opponents were of high quality, including colleges like Michigan, Nebraska, Penn State, and Boston College. Some of the notice that went Goldman's way had little to do with events on the playing field: he was a rare commodity, in being a multisport Jewish athlete.

Since the latter part of the nineteenth century, Major League Baseball had been one of the few places where immigrants had a chance to excel. Initially it was an opportunity for men who had arrived from Ireland and found little opportunity other than grueling manual labor. Those who had some athletic skill discovered that ballplayers could earn a living with a professional baseball club. Near the end of the nineteenth century there were McGraws, Delahantys, McGinnitys, and Kellys in the National League. Irish folks would pack the bleachers to see one of their own perform. Next came the German wave, with the great Honus Wagner, Hans Lobert, and Henry "Heinie" Groh. All had certain difficulties with lowbrow fans who loathed immigrants, but over time there came a general acceptance.

Jewish athletes entered baseball at a much slower pace. There were wealthy Jewish men who owned baseball teams, including Andrew Freedman of the New York Giants and Barney Dreyfuss of the Pittsburgh Pirates. Be that as it may, ballplayers were few and far between. Moe Berg entered the majors in the early 1920s. Buddy Myer became a star for the Washington Senators, but there is still debate today as to whether or not he was actually Jewish: apparently his father was, his mother not. Now Jonah Goldman began to make headlines in newspapers around the country, mostly due to his religion. Almost invariably, articles would mention he was a Jewish boy trying to make good with the Indians. If that was not enough to contend with, he had to beat out Joe Sewell for a job. The veteran from Alabama was not about to step aside for anybody.

Editors and columnists from around the country weighed in on the prospect of Jewish ballplayers in the big leagues. For years, manager John McGraw of the New York Giants had searched the New York City area, trying to find a talented Jewish player for his club. McGraw believed that if he could locate the right individual the Polo Grounds would be overflowing with Jewish fans. In 1928 the Giants brought second baseman Andy Cohen to training camp. McGraw hoped he had found the player that the vast Jewish population in the New York metro area would embrace. If Cohen made the Giants roster for the upcoming season, a large spike in attendance would surely take place. Some writers called it a fad, others commercialization.

A sports editor in Mississippi wrote a column on the subject, saying that there truly was a fad going on in baseball with this turn toward Jewish ballplayers. He referred to the Yankees signing Jimmy Reese, whose actual last name was Goldsmith, the Giants and Andy Cohen, and the Indians with Jonah Goldman, and noted the "ballyhoo" accompanying these players, mostly because of their religion. Some writers were hopeful that the fans around the country would be enlightened enough to boo or cheer based only on how the players performed. Most acknowledged that there were times when Jewish ballplayers were harassed out of the game, but the hope was that people in the late 1920s were more tolerant and would not hold a man's religion against him.

Damon Runyon saw the lighter side of the issue. He wrote in a syndicated column that boisterous Irish fans could cheer the "Andrew" part of Andy Cohen while the Jewish fans could yell for the "Cohen" part. He suggested the name should be changed to O'Cohen to appease both factions.

The Cleveland papers picked up on the hot topic immediately. They made a strong point of letting the readers know the young shortstop was Jewish. Later they would publish stories about his playing ability, but for now his religion was selling the papers. Shortly after the signing was announced, a local reporter pulled out a telephone directory and located the page with the name "Goldman" listed. He called ten of the numbers for reactions to the signing. Some of those he spoke to had no idea what was taking place, while a few knew baseball and figured out why they'd gotten the phone call. The article probably triggered chuckles around the city, but if the name had been Smith or Johnson there simply would have been no story.

For his part, Jonah Goldman stayed as quiet on the sidelines as possible. Writers mentioned that he did not take part in the clubhouse banter, did not play cards, or even smoke. He enjoyed going to the picture shows and seeing the sights. Whether or not he did these activities alone is purely a matter of speculation. His teammates may have accepted him on the playing field, but social activities could have been another matter. When asked about how the other players treated him, Goldman praised his teammates for all the help they provided on the diamond. He expected to get the cold shoulder, but was pleased to be treated as just another ballplayer. Although recently out of college, he had ample maturity and the good sense not to give sportswriters any more headlines than necessary. Though the Cleveland players may have been tolerant to a degree, it would be years before all of baseball followed suit.

Spring training went along as usual with the workouts and exhibition games. Those pitchers trying to overcome arm troubles would tell the press they had never felt better. Hitters who had had an off year would remark how well they were seeing the ball. Manager Peckinpaugh needed to study each player to determine who would take the trip north to open the season.

As the weeks rolled by, Peck sensed he had found lightning in a bottle in second baseman Carl Lind. The newest recruit had played his collegiate ball at Tulane University. He got a timely opportunity when Joe Sewell fell injured and there was some shuffling done in the infield. Lind seized the moment and earned himself a place on the roster. Not so for shortstop Jonah Goldman. He displayed a lot of promise, but Peckinpaugh believed he would do better with a year in the minors. His time would come, just a little bit later.

With Opening Day on the horizon, the Indians left New Orleans and traveled north for Chicago. They were eager to start a new season and prove the previous year's sixth-place finish was the exception to the norm. The White Sox were not expected to do much in the pennant race, which gave Cleveland a fighting chance to win a few early. Peckinpaugh opted to go with his veteran, penciling in George Uhle as the starter. It proved to be a wise decision, as the Indians won the opener, 8–2. The Sewell brothers led the way, with Joe (recovered from a sore knee) bashing three hits and Luke two. Uhle added three hits and a sacrifice for a perfect day at the plate. The game was not without plenty of excitement. In the bottom of the third inning, the White Sox had runners on first and third with two out. Willie Kamm, the Chicago captain, lifted a fly ball to short right-center field. Eddie Morgan raced in from center while second baseman Lew Fonseca drifted back. The ball was seemingly too far to reach and neither yelled they had it. Fonseca stretched out at the last instant and speared the ball. Morgan could not stop, slamming into his teammate at full speed. Somehow, Fonseca held the ball while both players fell to the ground. After a few minutes both stood up and walked slowly to the Indians dugout. Morgan came to bat in the fifth inning, took a big cut at Ted Lyons's pitch and crumpled to the ground. He was helped to the clubhouse, then straight to a Chicago hospital for X-rays. Nothing was broken, but the doctors noticed a blood clot right below the heart where the impact had occurred. Morgan had to remain in the hospital for several days. He would later say that he could not remember anything that happened before the fifth inning.

Despite the temporary loss of Morgan and Fonseca the Indians continued to win. They easily beat Detroit, 8–1, with Joe Shaute pitching a fine game. Willis Hudlin pitched well for his first win and Cleveland found themselves on top with a 3–0 record. They would arrive back in Cleveland filled with confidence for the long-awaited home opener.

The day before the League Park gates were unlocked, Alva Bradley spoke to members of the local Building Exchange. Bradley told the businessmen, "No big city is really a big city anymore unless it has a stadium and we want the biggest and best one here." Bradley challenged the city to get going on the plans, or he and his partners would build it themselves. Billy Evans spoke up as well. He said, "At the opener [this] Wednesday we could have enough paid admission to fill this proposed stadium." The new ownership was clearly making a strong statement that they wanted the new facility built now or they were prepared to go private and cut the city out of any lease revenue. William Hopkins quickly made a comment for the newspapers, saying, "The Cleveland Baseball Club Company will lease the stadium and be our largest tenant." He reminded fans that he would bring football and boxing in as well, which would take care of the bond interest and carrying charges. Whether or not Bradley was appeased by this declaration would remain to be seen.

April 18 finally came around and the excited Cleveland fans converged on League Park, ready to watch the Indians battle the White Sox. Many of them were using automobiles to get to 66th and Lexington. When Frank Robison built the stately park in 1891 he could not see the future and the coming of the horseless carriage. There was no room anywhere near his park for cars and buses, so fans parked on both sides of area streets and even used up large amounts of the sidewalks. Many of the folks who lived on Linwood and Lexington Avenues opened their front lawns for parking. Fees were not reported, but we all know about enterprising people and the economics of supply and demand. No doubt the car owners paid through the nose for prime parking.

Morning temperatures hovered in the frigid low thirties, and fans who arrived early brought their overcoats with them. The game-day forecast called for a chance of rain with highs in the low sixties. For those who knew Cleveland weather, anything near fifty degrees would be more than acceptable. Freezing temperatures notwithstanding, the fans lined up early at the ticket windows. Many would have taken a glance at the Terminal Tower to make certain the American flag was flying. If the flag was up that meant the game was on. All the reserved seats were taken but plenty of grandstand seats were available. By game time the stands would be completely filled.

The man in charge of concessions, Robert Hamilton, anticipated an enormous day for himself and his vendors. The night before they had roasted a massive amount of hot dogs. Once the game started, Hamilton had twenty-five boys standing by to reheat the dogs and slap on the mustard. As soon as the food was ready, there were seventy-five men and boys to peddle it around the park. All told, there were six hundred pounds of hot dogs ready to be devoured. For those that needed a coffee fix, Hamilton brewed over two hundred pounds' worth. To complement the hot dogs and coffee, roasted peanuts, popcorn, and potato chips were stored in hefty containers.

A number of fans were disappointed when they were told that soda pop was not on the menu. Concessionaire Hamilton decided that the receipts from previous years did not warrant serving any Coca-Cola. This news was happily welcomed by the American League umpires working League Park. Baseball fans had a long tradition of showing what they thought of bad calls by the umpire. After a few minutes of loud boos, the people in the stands took aim and heaved empty pop bottles at the hapless men on the field. An umpire had to be nimble to avoid the shower of glass coming at all speeds. At least for 1928, the men in blue at League Park could relax and worry only about flying peanut shells or an occasional hot dog.

Opening Day always featured various ceremonies before the teams took the field. Brass bands played, certain city officials were introduced, and the American flag was raised near the center-field scoreboard. Manager Peckinpaugh received a six-foot floral arrangement shaped like a horseshoe. The fans cheered while Peck waved to the grandstand. The longstanding custom of throwing out the first pitch went to City Manager Hopkins. He made an awkward throw, and it was time to play baseball. The Indians lineup went as follows:

Charlie Jamieson (left field)
Carl Lind (second base)
Sam Langford (center field)
Joe Sewell (shortstop)
George Burns (first base)
Homer Summa (right field)
Johnny Hodapp (third base)
Luke Sewell (catcher)
Joe Shaute (pitcher)

Johnny Mostil led off for the White Sox and grounded to George Burns. Pitcher Joe Shaute gave up a base on balls and hit a batter, but kept Chicago from scoring. The Indians got rolling in the bottom of the first. With one out, Carl Lind singled. Sam Langford lined a ball off the short right-field wall but was held to a single. Veteran outfielders like Johnny Mostil knew how to play balls that caromed off the imposing wall. He played the bounce perfectly, wheeled and threw to second to keep Langford from advancing. Joe Sewell got the crowd shouting by lining a double to right field. Lind crossed the plate with the first run of the home season. George Burns flied to right, scoring Sam Langford with the second run. Those would be all the runs needed by Shaute to win the home opener, although Cleveland scored five more times in the seventh inning. The big hits were a bases-loaded single by Johnny Hodapp and a double by Luke Sewell. The Indians cruised to a 7–1 victory.

It had been quite a successful day for Alva Bradley and his partners. They watched an exciting game with loads of action. Everywhere the new owners looked, there were fans yelling and applauding, thrilled to see the home season get off to a rousing start. There was still a great deal of work to do in making the club a contender, but Bradley saw the potential of putting a quality product on the field—including justification for building a new ballpark that could seat more than three times the amount of fans squeezed into League Park.

The game ended right around 5:00 p.m. Fans madly dashed to their automobiles, intent on getting ahead of the traffic. Within minutes one of the all-time traffic snarls in Cleveland history took place. The fifty police officers on duty whistled and yelled at hundreds of autos trying to get out of the neighborhood and find their way to Euclid and Carnegie Avenues. Any sense of protocol and orderly behavior was forgotten. Cars were everywhere, flying down alleys and side streets. The streetcars, special buses, and taxis moved in to pick up the thousands of people needing rides. Soon they were literally stopped in their tracks, blocked by the onslaught of Model T's and the like. Police estimated the delays at forty minutes and climbing. The cars that somehow reached Euclid Avenue ran directly into the normal traffic jam that had begun a half-hour earlier. Motorists were able to move about three feet, then stop and wait a few minutes to move another three. The fender benders were too numerous to count. One driver shouted to police to stop the car behind him that had already rammed him twice. An officer screamed back to write it down and mail the complaint to headquarters.

At one point a streetcar managed to reach a large group of fans. Within moments it was filled. Those who hadn't managed to climb aboard stood defiantly in the street, holding back the traffic until they spied another streetcar. To add to the chaos, a woman driver in a large auto attempted to make a left turn in the middle of Euclid Avenue. She got about halfway across, then stopped suddenly, unable to drive any further. This daring move stopped traffic in both directions, causing the male drivers let go with obscenities. Women had made significant strides by the late 1920s, but equality was still many decades ahead. The fact that the woman sat calmly in her car and chewed gum really aggravated the guys on both sides of her. It would be more than a full hour before the streets began to clear. This was Opening Day at its finest.

The following day, Willis Hudlin kept the good feelings alive by defeating the hapless White Sox, 9–2. Johnny Hodapp and Carl Lind had three hits apiece. The new second baseman was off to a blazing start, knocking in three runs with a single, double, and triple. All this winning was something new, prompting Gordon Cobbledick of the *Plain Dealer* to write, "If you will glance at the table of American League standings this morning, you will observe that the first team on the list is Cleveland and that New York and Washington were tied for second place." Cobbledick had taken the place of Henry Edwards, who moved to Chicago to work in the American League office. For the next forty years Gordon Cobbledick, a native Clevelander, would be regarded as one of the best sportswriters in the business. He may have been overly optimistic given that it was still only late April, but for a short time the Indians were playing like contenders.

In the beginning of June the Indians dropped seven in a row to the Red Sox, Yankees, and Senators. No doubt many of the sceptics were waiting for this. The team did not have much pitching and defense, and the lack of a real power hitter began to show. In the middle of July they dropped five straight to New York. As the months continued Cleveland sank deeper and deeper in the standings. Another sixth- or even a seventh-place finish was looming.

The Indians' inexperienced front office was making mistakes as well. On July 14 the newspapers reported the team had claimed pitcher Johnny Miljus on waivers from the Pittsburgh Pirates. Miljus was a journeyman at best, not a star by any means. Almost immediately a controversy arose. The front office had neglected a rule which stated that a player who had been bought by a Major League team, if waived within a year, must pay the purchase price and not the waiver fee. The Pirates had bought Miljus from Seattle for $17,500 the previous July. That meant the Indians had to pay $17,500, not the waiver price of $7,500. The front office, likely covering for an embarrassed Billy Evans, issued a quick statement that a clerical employee had made an error and was not authorized to act on the waiver deal. The office wanted to withdraw the claim and pretend it never happened. The identity of the phantom employee was never revealed. The Pirates front office appealed to Commissioner Landis to oblige the Indians to cough up the money. Landis took one week to render a decision. It was a terse one, to the effect that the Indians had bought Miljus for $17,500. Evans tried to save face by issuing another statement to the press, saying, "We took a licking but we don't feel bad about it. We rather think the acquisition of Miljus is a good thing for us." From July through September, the new pitcher would win one game for his new team.

Just two weeks after the Miljus fiasco, Alva Bradley made a decision that launched Cleveland baseball into the modern age: he gave the green light to WTAM Radio to start broadcasting the Indians home games every day except Sundays. For some time

Bradley had agonized over the decision. He, like other owners, was concerned that the broadcasting of games would result in a significant reduction in attendance. Why pay money to see the games when you could hear them for free in your office or home? There were no statistics to analyze involving any trends in attendance versus broadcasts. In the end, Bradley came to his decision by putting the interests of the Cleveland fans first.

Radio had been around in baseball since 1921, when station KDKA broadcast a Pittsburgh Pirates game. The World Series was next, with Grantland Rice behind the microphone. A few years later, Graham McNamee joined Rice and quickly established himself as a fan favorite. McNamee was not a student of the game, but his colorful and lively descriptions endeared him to listeners. If he made an obvious mistake or two, the fans just smiled and did not complain.

On Wednesday, July 25, 1928, WTAM broadcast the first Cleveland Indians game. Billy Evans started the play-by-play along with former public-address announcer Tom Manning. Fans chuckled at Evans's attempts to describe the action. Manning had suggested that the general manager use a diagram of the field, with names included, so he could quickly note who was making the plays. Evans scoffed at this but soon found that he did not recognize the players as well as he thought. To make matters worse, he had a sore throat which deteriorated as the game progressed. He tried lozenges and sucking on a lemon but nothing helped. After a few innings he turned the mike over to Manning and retired from broadcasting. The Indians, perhaps inspired by the new technology, clobbered the Red Sox, 10–2. A happy Evans bought a round of lemonade and orangeade for all the sportswriters in the press box.

The radio broadcasts were welcomed by the Cleveland fans. WTAM received a large number of letters from fans who were blind or otherwise handicapped. These people could not say enough kind words in thanking both the Indians and the radio station. One letter in particular really pulled on the heartstrings. It came from a veteran of World War I who had lost his sight in battle. He told the WTAM station manager that he had faithfully attended games at League Park for sixteen years, but after the war and his blindness there was no point in going to the ballpark. Now he could follow the Indians as before.

There would be one more remarkable team effort before the total collapse. On July 29 the Yankees were in town. Ruth, Gehrig, Lazzeri, and the others were a major draw in whatever city they played in, and the fans came in great numbers. By game time, the total attendance swelled to over 25,000, the biggest crowd of the season. The ushers brought out the ropes and let fans on the field, primarily in left and center. The Indians' hitters went crazy, scoring an incredible eighteen runs in the first three innings. Yankee pitcher George Pipgrass was removed in the opening inning without retiring a batter. The entire Cleveland lineup, except for pitcher Joe Shaute, had a least two hits apiece. Luke Sewell and Johnny Hodapp both had five hits, while Carl Lind had a day to remember, collecting four hits and driving in five runs. Hodapp dazzled the crowd by banging out two hits in the second inning, then two more in the sixth. The Indians bashed twenty-seven hits, twenty-four of them singles. The final score was 24–6, one of the most lopsided games in Major League history to date. And it came at the expense of the powerful Yankees!

Regardless of it turning out to be another disappointing season, Alva Bradley had not lost any of his enthusiasm. He told the newspapers that Roger Peckinpaugh would return for a second season, saying, "We want Peck to feel free to do whatever seems to him to be necessary to produce a winner or at least an improved team next year." Bradley went on to say that in September a number of minor-league prospects would join the club and get an audition with the team. The names mentioned were Jonah Goldman, playing at Decatur, Johnny Burnett, a flashy shortstop from the Terre Haute club, and his teammate, pitcher Wes Ferrell. Peck planned to take a long look at the up-and-comers to see if any of them might help the team in 1929. Bradley was showing the fans and sportswriters that he had a firm grasp of the situation. He gave his manager an early vote of confidence, which let the players know there would be no shakeups in the front office, at least for another year. Bradley preached stability, the best course of action for his franchise.

Chapter 3

THE VOTE IS YES

The conclusion of the 1928 season and the winter months ahead were critical for Bradley and Evans. The stadium bond issue was coming up in the November election, while Evans had a blank checkbook to find some extra talented ballplayers. The outfield was a prime concern as well as the need for pitching and infield help. The men in charge, including Roger Peckinpaugh, shared their ideas to improve the club. They took a hard look at the current roster to cull the weak ones from the herd.

First to come under scrutiny were the long-term veterans. Joe Sewell had lost a step in the field, but his bat was as lethal as ever. He batted .323 with 190 hits, including forty doubles. In 588 plate appearances, the shortstop fanned only nine times. His ability to get the bat on the ball was simply way off the charts. Brother Luke caught 122 games while batting a respectable .270. He shamed the Sewell family, though, by fanning a grand total of twenty-seven times. Left fielder Charlie Jamieson managed to hit .307, which kept him in the starting lineup for the ninth consecutive year.

On September 17 the Indians placed George Burns on waivers. Initially, Burns was on board with the decision. He was thirty-five years old and had been in the Major Leagues for fifteen years. Burns wanted to manage in the minor leagues and play some first base as well. He hoped none of the ball clubs would put in a claim, allowing him to find a place where he could manage. As a ten-year veteran, Burns was entitled to become a free agent if nobody claimed him on waivers. In spite of this, the New York Yankees unexpectedly claimed Burns, ruining his plans for the immediate future. Why they would need a backup to a young Lou Gehrig is hard to understand. Burns was quite angry with the decision, venting his frustration to the Cleveland papers. He told reporters, "I wouldn't say the Cleveland club handed me a raw deal. I suppose it is good business for the club to get $7,500, but it is a hard blow to me and smashed my plans for grabbing a good berth with a minor league club." Despite all the years of good service in the American League, Burns had no recourse but to report to New York. He played in just four games and was not eligible to receive any World Series money. Of course, the Yankees won another crown, beating St. Louis four games to none.

One of the strangest actions taken by the Indians occurred during the season on September 9. Manager Peckinpaugh announced that pitcher George Uhle was suspended for the remainder of the year. The explanation given was that Uhle was out of condition and not in shape to play baseball. There had to be more to the situation, as Uhle had already appeared in thirty-one games, starting in twenty-eight of them. How could a ballplayer not be in condition after playing for five months? There was no question that Uhle was having a poor season, with twelve wins and seventeen losses, but a suspension? A few months later the mystery was revealed. At the winter meetings, Billy Evans sent Uhle to the Detroit Tigers in exchange for shortstop Jackie Tavener and pitcher Ken Holloway. Evans revealed that the suspension was due to Uhle being a bad influence on several of the young players. For that reason, the former ace of the Indians pitching staff was banished from the club. Ironically, Uhle would return to Cleveland in 1936 and, at the age of thirty-eight, make a few token appearances for then-manager and old friend Steve O'Neill.

While the Cleveland front office tinkered with the roster, the city prepared to launch the campaign for the new stadium. On Friday, October 19, an executive committee was announced to lead the important battle. The chairman was Charles Otis, one of the most well-connected men in Cleveland and possibly the entire United States. Charles was born on July 9, 1868, to one of the wealthiest families in northeast Ohio. Otis's grandfather William came to Cleveland in the 1830s and immediately started a shipping enterprise linking Cleveland to New York City via the Erie Canal. He became one of the original men to invest in the fledging railroad business and later was a pioneer in the iron industry. Charles's father was a well-known local businessman who founded Otis Steel in the latter part of the nineteenth century. In the 1870s the elder Otis served one term as mayor of Cleveland.

Young Charles enjoyed a life of exceptional privilege, attending the best schools and frolicking in Europe with his closest pals. In the 1880s his brother owned a cattle ranch in Colorado where Charles rode horses and carried a six-gun in his belt. After attending Yale, Otis started his own steel business in Cleveland. He used his status as a member of the elite to solicit all the business he could handle. When he grew tired of the steel industry he hired more executives and left the business to others while he bought a seat on the New York Stock Exchange. In 1899 he founded the Otis & Hough Company, one of the initial brokerage houses in Cleveland. As might be expected, he had well-off clients with rolls of cash to invest. Soon after, he formed the Cleveland Stock Exchange, where he was elected its first president. Six years later it was time to explore new opportunities. In 1905 he bought the *Cleveland News*. Charles had great fun writing editorials and trying to boost the paper's circulation. He is credited with hiring a young Grantland Rice for his sports department. Rice went on to become one of the most respected sportswriters in all of America.

Charles Otis could boast of friendships with John D. Rockefeller, comedian Will Rogers, and his distant cousin Amelia Earhart. He knew many United States presidents, from fishing trips with Grover Cleveland to card games with Warren G. Harding. He debated with Teddy Roosevelt on whether the *Cleveland News* would support TR's Bull Moose Party. When America entered World War I, Charles was appointed to the War Industries Board, where he worked closely with future president Herbert Hoover. Regardless of being active in Washington, he found the spare time to sell a huge amount of war bonds in Cleveland.

In late 1919, when Prohibition was about to come into effect, Charles and close friend John Sherwin, the banker and future stockholder of the Indians, went on a buying spree. They spent the enormous amount of $30,000 on cases of Old Crow bourbon, whiskey, gin, and champagne. Trucks were hired to load the cases and deliver them to Sherwin's lavish home in Cleveland Heights. Whenever the rich folks threw a high-powered party, Charles was there with all the booze needed. If you wanted something of importance done, there was only one man in Cleveland to call.

Otis and his committee got on the job without delay. To assist, he had the leaders from the Rotary Club, Cleveland School Board, Cleveland Athletic Club, and John Carroll University. They sent 125,000 envelopes promoting the bond issue to the voters of Cleveland. Stadium badges in the amount of fifty thousand were distributed all around the city. Posters by the thousands were printed to be displayed in store windows and downtown offices. A total of thirty thousand letters were sent to organizations that might have a potential need to use the stadium.

The committee assured voters that the Cleveland baseball club favored a lease that would be in effect for the duration of the bonds. They estimated the baseball lease revenue would take care of 50 percent of the bond interest the city would eventually have to pay out. A diverse list of other possible events at the stadium included boxing, football, soccer, track, carnivals, opera, and community Christmas celebrations. Mentioned specifically was the possibility of bringing the college football powerhouses to the proposed stadium, including Navy, Notre Dame, and a small school in Columbus named Ohio State.

Charles Otis and his committee knew exactly how to reach the voters. Banners were put up at local high school and college football games. Slides were created to be shown before movies at the downtown theaters. An army of speakers hit the ground running to plead their case at every possible club available. The campaign could not advertise on radio, nor could they attach signs to the many streetcars gliding up and down the east and west side avenues. Both means were prohibited at the time.

In spite of this, on November 1 they did manage to get Billy Evans and William Hopkins on WHK Radio. This was an informational discussion that would enlighten voters on the pros and cons of building a new stadium. With these two speakers, there were probably quite a few more pros than cons.

The committee had the support of the three major Cleveland newspapers. Though Charles Otis had long since sold the *Cleveland News*, he still had influence there. The *Plain Dealer* published editorials appealing to the voters to mark an *X* next to the "yes" box. Sam Otis (not a relative), the *Plain Dealer* sports editor, strongly endorsed the bond issue, writing, "We want a touchdown, we want a touchdown IN A STADIUM ON THE LAKEFRONT! Cleveland must have the stadium. It means more to sports here than any other project launched."

Stuart Bell, the sports editor for the *Cleveland Press,* had a different angle as to why voters should support the stadium initiative. He wrote, "One argument we haven't seen put forth in behalf of the proposed stadium on the lakefront is that it would be the first perfect baseball stadium in the history of the game." Bell asserted that this would be the lone baseball park that would not be crammed onto an inadequate piece of land. There would be no short fences or sun fields, no entrance or exit problems, and parking spaces for everyone. Bell added, "There will be plenty of room on the lakefront. The stadium can be symmetrical and mechanically perfect as far as the outfield barriers are concerned. Best of all there would be no short fences to assist the manufacture of cheap home runs."

The campaign for the new stadium did have its share of detractors. Several members of the Citizens League expressed stout opposition to the plan. They submitted a minority report that claimed revenues generated by the facility would not be ample enough to cover the costs. They questioned the estimated revenues of $250,000 and where they would come from. The gentlemen acknowledged that about $125,000 was expected from the Indians lease, but where was the remainder going to be produced? John Gourley, the Cleveland recreation commissioner, had sharp words for the dissenters, replying that "There are powerful influences favoring the stadium that are in a position to guarantee the appearances of great sporting events other than baseball." When pressed for names, Gourley refused to comment.

On Friday, November 2, the Cleveland Baseball Commission held its annual banquet at the Statler Hotel. In the audience were 190 amateur ballplayers to accept awards and wolf down a gourmet dinner. City Manager Hopkins delivered a brief speech on the merits of a new stadium. He was followed by Max Rosenblum, the commissioner of amateur baseball and a longtime booster of Cleveland sports. Rosenblum urged all in attendance to get behind the stadium issue. Attending on behalf of the Indians were Alva Bradley, Billy Evans, and Roger Peckinpaugh. They sat at a special table and did their best to talk up the project.

The Cleveland Umpires Association held a special meeting at city hall to marshal the forces of the amateur ballplayers and coaches. It was their goal to assign at least one person to canvas every precinct and voting booth the day of the election. Not everybody was twenty-one, but the younger guys could hold signs and encourage voters.

The day before the election, twenty-five hundred people lined up attempting to register to vote. There was a presidential vote to be held the next day, but the last-minute registrants were likely more interested in the stadium issue than in who would be running the country. Estimates were that 250,000 people would cast their ballots in the city. There were no predictions made, but most of the big names of Cleveland publicly urged a yes vote.

At 8:30 a.m., November 6, the polls were opened. In the general election nearly two hundred thousand people cast their votes. In less than four hours, half of the voting was completed. Results were tabulated and the bond issue passed by a comfortable margin, with 55 percent voting yes, 45 percent no. It was quite a vindication for William Hopkins. He had worked tirelessly to get the project on the ballot. Now he could celebrate with all the people who had devoted their time and energy to make the new stadium a reality. Cleveland was getting a world-class stadium; all it needed was a baseball team that could fill the seats. It was now up to Bradley and Evans to make that happen.

The next few weeks saw the Cleveland general manager and his scouts pick their targets for the 1929 team. By the middle of November they had zeroed in on two of the best outfielders obtainable: Dick Porter and Earl Averill.

Dick Porter was born in Princess Anne, Maryland, on December 30, 1901. A left-handed hitter with some pop in his bat, he played his collegiate ball at St. John's College in Annapolis. His outstanding play there got the attention of Jack Dunn, the owner-manager of the Baltimore Orioles. Without much hesitation, Porter signed a contract to play for Dunn's ball club.

At that time the Orioles were a member of the International League and not affiliated with any Major League teams. As a result, Dunn held onto his best players without any real pressure from the big-league teams. As long as he was doing swell with the gate receipts, his players stayed where they were. Dunn had a knack, though, for signing and developing future Major League ballplayers, including Babe Ruth, Ernie Shore, Max Bishop, Robert "Lefty" Grove, and George Earnshaw. The only problem with Dunn was his reluctance to sell his stars, even when they were ready to move up to the American or National League. To placate the frustrated players, Dunn reportedly paid them well above the minor-league standards. It was said he paid them nine o'clock salaries in a two o'clock town.

Porter had to wait eight long seasons before he got his chance to leave the Orioles. The Cubs and then the Yankees tried several times to pry him away but to no avail. It was not until Jack Dunn passed away in October 1928 that Porter became obtainable. Charles Knapp, the new Orioles president, had no qualms about selling players. As a consequence, Billy Evans swooped and bought Porter for $30,000 plus two players, the total value of the deal coming to $40,000. Before he died, Jack Dunn had told reporters that Porter was worth considerably more. Dunn remarked, "Porter is worth $65,000 of anybody's money. He can bat like a demon, field finely and is fast. He can improve any club."

The twenty-eight-year-old Porter had an incredible career at Baltimore. In 1927 he led the league with a .376 batting average, 225 hits, twenty-five home runs, and 153 RBIs. The next year he played almost as well, batting .350 with 216 hits and sixteen triples. Evans would say later that Porter had been ready for the majors at least three or four years before. He would join the Indians right in the middle of his peak years.

One of the great things about the left-handed-hitting Porter was his unique batting style. He could not stand still in the batter's box, moving and fidgeting until the ball was delivered, with very quick wrist and arm movements similar to cracking a whip. Over the years he'd had a number of nicknames, including Wiggledy,

Twitchy, and Wiggles. During an exhibition game between New York and Baltimore, Yankees manager Miller Huggins had tried to get Porter to change his style and relax at the plate. The experiment proved a failure as "Twitchy" started to roll up the strikeouts. He soon reverted back to fidgeting and the strikeouts diminished.

Not only did the Indians pay out the $30,000 for Porter, they had to award him a decent salary. At Baltimore he was collecting $5,000 a year. Evans would have to up the ante to get Porter to sign his new contract. In addition to his baseball salary, Porter had a sausage manufacturing business he ran in the off-season. He was not a starving ballplayer by any means.

While the Cleveland faithful were buzzing about their new outfielder, Billy Evans was on a train to California. His mission was to have a conference with Charlie Graham, the president of the San Francisco Seals. There were two star ballplayers on the Seals that had caught Evans's eye. Number one was Smead Jolley, a power-hitting left fielder who batted .404 during the 1928 season. Due to the favorable weather, the Pacific Coast League played a considerably longer season than the Major Leagues, and in 191 games Jolley had pounded out forty-five home runs. The other player, Earl Averill, was not as prolific but did bat .359 with 33 home runs and 270 hits. Evans had some trouble deciding which man was a better prospect, but a letter from former Indians pitcher Walter "Duster" Mails had urged the team to pick Averill. Mails had been one of the stars of the 1920 World Champion team. He pitched tremendously in game six, beating the Brooklyn Robins 1–0. The next day Cleveland won it all. Mails did not last long in the big leagues, but knew talent when he saw it. In the letter he told the club Averill was a fantastic hitter, especially when he had two strikes on him.

Evans took the letter quite seriously. Manager Peckinpaugh reminded him that the Indians would soon be in a new stadium with a mammoth outfield. Jolley was at best an average outfielder. Earl Averill was fast and could cover a lot of ground. When Evans arrived on the West Coast he came to a decision to go after the better fielder. Averill was his man.

Just three days after the acquisition of Dick Porter, the announcement came over the newswires that Earl Averill was purchased by Cleveland for $40,000 and two players. As in the Porter deal, the two players to be named later were worth $5,000 each. If San Francisco was not keen on the players chosen, the Indians would pay an additional $10,000 instead. That made the total value of the two separate deals a whopping $90,000. Newspapers all around the country had a field day writing about the money shelled out by Cleveland. There was no doubt that Alva Bradley and his partners were playing for keeps.

Earl Averill came from the small town of Snohomish, Washington, in the northwestern part of the state. He was born on May 21, 1902. His father died when Earl was only eighteen months old. The Averill family, mother and sons, all went to work to scrape out a living. As a young boy, Earl would play baseball in a converted potato patch. The neighborhood boys had pulled out the stumps, cleared the rocks, and there was a perfect diamond to play on. They fashioned baseballs from old shoes and played until the makeshift balls fell apart. Snohomish did not have any organized baseball for Earl to get involved with. As a freshman in high school he attempted to make the team, but a problem with his throwing arm kept him on the sidelines. Soon Earl would quit high school and go to work on road crews, hauling lumber, and anything else he could find to earn a few bucks. All the physical labor helped him develop a large set of shoulders and strong arms that would come in handy in the near future.

A few years later, the owner of the local pool hall determined that the town should have a baseball club. Averill got a chance to play and immediately earned a reputation as a tremendous hitter and outfielder. The Snohomish Bearcats did not pay their players, but the pool hall owner passed the hat after games. He kept most of the money for himself, but Earl usually pocketed a small share when the hat was full. There is a story that one day Averill belted an important game-winning home run. Before he left the field the excited spectators presented him with a total of fifty dollars in coin. No doubt, the men in the stands had a few bets out on the winning team.

In the early days of the twentieth century, few baseball scouts found their way to Snohomish. The scouting business was fairly unorganized and likely to be hit-and-miss. If you played baseball in places like Bellingham, Everett, and the surrounding area, chances were you were likely to stay there. Team officials and managers relied on tips from fans, former players, and sportswriters to augment any scouts they may have had on the payroll. The likelihood of a team in Chicago, Boston, or New York discovering a prospect hundreds or thousands of miles away was slim.

Earl Averill found himself in a difficult situation. No matter how well he played for the Snohomish Bearcats, he had little chance of being noticed. The local folks realized Earl had a rare talent that might just enable him to earn a living playing professional baseball. In the early 1920s they took up a collection and gave Earl enough traveling money to get him on a train to Seattle. Once there, he would report to the ball club for a tryout. The Snohomish fans believed it would be just a matter of time for Earl to be in Major Leagues.

To everyone's shock and anger, the Seattle manager deemed that the new kid was another small-town boy and sent him packing. Averill was just about average height and weighed somewhere between 150 and 160 pounds. The Seattle boss took a quick glance and believed Earl did not have the look of a ballplayer. Several years later he would kick himself for the hasty decision. Averill hopped on a train back to Snohomish, wondering if he would ever get his chance.

Even though the Seattle trip went poorly, Averill was not the type to throw in the towel. In 1924 he saved a few dollars and loaded his ancient Oldsmobile for a trip south to San Francisco. He brought his glove, bats, and uniform in hopes of getting another tryout, this time with the San Francisco Seals. Regardless of his skills, Earl did not have any formal training in the art of baseball. He knew little of fundamentals, which the Seals coaches noticed right away. They did recognize his skill at driving a baseball and his cannon of a throwing arm. He was not ready for the Pacific Coast League, but he was signed to a contract and sent to the Bellingham club for the summer. Back in a familiar setting, he played well, learning how to throw to the right base and hit the cutoff man. For his efforts he received fifteen dollars per game.

The next year, the Seals retained their rights to Earl, transferring him to a club in Montana. He blossomed there, hitting .430 for the season. San Francisco had Lloyd Waner, the younger brother of Paul, playing center field. Waner did not hit well there, which led the Seals to seek another outfielder to replace him. In 1926 it would be Earl Averill.

The fans back in Snohomish had to be ecstatic that one of their own was a step away from the big leagues. Earl became one of the best all-around players on the West Coast. The Seals had a superb outfield with Averill, Smead Jolley, and Roy Johnson. Before long the trio began attracting scouts by the dozens. Billy Evans did not hesitate, and the Indians finally got a center fielder the likes of which they had not seen since Tris Speaker.

While those in the Cleveland front office were congratulating themselves, a slight problem developed. Averill informed the Seals he wanted a piece of the action: part of the sale price. Some ball-players who were sold for a considerable amount of money took a hard stand with management. A number of them believed they were responsible for the sale in the first place and should be cut in on the deal. The ones who had been around a while knew to ask for a clause in their contract that guaranteed part of the sale price. This was done in the event the player was sold to a Major League team. Ultimately, most of the players had almost no leverage with the owners on anything and a situation like this was one of the few chances to cash in.

Averill made it absolutely clear to the Seals he was not reporting to Cleveland until he got his share. One point in his favor was that the Seals had originally signed him without having to pay another club. Averill came to them as a free agent and real bargain. On the Seals' side was the contract, which did not have any language spelling out that they would have to pay Earl extra if he landed with the big leagues.

The uncomfortable situation prompted action from Billy Evans. Once again he boarded a train for the demanding cross-country trip to San Francisco. Upon arrival he met with both parties and found a way to end the crisis. With the Seals now out of the picture, Evans went over some spring training details with his new player. He needed to order bats for Averill and rolled his eyes when Earl told him he only used a forty-four-ounce bat. The heaviest bat in the American League was owned by Babe Ruth and that weighed forty ounces. Evans tried to explain that a lot of the pitchers in the majors threw fairly hard and a forty-four-ounce bat would not cut it. Averill would not be moved. He told his boss that, if anybody could throw the ball by him, maybe he would consider a lighter one. Averill did not lack confidence in his ability, a trait that would carry him a long way.

In the first week of December, Evans and Peckinpaugh traveled to Toronto for the minor-league winter meetings. It was a time to catch up with old friends and maybe buy a player or two. Evans did not waste a moment in purchasing thirty-four-year-old pitcher Jimmy Zinn from Kansas City. The Indians wanted to add an experienced pitcher to the staff to complement such youngsters as Willis Hudlin and, possibly, minor-league hurler Wes Ferrell. Zinn had won forty-eight games the previous two seasons and did have some big-league experience with Pittsburgh and Brooklyn.

With the business completed, Evans and Peckinpaugh spent time chatting with old friends, including Tris Speaker, Steve O'Neill, and former Cleveland Spider Jesse Burkett. Speaker was present as the new manager of the International League's Newark Bears, while O'Neill was set to manage the same league's Toronto Maple Leafs. They swapped humorous stories about their playing days and incidents that had happened on the diamond. The best story told was about Joe Cantillon, the former umpire and manager. One day Cantillon brought two friends with him to Comiskey Park in Chicago. When they reached the ticket taker Cantillon said, "These are two friends of mine. I'd like you to pass 'em in." The ticket man yelled upstairs to Charles Comiskey, "How about passing a couple of friends of Mr. Cantillon?" The reply came down for everybody to hear: "It's a lie! No umpire has got two friends!"

Attending the Toronto meeting were the Cleveland scouts, Cy Slapnicka, Bill Rapp, and former Naps Bill Bradley and Charlie Hickman. Bradley was an excellent third baseman, while Hickman was a good-hitting slow runner nicknamed "Piano Legs." These four gentlemen were responsible for covering the entire United States. Despite their enormous territories, each scout would find some first-rate prospects in the coming years.

The Cleveland club either owned or had working agreements with four minor-league franchises. They owned outright the Frederick, Maryland, team of the Blue Ridge League. This was Class D ball, where the most inexperienced recruits would go. They had working agreements with Terre Haute and Decatur of the Three-I League, which was Class B, and with the New Orleans club in Class AA, or one step from the majors. With these four clubs, the Indians could shuttle players back and forth and keep close watch throughout the season.

Once the Toronto gathering ended, the Indians contingent moved on to Chicago for the American League meetings. Alva Bradley was already there, waiting for his top men to arrive. Here in the Windy City was where any possible major trades might occur. Dozens of names were thrown about, but nothing eye-opening took place. The Indians announced the George Uhle trade to Detroit, and that was the big moment for them. The team owners did reach an agreement to start the regular season on April 16, a week later than the previous year, and set a date of September 29 to finish the campaign. The late start was agreed upon due to the poor weather in early April. A week's delay might not help much, but the owners hoped there might be a few days of sunshine rather than Midwest snow flurries: a few degrees up the thermometer would likely bring out more fans. The owners rarely failed to find ways to improve the take at the gate.

While the Indians continued to improve their club, news came that Western Reserve University had invited Yale to play a football game in the new Cleveland stadium. Ground had not been broken yet, but the proposed game was to be played in 1930. The local college was rumored to be negotiating a home-and-away series with the mighty Ohio State Buckeyes. Ambitious college grads in the area were contacting their former schools to schedule games at the new stadium. Among the colleges being courted were Syracuse, Nebraska, and Cornell. City Manager Hopkins was elated at the news. He had visions of 80,000 fans packing his new facility, not to mention the downtown hotels and restaurants. His stadium plan might just be exactly what his city needed.

Near the end of December, Hopkins announced some details about the new facility He wanted a study done to preserve the harmony of the lakefront. He had no intention of the stadium being built at a crazy angle that might detract from the buildings and pedestrian mall that extended north from Public Square. He contracted with Osborne Engineering Company, the builders of League Park, to provide the city with exact dimensions of the stadium. Once those were completed, the city engineer could determine the amount of excavating needed for the foundation. All those involved believed it would take one to two years to complete the project. Soon the bonds would be put up for sale, funds accumulated, and the digging would commence. The probability of any last-minute roadblocks to delay the project seemed remote at best. It seemed that 1929 would be a good year for the city of Cleveland.

Chapter 4

TROUBLE AHEAD

The new year in Cleveland was like most new years of the past: loads of snow and temperatures falling below twenty degrees, although it was plenty warm inside the offices at League Park. The office staff of the Cleveland Indians had much to do, including the mailing of the 1929 player contracts. Most would be returned with signatures on them, a few would not. Holdouts in baseball were quite common, dating back to the National League of the 1890s. Players knew they were in for a difficult fight with management if they refused to sign. The guys that held out had few alternatives. The reserve clause kept them property of their club year after year, so owners simply had to reserve rights to each player on their roster on a yearly basis. The owners held all the cards and the players had a simple choice: sign, or don't play at all. Those who were in the superstar category—a Babe Ruth or a Rogers Hornsby—had some leverage to squeeze a few more dollars by holding out. The average Major Leaguer had little clout, with no agents or players union to assist them in negotiating. The great majority of disputes ended at the start of spring training, when an unhappy ballplayer would reluctantly sign and report to camp. Most had to play baseball to support their families and pay the mortgage. Other than Ty Cobb, who made a fortune in the stock market, there were few independently wealthy ballplayers.

A good example of an unhappy player was Cleveland pitcher Joe Shaute. He sent back his 1929 contract despite getting a raise. A year earlier, Shaute had an incentive-based contract. Any wins he registered above thirteen meant an additional $400 for each victory. Shaute argued that, by the time he got win number thirteen, the Indians had thrown in the towel for the season. Roger Peckinpaugh was playing rookies and minor-leaguers to see who, if anybody, might provide more help next year. Shaute did not win any further games in 1928 and blamed the makeshift lineups as the reason. He had expected to win several more games and cash in on his incentives. He wanted the Indians to make up for the situation by raising him another thousand or two. That would not happen, and Shaute gave up the fight in early March and reported to spring training. He simply had no other action to pursue.

Alva Bradley had developed a progressive approach in contract disputes. If a player refused to sign, Bradley would take the necessary time to study the previous year's stats and contributions of the holdout. This meant both on the field and off. If the player was a good citizen and had made positive contributions at the ballpark, a raise would be offered. As part of this policy, the Cleveland owner made it utterly clear that there would be no more negotiating: the new contract was final. Billy Evans claimed that the majority of players who quickly signed their contract, indeed got a raise from Bradley. The owner was, in any case, decidedly more generous than his counterparts in the American League. As a result, the Cleveland players understood his policy and thought twice before staying home.

In addition to handing out raises, the Cleveland front office had paid out a huge amount on new players. Gordon Cobbledick wrote in his column that the team had spent major dollars: "When Bradley and his associates took over the Cleveland club last winter he said he would spend money and he has spent plenty. A considerable estimate would place the Indians' expenditures for new players in the past year at a quarter million dollars." A chunk of that money went for Earl Averill and Dick Porter, but the team signed a total of twenty new ballplayers for the 1929 season. Cobbledick claimed his sources revealed that Cleveland had spent $20,000 for Jimmy Zinn, who was a gamble at best. The Johnny Miljus debacle of the previous season had cost $17,000. Prospects from college and minor-league rosters made up the remaining costs. If that was not enough, the Indians' agreement with Terre Haute called for them to make up any of the farm club's deficits, which in 1928 amounted to $14,000. By all accounts, Alva Bradley had truly made a serious commitment toward building a winning baseball team.

In February, Billy Evans announced that his team would remain in New Orleans for the duration of spring training. After consulting with manager Peckinpaugh, it was decided the team would be in better shape by not doing any traveling until the regular season. The Indians had only six exhibition games scheduled, two each against Cincinnati, Brooklyn, and the New York Giants. A handful of games were also arranged with the New Orleans Pelicans. Any other contests would be intra-squad. Evans thought the train rides and traveling in general were tiring for his ballplayers and he wanted them at peak condition by the season opener on April 16. Some of the ball clubs trained out west in Arizona and California. The temperatures were great, but Evans believed the thousands of miles of travel negated the positive effects of ninety-degree weather. Sportswriters and fans alike were curious to see if Evans's innovative theory would pan out in the campaign ahead.

A day before the journey to New Orleans, Evans orchestrated another major deal. He sent third-string catcher Chick Autry—and cash—to the Chicago White Sox for left fielder August "Bibb" Falk. The trade surprised the baseball world, as Falk had been a star in Chicago since the 1920 season. He was a bona fide .300 hitter with a high of .352 in 1924. Falk was now part of a talented outfield that included Charlie Jamieson, Earl Averill, and Dick Porter. These players had a real chance to surpass the great Cleveland outfield of 1920 consisting of Tris Speaker, Elmer Smith, Joe Wood, and the now-veteran Jamieson.

Bibb Falk was born in Austin, Texas, on July 5, 1899. As a young man he carried bats for several Texas minor-league clubs. In 1917 he enrolled in the University of Texas, where he played tackle on the football team and pitched and played outfield for the baseball squad. He was all–Southwest Conference in football and batted over .400 in baseball. The White Sox signed him in July 1920 and brought him directly to Chicago. He sat on the bench for two months but became the regular left fielder when Joe Jackson was suspended for his part in the Black Sox scandal. Falk soon developed into a .300 hitter for the Sox with banner seasons in 1924 and 1926. In the latter year he batted .345 with eight home runs and 108 RBIs. Falk had some bad moments in 1928 and started telling anybody who would listen that he wanted out of Chicago. Billy Evans had attempted to acquire Falk after the 1927 season, and a year later the White Sox were listening. Evans offered $20,000 and catcher Autry. Faced with a likely holdout, Chicago agreed to the trade, giving the Indians a terrific outfield. The Indians were no longer a bottom feeder in the American League.

With an active off-season concluded, the Indians boarded a train on the Nickel Plate Railroad bound for New Orleans. For the first time in many seasons there was a degree of optimism among the players. Catcher Luke Sewell told reporters, "If I could choose from the sixteen clubs of both major leagues, I'd want to play with the Indians. They are going somewhere." They were certainly headed to New Orleans, but Sewell believed his club had a chance to move up in the American League standings. It would be a monumental feat to pass the Yankees or the Athletics, but a higher place in the standings was possible.

The early days in Louisiana were drenched with rain and Heinemann Park turned into a lagoon. The team stayed off the field and started in on calisthenics. One day, the boys got a heavy medicine ball and began heaving it at one another, and Luke Sewell fired the ball at the stomach of Joe Shaute. On impact, the oversized ball exploded, showering everybody with the stuffing. That ended the calisthenics for the afternoon.

The new players in camp slowly got acquainted with their teammates. They were a diverse bunch from all parts of the United States. Ballplayers of the 1920s were more educated than their counterparts from previous eras. Each season, more and more players were coming from the college ranks instead of working their way up in the minor leagues. There were fewer stories of country boys who had never seen a big city before or ridden on a train. On the Cleveland roster there was pitcher Walter Miller, a civil engineer, Bibb Falk, an expert in the stock market and active investor, and Luke Sewell, who had his undergraduate degree from the University of Alabama and was just one semester away from completing his master's degree.

Ken Holloway owned a ranch in the southwest. Willis Hudlin built ham radios for amateur operators around the country. The modern baseball player was beginning to emerge, a much different figure than the older generation of hard-drinking and hard-fighting men who shocked the crowds with their colorful language.

The new method of training seemed to be working for the Indians. There were few injuries, and regular poundings of the New Orleans Pelicans. At the end of March they destroyed their minor-league club, 19–7. Carl Lind had two doubles and a triple. Wes Ferrell, the twenty-one-year-old pitcher, threw four innings of relief. He was unbelievably wild, walking eight batters. Even so, he managed to wiggle out of trouble, something noted by Roger Peckinpaugh. A later exhibition appearance against Cincinnati convinced Peck he had a new pitcher to add to the staff. In four innings of work, Wes gave up one run on two hits in a 7–6 loss. The other Indians pitchers were hit freely, but the Reds could not get to Ferrell.

While the Indians were gearing up for a new season, a troubling event occurred in the United States. On March 25, the stock market took a deep plunge, which caused a panic among investors. For years, Wall Street had been sailing along with positive results. For most of the 1920s, investing in the stock market was almost a guarantee to make money. People who knew little about stocks and bonds put their money in the market. If you did not have the cash to invest, you could buy on margin, putting in a down payment of 10 to 20 percent of the stock's value and owing the rest. The risk was that if the stock did not perform well and dipped below the value of the purchase price, the buyer was responsible for the entire amount. Despite the chance of a margin call, buyers ignored the peril and continued to purchase on credit. When the twenty-fifth rolled around and stocks fell, a considerable percentage of investors could not pay what they owed. To avoid a serious crisis, National City Bank in New York announced it was allocating $25 million in loans. This action stopped any further panic, but did not serve as a warning to people heavily over-financed. The thrill ride continued, even though it had hit a serious bump in the road.

Spring training eventually turned into Opening Day, much to the delight of the eager Cleveland fans. League Park was again completely sold out. The oddsmakers in New York had the Indians listed as a 50-to-1 shot at the pennant, with 10-to-1 odds to finish in third place. As expected, the Yankees and Athletics were the favorites to claim the top spots. If you were an audacious gambler you might put money down on the Boston Red Sox, who came in at 1,000-to-1 odds to end up on top. Damon Runyon, in his syndicated column, offended the Cleveland fans by picking the Indians to finish seventh. Runyon was clearly not a first-class handicapper. He had the Philadelphia Athletics in fourth place while most writers had them fighting for the pennant. Stuart Bell of the *Cleveland Press* believed the locals would win eighty games. He based that on the new pitchers, who he figured on bringing another fifteen to twenty wins to the table.

Billy Evans sat in his upstairs office, dreaming of the new stadium and the prospect of filling double or triple the number of the twenty-five thousand seats available at the current home grounds. A full house at League Park would net the club roughly $20,000, but a crowd of just forty to fifty thousand at the new site would bring the team $35,000 to $40,000. No wonder Evans had dollar signs floating around his brain.

Alva Bradley took out a newspaper ad urging Clevelanders to support their team. The three-quarter-page ad spoke of all the changes his regime had made: "In all probability Never In The History Of Baseball has the personnel of a team been so changed from one year to another as the Cleveland Club of 1929. A dozen old faces eliminated and a dozen new ones added. Come out and help us put it out!" Bradley had really done his part. Now the focus shifted to Roger Peckinpaugh and how he would guide his team.

WTAM Radio reached a deal with the Indians to broadcast all the weekday games, beginning with the opener. Tom Manning was back in the booth to do all the play-by-play. The station had found a sponsor for the entire season, the automobile dealership Reeke-Nash Motors. The advertising element was fast becoming a staple of radio broadcasts. Soon, Manning would have his hands full trying to squeeze in the numerous commercials.

Radio listeners in Cleveland also had the choice of tuning in WHK, which was carrying Columbia Broadcasting's national feed of the Yankees–Red Sox opener. As an added bonus there would be a cut-in to the Washington-Philadelphia game in the nation's capital. Fans could hear the description of President Herbert Hoover throwing out the first pitch. Avid fans were taking the initial steps toward the concept of channel surfing.

The weather for Cleveland's Opening Day against Detroit was better suited for a football game, with gray skies and temperatures in the upper thirties. To protect against the wind and cold, the fans arrived wearing heavy coats (including fur in the more expensive seats) and carrying blankets. There were unconfirmed reports of flasks being passed around the stands. At game time there were nearly nine thousand empty chairs: many fans decided to stay home rather than freeze to death. The left-field bleachers were all but deserted. Those staying home missed a rousing contest between the Tigers and Indians.

After the ceremonial first pitch and flowers for Peckinpaugh, the Indians jogged onto the field in crisp new uniforms. The jerseys had black piping and a black *C* on the chest. Each player had a ferocious-looking Indian on the left sleeve. The socks were black with narrow white stripes. Meanwhile, it wasn't just the uniforms that had changed. The Indians lineup bore little resemblance to the one in the previous year's opening game. Only Joe and Luke Sewell and Charlie Jamieson had started the previous season. Joe was now playing third base, as he could no longer cover the ground at shortstop. There were three new infielders and two more in the outfield.

The Tigers opened the scoring against Joe Shaute with a run in the top of the first inning: Harry Rice singled and went to second on a walk to Charlie Gehringer, then a sacrifice fly and an infield out brought him home. The excitement really began in the bottom of the inning when Earl Averill came to bat. There were two outs when Averill walked to the plate for his first Major League appearance. Detroit pitcher Earl Whitehill threw two strikes past the highly touted rookie. The third pitch was over the plate and Averill smacked a rising line drive over the right-field wall. The Cleveland fans jumped out of their seats when the baseball cleared the high screen by six feet and landed far up Lexington Avenue. Averill trotted around the bases to thunderous applause. He would always remember this trip to the plate as his finest moment while playing for Cleveland. Detroit scored two more in the third inning: Harry Rice was on first when Charlie Gehringer blasted a home run. Cleveland came back with a run in the fourth on a single by Charlie Jamieson. The Tigers added another run in the sixth to go up 4–2.

The score remained there until the eighth inning, when the Indians pushed across a single run. Willis Hudlin entered in relief and Detroit went out in the top of the ninth still holding a one-run lead. With three outs left, the home crowd began to make a significant amount of noise. Lew Fonseca drilled his third hit, a double off the right-field wall. Jamieson reached on a bunt single, Fonseca advancing to third. Luke Sewell drove a clutch base hit to center field, sending the game to extra innings. Neither team did anything until the bottom of the eleventh when Luke Sewell singled. Willis Hudlin flied to center. After a walk to reserve shortstop Ray Gardner, Carl Lind lined a double to deep left field, scoring Sewell with the game winner. Derby hats went flying through the stands as the fans celebrated a thrilling 5–4 win. This was not looking like a seventh-place ball club.

That night, the Hotel Winton hosted a meet and greet with old-timers from the Spiders and Naps. The honored guests in the chic Rainbow Room included Cy Young and Chief Zimmer from the Spiders. Representing the Cleveland Naps were Bill Bradley, Elmer Flick, Terry Turner, and Earl Moore. Two of the Delahanty brothers, Frank and Jimmy, were on hand, along with Patrick "Paddy" Livingston from the old Athletics and the Naps. A full orchestra provided the dance music while fans mingled with the popular stars of the past. The much-admired Jack Lynch's Rainbow Girls performed during the evening. It had been a great day in Cleveland with hopefully many more to come.

The next day featured a matchup of the two recently traded pitchers, George Uhle and Ken Holloway. Uhle showed his old team a thing or two by beating the Indians 15–3. The only difficulty he had was giving up another tremendous home run to Earl Averill. The Tigers drove Holloway from the mound by scoring seven runs in the first two innings. Manager Peckinpaugh went to the bullpen early, calling for Wes Ferrell to relieve. In his first significant action as an Indian, Ferrell pitched a strong four and two-thirds innings. He did not allow a run, giving up only three hits. Gordon Cobbledick marveled at what he saw. He wrote in his column, "The big kid has a terrific fastball and a fine curve together with excellent control. Moreover he uses his head when he's out there in the box." Manager Peckinpaugh indicated Ferrell would soon get his chance to join the starting rotation.

Even though the season was just two days old, Cleveland fans were starting to notice Averill and Ferrell. One was pounding out line drives all over League Park while the other showed some exceptional pitching. The new players brought instant excitement to the field, which was surely good for business. With these young stars in the lineup, the Indians really had a chance to win their share of games. Over the course of the season, the American League would feel their impact.

Wes Ferrell was born on February 2, 1908, to Rufus and Alice Ferrell. The family lived in Greensboro, North Carolina, where his father worked for the Southern Railway. After twenty-five years of devoted labor, Rufus bought a large allotment of land just outside of Greensboro. In 1914, after some fiddling with the land, he added a herd of cows and started a dairy farm. The property had a great quantity of wide-open spaces where the seven Ferrell brothers learned to play baseball. They had an amazing team, with older brother Rick catching and other brother George in the outfield. Later, Rick would begin his Major League career with the St. Louis Browns. George played many years for Memphis in the Southern Association, compiling over two thousand hits before he retired.

Wes played high school basketball and baseball, then enrolled in the Oak Ridge Academy in Guilford County. Soon he drew the attention of scouts, including Bill Rapp of the Cleveland Indians. Initially Rapp traveled to Oak Ridge to see another player, but quickly turned his attention to Ferrell. A contract was offered to Wes, but he turned it down, saying he wanted to attend college. For one reason or another, the college plans did not materialize. In the summer of 1927, Ferrell was in Massachusetts, pitching for East Douglas, a highly regarded semipro team. The Detroit Tigers looked at several of the players, including Wes. They did not offer him a contract, a mistake that would come back to haunt them. Later that summer, Cleveland scout Charlie Hickman stopped by East Douglas and offered him a deal. Wes was ready to sign, but told Hickman he would only do business with Bill Rapp. Apparently the other Cleveland scout had made a good impression when he visited Ferrell in North Carolina. Arrangements were made, Rapp caught a train to Massachusetts, and the Indians signed a great prospect.

In the spring of 1928 Wes reported to Terre Haute. From the start of the season it became quite evident he was on his way to stardom. He won twenty games for the Tots while losing only eight. He pitched 240 innings and was good with the stick, hitting two home runs and batting .267. At the end of the Three-I season the Indians brought Wes to Cleveland, where he made several mop-up appearances. The following year he joined the Indians veterans working out in New Orleans. He showed a wealth of promise, but Billy Evans thought another year in the minors would make Wes a "wonder." The young stud would have none of it. He told Evans, "Wonder nothing. I am up here to stick and before June you'll be glad to have me stop some of these big league hitters." Bravado, yes, but Evans had to be impressed with the attitude. He agreed with Peckinpaugh to send Ferrell north to Cleveland.

Wes rented an apartment near League Park where many of the newsboys gathered to sell their papers. He became friendly with the boys, playing baseball with them in the evenings. Each member of the Indians got free tickets to all the home games, and Wes made it a point to give his passes to the boys in the neighborhood. Even before he established himself on the mound, he gained a loyal following. When he had free time he played the guitar, singing the popular country songs of the day. At times he brought the guitar to the clubhouse, where he entertained his teammates and sportswriters. Ferrell was the All-American boy, except for one shortcoming: he had an explosive temper.

Though nobody had seen it yet, Wes had difficulty accepting any setbacks, particularly those that happened on the mound. He would routinely tear his glove to shreds when he gave up a key hit or somebody behind him committed an error. His tirades in the locker room became legendary. A story circulated that Ferrell was in the clubhouse attempting to rip a new glove. While the rest of the Indians watched with amusement, Wes yelled for the clubhouse boy to get him a pair of scissors. He cut up the glove until he could tear it up properly. For the moment, his bad temper was somewhat harmless, but in later years the outbursts would become a real concern.

With the season underway, City Manager Hopkins issued a statement that Frank Walker, a prominent local architect, would design the plans for the stadium. Walker and his firm had conceived most of the important city buildings, including the Cleveland Public Library, city hall, and the Public Auditorium. The architect was a longtime member of the City Planning Commission and the logical choice for the ultra-important assignment. Still, a hitch in the plans developed when it was discovered that Walker had a conflict of interest. As a member of the City Planning Commission he was a city employee, even though he received no compensation for his work. The city charter stated, "No employee of the city shall have a financial interest direct or indirect in any contract with the city." Walker offered his resignation to Hopkins, who refused it. His idea was that all monies for the stadium would be paid directly to Osborne Engineering, which in turn would pay Walker. This raised some eyebrows, and Walker offered his resignation a second time, which Hopkins accepted. Now the architect was free to design the stadium without any repercussions.

With Walker no longer working for the city, the Planning Commission approved the specific site for the stadium. Its west end would be behind the county courthouse in line with West 3rd Street. This position left a view of the lake from the pedestrian mall north of Public Square, while blocking from view the unsightly railroad tracks that detracted from the lakefront. The structure would be 720 feet wide and 1,102 feet in length. Two walking ramps were being considered, one leading down to West 3rd Street and another to West 9th. The process began moving forward without any serious issues, with plans for beginning construction in the summer.

At the end of April the Indians announced a day to honor Charlie Jamieson, planned for Saturday, May 11. Fans were asked to send cash or checks to the Cleveland offices at League Park or to the *Cleveland Plain Dealer, Press,* or *News.* Alva Bradley approved a $500 donation to kick things off. Within days the fund soared to the $3,000 mark. Most of the contributions were between one and five dollars, but the volume was overwhelming. Jamieson was tremendously popular with the Cleveland fans. He played a big part in the 1920 season, when he batted .319 and established himself as a premier lead-off hitter. Jamie was a throw-in when Connie Mack sent

Larry Gardner and Elmer Meyers to Cleveland for outfielder Bobby Roth and a prospect. The Indians thought little of Jamieson, but by 1920 he had beaten out Jack Graney for the left-field job. The dimensions of League Park created a sun field in Jamie's territory, but he learned how to adapt to the blinding conditions. The left-field bleachers were home to the rowdiest fans in Cleveland. They paid their fifty cents each game and were quick to harass anybody who messed up on the diamond. On the other hand, they never booed Jamieson, as he played flawless ball in left. In 1923 he batted a sparkling .345 while leading the American League in hits with 222. The following year he upped the average to .359, second only to Babe Ruth. His 213 base hits were second to Sam Rice of the Senators.

Now at age thirty-six it was time for Cleveland to say thanks. Fans who attended Jamieson Day received a mini-pamphlet titled *Jamie*. One of the passages read, "Eleven years of loyal hustling service he has given to Cleveland, and the town is taking the opportunity at last to tell him his work hasn't gone unnoticed." The large turnout of fans gave him a thundering ovation, while Jamieson waved to the crowd and accepted his check for $3,200, just about a half-year's pay. Unfortunately, the Athletics were in town and Lefty Grove was pitching. The Indians trailed 4–1 going into the bottom of the eighth inning. With runners at first and second, hot-hitting Lew Fonseca came to bat. The infield was playing back, looking for a double play. Fonseca laid down a bunt and beat the throw to first base. The crowd was shocked when umpire William Campbell called him out. What the fans did not realize was that Fonseca had stepped out of the base line while running and was automatically declared out. Manager Peckinpaugh came storming out of the dugout to argue the ruling. Within a moment, Peck got thrown out of the game and later received a five-game suspension. The booing continued and then a lone fan heaved a soda pop bottle (they were back on the menu) at Campbell. Soon the bottles were flying all around the infield. One errant throw hit third-base umpire Emmett Ormsby square in the head, knocking him unconscious. A hurried phone call went from the League Park office to the 55th Precinct nearby. Within minutes a squad of police covered the infield. The bottle throwing quickly ceased, but the third umpire on the field, Clarence "Brick" Owens, picked up a bottle and waved it defiantly at the grandstand. This prompted a second assault of missiles, though no further targets were struck. The police stayed on the grounds to provide an escort for Campbell at the conclusion of the game. Billy Evans and trainer Max "Lefty" Weisman carried the dazed Ormsby off the field. The Indians' grounds crew seized wheelbarrows and dashed onto the field to pick up the three hundred or so pop bottles. The game continued, with Philadelphia winning 4–2.

The incident was déjà vu for Evans. Back in 1912, the former umpire was involved in a similar riot on the League Park grounds. In the bottom of the eighth inning he called two strikes on the Naps batter, Hank Butcher. Words were exchanged that resulted in Evans tossing the livid player. The fans booed, then a number of them climbed out of their seats to confront Evans. He fought three different fans before police could clear the field and haul Evans to the umpire's dressing room. What must have gone through his head when he carried off Ormsby he did not speak of.

Stuart Bell gave his opinion of the riot in the *Cleveland Press*. He took a lighthearted approach to the entire incident, writing, "We are not in favor of riots accompanied by assaults. If pop must be sold in ballparks it should be sold in soft rubber bottles so that when the containers are thrown they will bound but not injure." He believed the fans who threw the bottles were not the best sort of customer and only had the guts due to the high screen fence separating them from the players. Bell thought that the riots woke up the fans to a great intensity and believed each ballpark was entitled to one riot per season.

The Indians' team doctor examined the injured party and found no cuts or bleeding, probably just a mild concussion. Ormsby was able to slowly walk and take a deserved rest in his room at the Statler Hotel. He was back on his feet in twenty-four hours.

This was a day Charlie Jamieson would long remember. He received a large check and much applause from the fans and congratulations from his teammates. Jamie had a good day in the field and banged out two singles. It all went south in the eighth inning, though, when the bottle attack began, and Jamieson Day came to be remembered for the riot and not the ballplayer. The best-laid plans sometimes go awry, and this day was a prime example. Jamie really did deserve better.

While the Indians attempted to get over the .500 mark, some troubling events took place. On June 1, the price of wheat fell to below a dollar a bushel, the lowest price in sixteen years. There was a glut of wheat around the entire world, leaving American farmers with far too much product to sell. There were no quick solutions to alleviate the problem. The US government recommended farmers drop their production by 30 percent, which would eventually cause a world shortage and a rise in prices. But this could not be done overnight, and farmers throughout the country had an extremely difficult time of it.

The flooded wheat market had little effect in the Cleveland area. However, the market crash of the past March and the current wheat problem were indications that rough financial times could be ahead. Most of the population took scant notice and continued to invest and spend money all over town. The Roaring Twenties still had a ways to go before they came to an abrupt halt.

Another upsetting event occurred when the news of a lawsuit against the building of the stadium became public. On May 20, 1929, Andrew Meyer, with help from two attorneys, filed for an injunction to stop any construction of the facility. The suit was filed in Common Pleas Court, case number 318019. Meyer was a local political activist with an agenda that was certainly anti-Hopkins. He claimed to represent the people of Cleveland in their concern that the actual cost of the new stadium would exceed the $2.5 million figure promised.

Meyer and his attorneys listed eight points as the bulk of their argument. The first maintained that the city had no right to issue bonds for the construction of a municipal stadium. The second point claimed that the city did not own the land in question and therefore had no right to build there. They termed the ownership of lakefront land both "questionable and cloudy."

The next point asserted that, if indeed the city had title to the land, it had been designated per a previous ordinance for improvements to navigation and commerce only. A stadium had nothing to do with shipping or building ports and warehouses. Once the stadium was constructed, it would leave little space for any kind of new waterfront projects or activities. This argument did have some validity to it.

No Money, No Beer, No Pennants

The subsequent point was the most interesting of all. The plaintiffs argued that the original resolution for the stadium dated back to August 20, 1928. It had stated, "Provided for such bonds to construct a stadium on the lakefront for the proper accommodation of the public and the preservation of the public health and welfare." This language was removed when the resolution was placed on the November 6 ballot. Meyer and his lawyers believed that no consideration was being given to the public. One of the later points contended that the stadium was to be built for private enterprises only. The voters of Cleveland would not benefit in any material way, except if they wanted to watch a baseball or football game.

On July 18 the parties were in court before Judge Homer Powell. Opening statements were offered by Meyer's attorney, Marvin Harrison. He stated, "The city is without power to issue bonds for a stadium; the city is without sufficient title to the land where the city proposes to build the structure; if the stadium is built on the artificially filled land the city would be violating the provisions for the use of the land for 'the aid of navigation.'" City Law Director Carl Shuler refuted Harrison's claims and maintained the city had title to the land and had seen to it that the costs would not exceed the bond issue passed by the voters.

Depositions filed two weeks prior showed that part of the site chosen was on land that the city had contracted to sell to the New York Central, Big Four, and Pennsylvania Railroads. The city in spite of this argued that an agreement had been obtained by William Hopkins to modify the contract to cut the number of tracks from forty-four to sixteen to permit all the room needed for construction of the stadium.

City Manager Hopkins took the stand for a nerve-wracking interrogation by Harrison. The questioning concerned whether all costs were included in the estimate of expenses for building the pedestrian ramps and bridges to the lakefront, as well as the large parking lots that would be needed. Hopkins claimed the parking venues would not cost anything, and told the court that contracts had been drawn up with the railroad companies to handle the bridges at no charge to the city. If necessary, Hopkins believed, they could still funnel people to the stadium without building any ramps. Harrison then blasted the witness for making verbal agreements with the railroads for the sale and exchange of lands if needed. An angry Hopkins replied, "The agreement is a gentlemen's agreement and will be carried out. And the stadium would extend only 150 not 200 feet into railroad property, should the agreement fail."

The second attorney for Meyer, Edgar Byers, charged that the stadium was being built for the convenience of the Cleveland baseball club. Law Director Carl Shuler objected to the charge but was overruled by Judge Powell. Byers wanted to determine if a contract had been made with the Indians. Hopkins repeated what Alva Bradley had stated months before, that if the city council would draw up an agreement to lease the stadium, he preferred that approach rather than building his own park. Hopkins advised the court that he had no power to perfect a lease; only the city council could draw up the agreement. The city proposed to charge the Indians $50,000 annually, with an additional charge of fifteen cents for every admission over six hundred thousand. Hopkins stressed that amateur baseball clubs would have use of the stadium as well.

Hopkins was excused and Virgil Allen, representing Osborn Engineering Co., took the stand. Harrison was able to get testimony that the original cost estimate did not include the engineer's contract, insurance, and workmen's compensation costs. Allen estimated that the cost might well rise as much as 12 percent, or $300,000. This boosted the total to $2.8 million, which made a significant difference. The hearing concluded with Judge Powell advising both parties that a ruling could be expected in approximately one month.

Why would Andrew Meyer go to such great lengths to stop the stadium project? He had maintained he was representing the people who voted against the bond issue. One probable reason is that Meyer planned to run for city council in the November election. This was quite a way to get publicity. He would run on a platform dedicated to removing Hopkins from office. He required some clout to do so and the lawsuit would certainly embarrass the city manager to a great degree. Nevertheless, to stop construction of a stadium that the majority of voters had approved bordered on madness. There were public forums to address, letters to the three newspapers, and other means to express one's opposition. Meyer had made certain that construction was held up indefinitely, and in the likelihood he lost the suit, there was an appeals process. The stadium project might remain in limbo for a year or possibly longer. It all depended on how far Meyer was prepared to go. To his credit, the taxpayers of Cleveland were now aware that the costs for the structure probably were going up a significant amount. Even so, his method of spreading the word was most inappropriate.

Throughout all the thorny proceedings, William Hopkins put on a happy face. His public comments were evenhanded and optimistic. He believed the conflict would end shortly and construction could begin in a reasonable amount of time. At the end of July he spoke at a meeting of the Lakewood Kiwanis Club, saying, "The stadium is temporarily checked by a legal proceeding. I don't think it will be delayed long." Ever the salesman, he added, "It will be more favorably located than any other stadium in the country." He emphasized that the facility would be within walking distance of all the downtown hotels. Whether or not Hopkins was mortified by the lawsuit is a matter of conjecture. The lakefront stadium would represent Hopkins's greatest achievement as city manager. The municipal airport stood a close second, but the modern stadium plan showed vision and smarts few other city or county officials had. It is not known whether, privately, Hopkins wanted to throttle Andrew Meyer. On the surface he appeared to be only a tad perturbed by the injunction.

Going into August, the Indians were beginning to show signs of life. They returned home with nine wins in their last eleven games. There was a four-game sweep of Washington, three out of four games with Boston, and two wins in three contests with the Yankees. Cleveland now owned a record of 53–47, which left them just a half-game behind St. Louis for third place. The pennant race was all but over, with Philadelphia ten games ahead of New York and twenty-one over the Indians.

On Saturday, August 10, the Yankees came to town to open a four-game series. Babe Ruth already had twenty-eight home runs for the season, but of more importance was his career total of 498. Fans swarmed the ticket windows at League Park, hoping to be in the grandstand when Babe stroked number five hundred. Ruth and his teammates always brought a large crowd, but this weekend was going to be a sellout. Approximately fifty thousand people bought tickets for Saturday and Sunday. They were not disappointed when on Saturday Babe connected for number 499, a solo shot in the eighth inning. The Yankees won the ball game, 4–2. That set the stage for Sunday's game, with ropes set up in the outfield for standing-room-only tickets.

While the Yankees were taking batting practice, Ruth had a brief meeting with Clay Folger, the head of security at the park. The Bambino told the policeman that, if he managed to hit number five hundred, he wanted the baseball as a memento. Folger, who had been on the job for over twenty years, assured the Yankee slugger that he and his staff were on the case.

The game began with Willis Hudlin on the mound for Cleveland. With fans still piling in, New York went down in order in the top of the first. Ruth, batting cleanup, would lead off the second inning. Fans that came to see the once-in-a-lifetime moment had to fidget in their seats a trifle longer.

While the Indians batted in the home half of the inning, James Geiser arrived at the ballpark. The Indians fan had driven all the way from New Philadelphia, a town south of Cleveland and about a three-hour drive away. He walked to the ticket window, hoping to still get a seat inside. At that moment there was a huge roar from the grandstand. Geiser looked up and saw a baseball clear the right-field screen and go bouncing down Lexington Avenue. He ran down the street, picked up the ball, and put it in his pocket. James had no idea the ball he retrieved was the five hundredth home run swatted by the Yankee home-run king. The Indians still had a policy that any person who retrieved a baseball hit out of League Park could exchange the ball for a free ticket. Geiser wanted to pay for a seat, but the clerk behind the ticket window offered a ticket for the ball. While James mulled it over, Clay Folger and his security crew burst through the gate and headed straight for the bewildered fan. They explained to the young man that the ball he retrieved was hit by Babe Ruth and the Yankee slugger wanted it back. Apparently, Geiser knew he had a most historic item. He graciously agreed to hand the ball over. Folger escorted him into the park and led him onto the field, directly to the Yankees dugout. The game had been momentarily stopped for Ruth to take a bow and wait for the baseball. Geiser stood in awe while he was introduced to baseball's greatest star. The Babe politely explained that the baseball meant a lot to him and he would like to have it. Geiser produced the ball and handed it to Ruth. A fountain pen and a new ball were hustled to the Yankee dugout. Ruth signed the unused ball and gave it to James. They shook hands, and when Geiser pulled his hand away there was a twenty-dollar bill attached. The long drive from New Philadelphia was most definitely worth it. Imagine what the folks in New Philadelphia would say.

The fans in attendance were treated to more fireworks. In the top of the fourth Lou Gehrig clubbed another home run to give the Yankees a 2–0 lead. The Indians did not hit any homers but pushed across three runs in the fourth inning to go up by a run. The big hit was a single by Johnny Hodapp that scored two runs. During the course of the season Carl Lind had faltered and Hodapp was now the regular second baseman. New York tied the game in the fifth on two singles and an error. In Cleveland's half of the fifth inning Earl Averill got his second hit and scored on Bibb Falk's drive to right field. The Indians now led 4–3. The Yankees came right back in the top of the sixth. Lou Gehrig walked and Ruth singled to center. Lazzeri walked to load the bases. Wills Hudlin was still toiling on the mound and gave up a double to Bob Meusel. New York took the lead again, 5–4. The Cleveland fans were seeing baseball at its finest, with both teams battling like a pennant was at stake.

The Indians came charging back in the bottom of the sixth. The Sewell brothers both singled, and with two out Earl Averill doubled to right field, his third hit of the game. Now with a 6–5 lead, Hudlin righted himself and held the Yankees the remaining three innings for a come-from-behind win. It was a special day at League Park for the twenty-five thousand fans who came to see the mighty Bambino establish a record that would stand for many years. Ed Bang of the *Cleveland News,* now the dean of Cleveland sportswriters, penned his impressions of the memorable game: "It was the five hundredth time in the Bambino's major league career that he catapulted a ball either out of a ball lot or so far removed from outfielders as to be able to negotiate four bases. It was his thirtieth home run of the current campaign, but that itself didn't mean so much to Babe as to achieve the five-hundred mark, one which undoubtedly never again will be attained by a ballplayer in the big time."

Bang and all the other sportswriters would eventually note Babe's 600th and 700th home runs. There was no other ballplayer in that era who rivaled Ruth's home-run record. When Ruth clubbed number 500, Cy Williams of the Philadelphia Phillies was a distant second at 246. He retired after the 1929 season with 251. Jimmy Foxx reached the 500 mark in 1941. Babe's career mark of 714 would stand until 1974 when the great Hank Aaron broke the seemingly untouchable record.

The Indians beat the Yankees on Monday to take sole possession of third place. Alva Bradley had to be grinning from ear to ear at what his boys had accomplished. Usually at this point in the season it was time to wave the flag and bring in the prospects for next year. The Indians were not going to overtake New York, but the team was playing at a high level for the first time in three years. The new guys on the team were largely responsible for the surge. Earl Averill and Bibb Falk were not Ruth and Gehrig, but they were clouting home runs at a fast clip. During an August game with the Tigers, Averill blasted his thirteenth home run, which struck the roof of a company on Lexington Avenue. Moments later Falk hit his thirteenth in nearly the same spot. James Doyle, writing in the *Plain Dealer*, joked that Averill had a deal with a roofing contractor. Averill would hit a shot out of the park and damage a homeowner's roof. The contractor would lurk nearby, visit the home, do the repairs, and pay Averill half the fee.

Humor aside, Averill was on pace to break Tris Speaker's record of seventeen in 1923. Falk had never been a slugger before, but the short porch in right field was an easy target for him. The total distance down the right field line stood at a shade less than three hundred feet. The only trick was to launch the ball over the towering right-field wall. If a left-handed batter could master the technique, home runs would follow in short order. Lew Fonseca did not hit the long ball, but maintained an average over .340 to rank in the top five of the American League hitters. Joe Sewell was having another .300 season, while Dick Porter on a part-time basis hit well during the latter part of the year.

Another reason for the Indians surge was the pitching of Willis Hudlin, Wes Ferrell, and Walter Miller. In mid-August the *Sporting News* pointed out that the three pitchers had each won eleven ball games, and each was performing well enough to win a bunch more. Miller surprised the Indians by pitching as capably as he did, but big things were expected of Hudlin and Ferrell. Though only twenty-one, Wes handled himself like a true veteran. He learned the habits of the American League hitters rather than trying to overpower them with fastballs. He constantly worked on his game to become a better pitcher. With a month and a half remaining in the season he still had a shot at twenty games. Johnny Miljus, the $17,000 man, put together a string of victories that helped the Indians drive into third place. It was a team effort, with clutch hitting and reliable pitching that gave Indians fans hope for the seasons ahead.

While Cleveland played good baseball, the court battle over the stadium nearly ended. On August 15 Judge Powell issued his ruling in favor of the city of Cleveland. He dismissed the complaints filed, allowing the construction to begin. Before William Hopkins and city officials could slap each other on the back, though, Andrew Meyer filed an appeal on August 19. The bond issue had passed nine months before, yet another long delay seemed quite probable. In all likelihood the issue would drag on to at least the end of the year. Hopkins once again put a positive spin on the situation. He remarked that Meyer and his lawyers had stated that they would abide by the ruling of the appeals court and bring no further action. Edgar Byers contradicted Hopkins, telling the newspapers they had made no promises to accept the ruling as the last word. There appeared to be no end in sight for the ugly state of affairs.

The Indians finished the 1929 season in third place, behind the champion Athletics and the dethroned Yankees. Cleveland had won eighty-one ball games while losing seventy-one. Wes Ferrell won ten of his last twelve starts, for a grand total of twenty-one for the season. That gave him the second-best record in the American League, behind Philadelphia's George Earnshaw. Few pitchers in modern baseball were able to win twenty games in their rookie season. Wes was in elite company, with immortals Christy Mathewson and Grover Cleveland Alexander. He still had much to prove in order to be mentioned with such all-time greats, but he certainly was off to a fast start. On September 14, Ferrell won his eighteenth game, beating Washington 4–1. Leaving nothing to chance, he knocked in three runs himself with a double and a single. The big day came on September 29 at League Park. Wes was fantastic, throwing a two-hit shutout to top St. Louis, 4–0. Over 15,000 fans turned out to witness Cleveland's first twenty-game winner in three seasons.

Along with Ferrell's terrific pitching, the fans were treated to the Indians' only batting champion since Tris Speaker in 1916. The improbable Lew Fonseca took the American League lead in mid-September and held off Al Simmons to win the crown. Just three years prior, the Philadelphia Phillies had given up on Lew, sending him outright to Newark. There, he reinvented himself by changing his batting stance and spraying the ball to all fields. In 1927 Cleveland was in the market for a reclamation project and bought the well-traveled ballplayer. The Indians hoped Fonseca could be a competent utility player, filling in at second and first base. They were quite pleased when in the 1928 campaign he went miles beyond their expectations and hit .369 for the year. Lew collected 209 hits, scored 97 runs, and had 103 RBIs. For much of his career he had battled injuries that significantly limited his playing time, yet in 1929 he only missed a handful of games. In mid-September he dislocated his shoulder but came back two days later. At the end of the month he got a nasty spike wound but stayed in the lineup. Fonseca had a season players dream about. This would be his finest moment in baseball.

Earl Averill, with eighteen home runs, did break Tris Speaker's Cleveland home-run mark. It was a bad year for Spoke, being erased from the record books in two separate categories. Averill had a tremendous rookie season with a .331 batting average, 110 runs scored, and 97 RBIs. The Indians' investment in Averill was already paying big dividends. Finishing in third place meant the Indians were due for a share of the World Series money. After the Athletics polished off the Cubs, each member of the Cleveland roster received a check for $700. It was an encouraging year for Cleveland baseball.

Chapter 5

AN IMPROVED BALL CLUB

W hile the Indians players left Cleveland for some rest and relaxation, shocking news from Wall Street made national headlines. On Thursday, October 24, 1929, the stock market endured a severe crash that jolted investors around the United States. Nearly thirteen million shares were traded as stockholders panicked and sold their investments at a staggering rate. Margin calls went out, wiping out the bank accounts of people who had bought on credit. Wild stories circulated of businessmen committing suicide by jumping out of office windows all around New York City. Actually, relatively few did jump to their deaths, but investors were shaken to the core.

Five days later it happened again. An unheard-of sixteen million shares were traded, pushing the Dow Jones Industrial Average down thirty points, or a monstrous loss of 12 percent. Companies including General Electric and Westinghouse saw their share prices drop fifteen to twenty-five points. It was a disaster of epic proportions. Individuals and corporations saw their hard-earned holdings completely disappear. The end result was an enormous loss of jobs and a dire need for public assistance.

City leaders around the country were not prepared for such an economic disaster and had to scramble to find solutions. Cleveland had a difficult situation in spending much time and effort to make downtown a showplace for residents and tourists alike. The building of the new stadium, the recent Terminal Tower, and plans to develop the lakefront were all based on a stable economic situation. With the stock market imploding, how were the city leaders going to handle an exceptionally complex situation? City Manager Hopkins and the Cleveland City Council had an alarming task ahead.

Cleveland, like much of the Midwest, was an industrial city. Huge steel plants and automobile factories employed a large segment of the population. If there happened to be a slowdown in construction and a decrease in auto sales, thousands of workers were bound to be laid off. This meant the purchasing power of the blue-collar workers would diminish and adversely affect other industries, including retail stores, restaurants, and entertainment. Part of that entertainment was dollars spent at League Park, cheering on the Indians. Only time would tell how much of an impact the market crash had caused and how long it might last. Fears of a long-term depression spread to all parts of the United States. There had been serious depressions in the past. Still, this one, possibly fueled by the events of late October, might just surpass all others. Millions of Americans braced themselves for the likely hard times ahead.

Despite the shockwaves across America, Major League Baseball went about its business as usual. There appeared to be no worries about the recent activities on Wall Street. For the duration of the winter meetings, the only real area of concern was the radio broadcast of games. Team owners were split on whether or not to continue the play-by-play live accounts. Billy Evans indicated that the Indians were planning to go ahead with broadcasts regardless of what the other owners intended to do. There was no evidence to support the claim that ball games on radio had any negative effects on attendance. *Baseball Magazine* weighed in with two separate articles on the pros and cons. The naysayers believed that radio did not increase attendance and that a number of announcers were not sound baseball men. The article criticized certain broadcasters for mispronouncing player names and getting too excited at the action on the field. The article went on to question whether new fans introduced to the game by radio would feel the urge to see a game live.

The article in favor of radio emphasized the people who could not physically attend games. Those in hospitals or those with handicaps now had a box seat to hear all the plays as they happened. Another point focused on housewives bringing up children who could now follow their home team without leaving the house. The article defended the advertisements during the game as providing revenue needed for the airtime. Newspapers and magazines relied heavily on ads, why could radio not do the same? It was quite an interesting debate regarding the new media. The magazine gave Cleveland some applause for hiring a baseball man in Tom Manning. He knew the game just as well as the sportswriters and front-office people. The radio debate would continue, especially as the economic times worsened.

In January 1930 Alva Bradley organized the Terminal Club, a refuge for the elite businessmen of Cleveland. Mindful of the effects of the stock market crash, he limited the membership to sixty. The other barons would have to fend for themselves. Bradley built rooms on the tenth floor of the Terminal Tower, with easy access to the kitchens of the Hotel Cleveland. The walls of the club had oak paneling from floor to ceiling and several posh lounges for the members. Life in general was still good for Mr. Bradley.

A month later the Cleveland owner got the news that Wes Ferrell was holding out for more money. The Bradley method of analyzing player statistics and offering a fair deal did not impress the Indians' hottest pitcher. The newspapers reported that Bradley had already agreed to triple Ferrell's salary, which was believed to be approximately $3,000. However, the twenty-one-game winner thought he deserved even more. Spring training was still weeks away, but Roger Peckinpaugh did not want to leave for New Orleans without his young star. Wes was working out with his brothers at the YMCA back in Guilford County, North Carolina, and doing a little bowling. He told the local paper in Greensboro, "I don't think I am asking an exorbitant salary and they will have to come to my figures. I am asking only what I think I am worth." To add to the somewhat tense situation, news came that Willis Hudlin wanted a new deal as well. The Bradley contract method was coming apart at the seams.

More unwelcome news came from California, where Lew Fonseca was diagnosed with scarlet fever. The illness usually occurred in children, but the batting champ had the acute sore throat, high fever, and rashes that were common with the sickness. It was thought that Lew would need several weeks to recover, and then spend a week or two practicing with the San Francisco Seals. Unfortunately, after a few workouts it became obvious he was far from in baseball shape. Doctors on the case sent Fonseca to Palm Springs to rest at one of the many resorts there. Nobody had any inkling whether he would be ready to play baseball for the regular season.

The train bound for New Orleans came and went without Hudlin or Ferrell, the Indians' best pitchers. While the holdouts continued, a few of the young pitchers in camp put in several impressive workouts. One of the group had been with the team in 1929 but got few chances to show his stuff. With the big boys staying home, twenty-year-old Mel Harder got his chance in the spotlight.

The third child of Claus and Clara Harder was born on October 15, 1909, in Beemer, Nebraska, a tiny community located about eighty-five miles northwest of Omaha. The town was incorporated in 1886 and boasted a water tank for the railroads, a soap factory, a post office, and a mill. When Mel was two, the Harders moved to Omaha, where better-paying jobs were available. Claus found work as a machinist and bought a home on Seward Street. At a very young age Mel began playing with a baseball, preferring the round rubber ball to any other of his toys. He attended Druid Hill Grammar School, telling anybody who listened he was going to be a ballplayer. As a teenager he entered Omaha Technical High School. There he pitched his team to the city championship. Mel already had a lively fastball and curve that caught the attention of Barney Burch, the president of the Omaha club that played in the Western League. Harder had spent a great summer pitching for the amateur Carter Lake team when, as the story goes, Burch tracked him down in the local drugstore, where he was downing a chocolate sundae. At age seventeen, Mel agreed to pitch for Omaha. The professional club trained in Texas, which meant he would have to leave high school and report for spring training.

Harder pitched his first game on March 28, 1927, against the Waco, Texas, team. He went four strong innings without giving up a single run. It was an impressive debut for someone who had yet to complete his high school education. Soon, though, his inexperience began to emerge and president Burch optioned Mel to the Dubuque, Iowa, team of the Mississippi Valley League, a Class D outfit. Faced with lesser competition, Harder tore up the league, winning fifteen games in two months while topping all the clubs in the strikeout category. The other teams in the league were quite unhappy with Dubuque's superstar, and one team in particular checked how Mel was acquired. The Mississippi Valley League had a rule that required all players to be owned by their respective teams. Since Dubuque did not own the contract for Harder, a grievance was submitted to the league officials. The decision was a harsh one. Mel was ordered to return to Omaha and Dubuque would have to forfeit all fifteen games he had won. Mr. Burch tried to argue that he had sold Harder outright but his claim was quickly denied. The working relationship between Omaha and Dubuque came to an abrupt end.

Mel returned to Omaha to take his place in the rotation. He struggled through most of his starts but showed enough stuff for Major League scouts to stop by and take a look. Charlie Hickman traveled a long way to see the young pitcher. The Cleveland scout had a knack for spotting pitchers (including Wes Ferrell) and soon offered a contract. President Burch wanted a hefty sum plus players to give up his local star: in late August, after a bit of haggling, he agreed to sell Harder to the Indians for $18,000 and two players. This would be the last player signed under the Dunn ownership. Ernest Barnard handled the acquisition for Mrs. Dunn, then wrapped up the sale of the club to Alva Bradley.

On September 5 an extremely motivated Harder pitched his last game for Omaha. In his home park, Mel dazzled his neighbors by throwing a five-hit shutout, beating Denver 2–0. No runner from the visiting team got past second base. Mr. and Mrs. Harder, along with Mel's two older sisters, were quite thrilled to see how far he had come. From the little boy with his rubber baseball, he was now, at eighteen, a member of the Cleveland Indians.

When Harder reported to spring training he stood six feet in height but weighed only 150 pounds. Manager Peckinpaugh directed him to add some meat to his bones if he were to become a Major League pitcher. Regardless of the weight problem, Mel showed enough to earn a place on the roster. He rarely saw any action in 1928, usually getting the call in mop-up time. He did succeed in adding fifteen to twenty pounds over the course of the season. After games at League Park the older players let Mel tag along to their favorite speakeasies. There he would have a beer or two and gradually gained the pounds needed. It was not the standard way to add weight, but it worked nevertheless.

Two years later, Harder pitched well in New Orleans, which led to a chance for a spot in the starting rotation. The Indians were leaning toward a youth movement and the right-hander from Omaha was primed for his opportunity. Both Hudlin and Ferrell had ended their holdouts, giving the Indians one of the youngest pitching staffs in the American League. Most of the sportswriters slotted them for third place behind the two powerhouses, Philadelphia and New York. Where the Indians landed would depend on pitchers who were just out of their teens.

Despite missing a good chunk of spring training, Ferrell and Hudlin showed no signs of rust. On March 24 they both made their first game appearances in the exhibition season. Hudlin went five innings without giving up a hit. Ferrell entered in the sixth and promptly walked several New Orleans batters. He pitched his way out of trouble, though, and finished the game for a combined no-hitter. Both hurlers were likely a bit smug after proving that skipping a few weeks of training had no ill effects. In truth, Ferrell had a world of ability that did not need a lot of work. Hudlin was not quite on the same level but clearly was a cut above the remaining Cleveland pitchers.

When the Indians headed north to start the regular season, a new shortstop would be in the starting lineup. Jonah Goldman, after two years of minor-league ball, had won the job. His fielding skills were Major League–ready, but his hitting was still a question mark. The newspapers welcomed back Goldman, referring to him as "the little Jewish shortstop" or "the little Jewish kid," or even "the stocky little Hebrew boy." At times they anglicized his name, changing Jonah to "Johnny." It remained to be seen how the fans in the opposing teams' parks would treat him.

In the off-season, Gordon Cobbledick wrote many profiles of the current and future Indians players. In January 1930 he wrote one about Goldman. There were the usual facts about batting and fielding and the shortstop's time at Syracuse University, but there was also a curious paragraph about Goldman's 1928 season at Decatur, Illinois. Cobbledick wrote, "Goldman isn't very big—he stands five feet seven inches and weighs one hundred seventy pounds—but he is a scrapper. In his season at Decatur he licked half of the league and challenged the other half including a 260 pounder on his own club."

Cobbledick did not elaborate on why Goldman got into a ridiculous number of brawls. Baseball players did have occasional fights, but more than one a year was considered excessive. Why would a college-educated ballplayer need to defend himself on the field time after time? It is likely that Jonah Goldman received a considerable number of insults due to his religion, and was provoked into standing up for himself. There were no other Cleveland player profiles that mentioned scrappers.

In mid-April the Cleveland ball club arrived home for a brief workout, then boarded a train for the season opener at Chicago. They probably had no idea that a new Cleveland city manager had been chosen. Back in January, the Republican majority in the council had ousted William Hopkins by a vote of fifteen to ten. The move could not have come at a worse time. There was great uncertainty about the local economy, rising unemployment, and the still-pending lawsuit regarding the new stadium. After losing his appeal with the circuit court, an undaunted Andrew Meyer had his attorneys file for a hearing with the Ohio State Supreme Court.

Despite the serious issues, the Republican leaders forged ahead, charging Hopkins with being negligent, reckless, stubborn, and, strangely, un-American. The whole point of having a city manager was to have a leader who was not a politician. Be that as it may, the movement to remove Hopkins had partisanship all over it. The Democratic minority supported Hopkins, but after six years of his ruffling some feathers, the Republican majority decided to use their numbers to find someone else to their liking. Several thousand folks protested at city hall, but the decision stood and Hopkins was out.

The Republicans had their man in State Senator Daniel Morgan. A thirty-year resident of Cleveland, Morgan was a lawyer with a reputation for being honest and fair-minded. Fellow state senator George Bender lined up the support and the vote was decidedly in Morgan's favor, nineteen to six. The new city manager quickly studied the stadium situation and told reporters he was leaning toward reducing the seating capacity by twenty thousand. He believed sixty thousand seats were adequate and the money saved could be used to build the bridges needed for access to the site. He overlooked the fact that, to bring in big-time college football, eighty thousand seats were the norm. Schools like Ohio State and Notre Dame were not likely to schedule a game away from home unless they could maximize the gate receipts. Lowering the seating capacity for baseball was not a problem, but the influential Clevelanders wanted their alma maters to play there. Morgan would have to reassess his position.

In early April the Ohio State Supreme Court denied Andrew Meyer's petition, ending an almost yearlong battle to stop the building of the stadium. Even though he had had nothing to do with the bond issue or the construction plans, Daniel Morgan was now the man behind the stadium. His leadership would be the determining force in whether or not the project went boom or bust. The next few months would be crucial in determining the fate of the stadium.

With the news of the stadium lawsuit off the books, the Indians began the 1930 season on the road against the White Sox. Heavy rains postponed the opener until Thursday, April 17. Cleveland had another new lineup:

> Dick Porter (right field)
> Joe Sewell (third base)
> Earl Averill (center field)
> Lew Fonseca (first base)
> Bibb Falk (left field)
> Johnny Hodapp (second base)
> Jonah Goldman (shortstop)
> Luke Sewell (catcher)
> Willis Hudlin (pitcher)

The Indians started fast, leading 4–0 going into the bottom of the sixth inning. Willis Hudlin was cruising along, setting down the White Sox hitters with ease. But Hudlin ran out of gas in the sixth and before the inning ended Chicago scored six runs to take the lead. Mel Harder came on in relief only to be hit hard by the Sox batters. All told, the White Sox had twelve batters come to bat in the fateful inning. The Indians added two more runs in the seventh but the Sox kept pace and led 7–6 at the top of the ninth. Cleveland kept their hopes alive when Joe Sewell singled. Johnny Burnett entered the game to pinch run. Lew Fonseca, still feeling the effects of scarlet fever, lifted a pop fly that fell safely down the right-field line. Burnett never stopped running and tied the game at 7–7. The two teams went to extra innings and Chicago scored a run in the tenth for the 8–7 win.

Dick Porter had three hits in the loss while Earl Averill drove in three runs. The Indians totaled fourteen hits in the contest. Manager Peckinpaugh probably glared at Hudlin as if to say, "That's what happens when you miss part of spring training!" Both managers pulled out all of the stops during the game, using a total of thirty-one players.

Cleveland bounced back, winning three out of four games against the Detroit Tigers. Wes Ferrell got the initial win, holding the Tigers to one run in a 7–1 triumph. Wes knocked in a run with a double while the rest of the lineup hit well enough to account for the other six runs. On April 20, Willis Hudlin threw a two-hit shutout to beat Detroit, 2–0. The game was scoreless until the top of the seventh, when pinch hitter Johnny Burnett lined a double to score Bibb Falk and Johnny Hodapp. The big surprise occurred the next day in the final game of the series. Roger Peckinpaugh elected to start seldom-used right-hander Clint Brown. The twenty-six-year-old had made a few appearances the last two seasons, but was not counted on to pitch regularly. The Indians scored four runs in the top of the first and Brown held the lead in a 6–1 win. Charlie Jamieson got a chance to start and responded with three hits and two RBIs. At thirty-seven, the team's oldest player still had some mileage left.

The Indians left Detroit for the relatively short train ride to Cleveland and another home opener at League Park, where fresh green paint had been applied to the ancient grandstand. The ushers greeted fans wearing snazzy new red caps. The Cleveland dugout had a portable heater that generated warmth for the players crowding around it: the temperatures barely reached into the forties, with a hefty wind swirling around the park. Many of the fans entering the grounds realized that League Park as a baseball facility was coming to an end. If construction began soon on the lakefront stadium, there might be only one or two home openers left for the historic old park. At any rate, twenty thousand fans bought tickets to see the Indians battle the White Sox.

For the third straight year WTAM had the broadcasting rights for the home games. Tom Manning was a very popular announcer, receiving over twenty thousand letters during the 1929 season. A number of them were from young women requesting a lock of the redhead's hair. Manning remarked that if he complied with the requests there would be no hair left to give away. Elgin National Watches was the new sponsor for the entire season. It was a smooth summer for the broadcasts, with one exception. In July, Manning was calling a doubleheader against the St. Louis Browns. By the middle of the second game, engineers back at the WTAM studios heard some loud noises coming from the on-field equipment. They called Manning's engineer, who discovered a faulty tube hanging out of its socket. The engineer adjusted the tube, but when he let go the noise returned. For the last three innings, the engineer was forced to hold the tube in place to keep the broadcast going. This skilled repair worked, allowing Manning to finish the play-by-play.

The ceremonial first pitch was thrown by former heavyweight boxing champ Jack Dempsey. Now a man of leisure, Dempsey enjoyed traveling around the country rather than taking punches to the chin. Just to be on the safe side, though, he grabbed a catcher's mask and put it on. The game began with Wes Ferrell on the mound, and quickly Cleveland trailed 3–0. The Sox had a runner in scoring position when Johnny Riddle lofted a high fly ball toward the overflow crowd in left field. Charlie Jamieson moved in as fast as his aging legs would carry him. The high pop drifted into foul territory, where Jamie reached to grab it at a dead run. At that precise moment a foolish teenager leaned through the ropes and got his hands on the ball, right where Jamieson was about to make the catch. The otherwise catchable ball hit the ground, allowing Riddle another chance. He took the gift and drove in the fourth Chicago run.

The police, along with Billy Evans, trotted to the left-field line and escorted the young man out of the park. The boy needed to leave anyway, as angry fans nearby were going to beat the daylights out of him. Order was restored and the game resumed. In the bottom of the seventh inning the Indians loaded the bases. Peckinpaugh looked down the bench and called on Earl Averill to pinch hit. The center fielder had the day off due to a sore ankle. The home crowd roared as Averill slowly stepped to the plate. With two strikes, Earl lined the next pitch off the right-field wall. Two runs scored, but the painful ankle kept him from advancing past first base. Averill was replaced by a pinch runner. Bibb Falk followed with a single that scored the third run. A healthy Averill would have easily reached second and scored on Falk's base hit. That was not to be, and the Tigers spoiled the home opener by a score of 4–3.

The 1930 season featured the Indians playing twenty-three games where they scored ten runs or better. In May, Eddie Morgan got his chance to join the starting lineup when hard-luck first baseman Lew Fonseca broke his arm. He responded with a career season, batting .349 with 26 home runs (a Cleveland record) and 136 RBIs. He finished the year fifth in the league in both total bases and slugging percentage. The only batters in front of him were Ruth and Gehrig of the Yankees and Foxx and Simmons of the Athletics. Even more astounding was the hitting of second baseman Johnny Hodapp. The man who drove hearses in the off-season led the American League with 225 hits and 51 doubles. He added nine home runs and 121 RBIs. These two unlikely heroes overshadowed fine seasons for Earl Averill and Dick Porter. Billy Evans had showed the Cleveland fans why he paid that large sum of money for the pair of outfielders. Porter hit well the entire year, batting a lofty .350. Averill followed with a .339 average with 19 homers and 119 RBIs.

The highlight of Averill's season took place on September 17, when the Washington Senators were in town for a doubleheader. In the bottom of the third inning, Earl detonated a bases-loaded home run. In the fifth inning he added a two-run homer, then hit another two-run blast in the eighth. Cleveland won the game, 13–7, with Averill batting in eight of those runs. Game two began with Washington scoreless in the top of the first inning. The Indians had two runners on base in the bottom of the first when Earl Averill stepped to the plate with a large ovation coming from the grandstand. He swung and sent a line drive to deep center field. The runners streaked for home with Earl close behind. The throw from the outfield was too late to catch the speedy Averill. He crossed home plate with a three-run inside-the-park home run. Four homers and eleven RBIs for the day! The rooters at League Park had never seen anything to match Averill's performance. Washington took the lead, though, and held it going into the bottom of the eighth inning. Once more, Earl Averill stepped into the batter's box. This time he slammed a high drive down the right-field line. Everyone in the park watched in stunned silence as the baseball soared over the right field screen, curving foul at the last instant. Reporters wrote that the ball was no more than a few feet foul. Previous to this at bat, the Washington pitcher had beaned Averill twice. Had they let him swing away there might have been a fifth or sixth home run. The Indians wrecking crew of Averill, Morgan, Hodapp, and Porter were largely responsible for the high-scoring ball games and the winning margins.

The pitching department lagged well behind the hitters. Only Wes Ferrell had another terrific season, winning twenty-five games against thirteen losses. The new Cleveland ace was among the leading pitchers in just about every category. Only Lefty Grove of the Athletics had more wins and a lower ERA. Ted Lyons of Chicago pitched an American League best of 298 innings to Ferrell's 297. Willis Hudlin had a disappointing season, winning only thirteen games, while Mel Harder in his first complete year had eleven wins and ten losses. Clint Brown added eleven wins but had an earned run average of 4.97. If not for the tremendous hitting, the Indians probably would not have won eighty-one games and finished in fourth place. The Athletics left everybody behind, totaling 102 wins for the season, just two shy of their 1929 mark.

For the past ten years, since the Indians' pennant year of 1920, the American League had been virtually a New York playground. The Yankees won the flag six times and the Washington Senators twice. Connie Mack completed a fifteen-year rebuilding project for the Athletics by winning in 1929. The remaining teams, including Cleveland, had their moments, but nobody could compete with the likes of Ruth, Gehrig, Meusel, and Lazzeri. Starting the new decade, the Athletics surged ahead. They had the pitching with

Grove and Earnshaw and fabulous hitting, including Foxx, Simmons, Bing Miller, and Mickey Cochrane. The Indians could only hope the Babe would slow down and Mack would break up the Philadelphia team as he had done in the past.

There were times, though, when Cleveland rose up to smite their enemies. On Sunday, May 11, 1930, the Indians completely destroyed the Athletics, 25–7. This was the third game in a series that had begun on Friday in Philadelphia. Strangely, there still remained a law in Pennsylvania prohibiting Sunday baseball. Through quirks in the schedule, the Athletics would have home games scheduled for Sundays, so the team had no choice but to board a train to play the contest in the visiting team's park. Such was the case here, and the Athletics and the Indians left Philadelphia on Saturday night to play the Sunday game in Cleveland. Connie Mack left Al Simmons and catcher Mickey Cochrane behind, as both were nursing minor injuries.

A crowd of 28,000 fans spilled into League Park to get a look at the reigning World Champions. The overflow was put on the playing grounds down the right- and left-field lines. Manager Peckinpaugh loaded his scorecard with left-handed batters who could knock the ball into the short right-field area and likely get a ground-rule double. The strategy paid off, with Cleveland batsmen getting a total of nine cheap doubles. They scored runs in the first seven innings, sending at least nine men to the plate in the fourth and sixth innings. Eddie Rommel, a veteran starter, did not survive the opening inning. His relief pitchers were bombarded as well. Roy Mahaffey, a fairly good pitcher, surrendered eleven runs in three and one-third innings. The Indians showed no mercy to untried rookie Al Mahon, rocking him for eight runs in two innings. Mahon would never pitch in the majors again.

The Cleveland fans could not get enough of the onslaught. They were razzing the Athletics outfielders throughout the game in an attempt to distract them into dropping fly balls. The *Plain Dealer* summed it up: "Did the crowd like it? And how! The mob was out for blood and got it."

Five Cleveland hitters had three or more base hits. Bibb Falk had fives all around: five at bats, five hits (including three doubles), five runs scored, and five RBIs. Earl Averill had three hits and two doubles and Jonah Goldman had four RBIs. Johnny Burnett had two hits and two RBIs. (Burnett was in the lineup due to third baseman Joe Sewell's illness. In Boston at the end of April, Sewell had played one inning and then had to leave the game. He developed a high fever of 102 degrees and was sidelined for several weeks. The illness broke his streak of appearances at 1,103 consecutive games, second only to the record set by shortstop Everett Scott during his years with the Red Sox and Yankees.) Wes Ferrell cruised to his fifth victory in six starts. He had allowed five runs, only two of them earned.

The Indians were not finished with the lopsided ball games. On August 14 they again pounded Philadelphia, 15–0. Eddie Morgan launched his twenty-fourth home run over the left-center-field roof of Shibe Park. The only other ballplayer to accomplish this was the Athletics slugger Jimmy Foxx. Cleveland notched twenty hits against three A's pitchers. Once again, Roy Mahaffey took the brunt of the onslaught, allowing six runs in one and two-thirds innings. The win marked Wes Ferrell's ninth in a row and twentieth of the season. Wes gave up seven hits, most of them coming in the first four innings, and struck out five. For his career he had seven wins against Philadelphia and only two defeats.

While the Indians periodically ran up the big scores, progress was being made on the new Cleveland stadium. In late April, Daniel Morgan announced construction would begin in June. Osborn Engineering had provided the information that bids to do the grading work had gone out and digging could start in about a month. Meanwhile, the site had moved a hundred feet east and ten feet south in order to avoid buying any land from the railroads. A part of the beautiful lake view from the north end of the mall would be obstructed, but the cost savings were important enough to move the site.

The actual construction began on June 24, nineteen months after the bond issue was passed. There was no fanfare to mark the occasion. City Manager Morgan believed all the delays did not warrant a celebration. Besides, the effects of the stock market crash were beginning to be seen, and a costly celebration was not appropriate. Just blocks from the site unemployed men were walking the streets, begging for a handout or selling apples to make a dime.

The time to celebrate was long past. Osborn Engineering now had the challenging assignment of building a new stadium and keeping the budget at the original cost of $2.5 million.

So, on that noteworthy day in June, there were no marching bands or flags flying. The 5th City Excavation Company of Cleveland brought two heavy steam shovels to begin leveling the ground. They began the job at the foot of West 3rd Street; finishing it would take about three months. Osborn Engineering would start the foundation work when the grading was a third of the way to completion. The city optimistically hoped for a completion date only one year away. They already had a request to rent the stadium in July 1931 from the national Shriners group. This meant a sizable rental fee in addition to substantial business for the downtown hotels and restaurants.

On July 24, Daniel Morgan announced the formation of a stadium advisory committee to oversee the plans and construction of the new facility. A number of sports-minded gentlemen were among the names listed. Ed Bang of the *Cleveland News* was a member. Stuart Bell of the *Cleveland Press* and Sam Otis of the *Plain Dealer* were also on board. Another prominent name was Max Rosenblum, Cleveland's premier supporter of amateur sports. These men, along with civic and educational leaders, would review blueprints and sketches, while offering suggestions and criticism as the project moved along. They were to meet with Morgan on a monthly basis until the stadium was completed.

The initial meeting of the advisory committee took place on July 31. There was a great deal of business for the committee to review, including the awarding of a contract to build a bulkhead off the Lake Erie shoreline. This massive retaining wall would keep water from eroding the shore and filtering underground to the stadium site. Great Lakes Dredge & Dock Company landed the contract at a cost of $73,000. The immense barrier was designed to be 1,200 feet in length and extend from East 3rd Street all the way to West 3rd.

Another issue discussed was whether to use concrete or bricks for the exterior walls. The bricks were yellow in color, something close to what was done at the new football stadium for the University of Notre Dame. Representatives from Osborn Engineering had visited South Bend and gave positive reports on the attractiveness of the outside walls. Frank Walker's architects were in favor of the bricks, but no decisions were reached during the meeting.

In the middle of September, Morgan announced an August 1931 completion date for the stadium. He had consulted with the major contractors and all agreed the August date was reasonable. Two weeks later the city manager authorized a ten-hour workday for the crews laboring on the foundation. This action was necessary to ensure the work would finish by December 1, as per the terms of the contract. The engineers determined that sixty piles had to be driven into the ground daily to meet the timetable. The only way to see this through was the extra hours. City officials believed the additional hours could still be financed under the original $2.5 million contract.

The first 120 days of construction moved along without any stoppage of work. With few problems to deal with, Morgan allowed bids to be mailed for the general construction work. This area included the stadium walls and pouring much of the concrete. A start date of October 15 was decided upon. This date ensured that a large part of the stadium bowl would be in place before winter set in. Although a latecomer to the project, Daniel Morgan was doing an exemplary job. There did not appear to be any backlash from the city council or further threats of lawsuits from concerned taxpayers. The stadium was going to happen.

Ed Bang was one of Cleveland's most respected sportswriters and editors. He wrote several letters to Daniel Morgan about the construction at the lakefront. Bang urged the city manager to have a running track built outside of the baseball field. Bang stressed that Cleveland had its share of outstanding runners who should be able to use the stadium track for championship meets. He added that, if a proper running track was built, perhaps the city of Cleveland could make a bid for a future Olympic Games.

For years afterward, many books and articles about the stadium maintained that one reason for constructing it was as a last-minute bid to land the 1932 Olympics. The Ed Bang letter was likely misinterpreted to mean that Cleveland was in fact attempting to bring the games to the new stadium, but elsewhere in the related correspondence and newspaper articles from the period there is no

NO MONEY, NO BEER, NO PENNANTS

mention of the city making such a bid. Meanwhile, Bang's request for a proper running track went unanswered.

By the end of October a frenzy of activity was taking place on the lakefront. City engineers announced plans for two steel pedestrian bridges to be built simultaneously. One bridge would span from West 3rd Street over the railroad tracks directly to the stadium. The second was designated for just east of the courthouse. At the same time, a load of giant girders arrived that would form the steel skeleton around the stadium. Bass Construction Company, another Cleveland firm won the bid for the job. The playing field already had a cinder base put down, along with a portion of the topsoil. The W. J. Schirmer Company, still another local outfit, had the general contracting job. They were in the process of hiring three to four hundred men to install fifteen thousand bleacher seats. The flood of action served a dual purpose in giving jobs to those who badly needed work. It was temporary employment, but it helped men pay their overdue mortgages and put food on the table. Ultimately, the stadium project became more than a means for future city income: it was helping with the unemployment problem rapidly spreading throughout northeast Ohio. Surely, it would only make a dent, but each man who reported for work was one less on the bread line.

The foundation work continued running two shifts. The first began at 7:00 a.m. and continued until 4:00 p.m. The second shift commenced at 6:00 p.m. and lasted until 4:00 a.m. For the evening shift, a series of searchlights covered the work area. Daniel Morgan assured anyone concerned that there were still adequate funds in the original budget to cover the overtime. The city manager seemed to have all the bases covered in managing the project, although soon he would let politics get in the way, and make a very questionable decision that provoked a controversy with members of the city council and the general public.

With the stadium project fully underway, Morgan determined that a stadium manager was necessary for the remainder of construction and beyond. The job would be a hands-on position, authorized to deal with contractors, workers, and any problems that developed. Once the stadium was open for business, the manager would have the job of working with the tenants, mainly the

Cleveland Indians. Of course, there were also football games, boxing matches, and civic events that needed attention. The position called for someone with experience in sporting events, promotion, and negotiating contracts. Many eyebrows were raised when Daniel Morgan nominated former state senator George Bender for the job.

This was the same George Bender who nearly a year before had lobbied hard for the votes needed to place Morgan in the city manager's office. This move looked to be payback for the political maneuvering, especially since Bender had recently lost his bid for a congressional seat and now found himself unemployed. Several years earlier, Bender had attempted to land the job as manager for the newly built Public Auditorium. He had no cards to play with William Hopkins and the position went to someone else. Now, it seemed, the former state senator was calling in favors to put him in the stadium manager's seat.

The opening shots were fired by the Federation of Women's Clubs of Greater Cleveland. This was an organization with much clout and a strong dislike of George Bender. In a statement to the newspapers, the members expressed their deep concern. The statement read, "The citizens who originally sponsored the idea and actively campaigned for the bond issue have a right to expect that the manager of the stadium will be a person whose training and experience fit him peculiarly for such managership." It went on to say that Bender's managing ability and business acumen were debatable.

The Women's Club did have an axe to grind with Bender. They had hired him six years before to publish their monthly bulletin. They believed money was owed to them by their former employee and the debate was still a live one. Bender would not comment on the allegations, leaving everyone involved to decide where the truth actually fell.

The organization proposed an alternative for selecting a stadium manager. The ladies wanted to see a commission formed with members who were heads of athletic associations, sportswriters, and representatives from the Cleveland Chamber of Commerce. They believed a group such as this could better determine the correct person for the job. Their logic was sound: a proper committee closely associated with sporting events and promotion might come up with the ideal candidate. Unfortunately, politics would rule the day, and the job had patronage written all over it.

The same day Morgan announced his choice for stadium manager, blueprints and sketches were forwarded to the Indians' front office. The plans illustrated the upper and lower tiers of the facility along with ideas yet to be implemented. The material was closely studied by Bradley, Evans, and Peckinpaugh. Discussions for a lease agreement were just around the corner and the team officials needed every bit of information before committing to anything. They knew that Daniel Morgan would be calling on them with pen in hand. Before any signatures were recorded, Bradley wanted to be absolutely certain the lease was favorable to his ball club.

Several days later, Councilman William Kennedy weighed in on the stadium manager debate. Kennedy reasoned that the Indians' occupation of the stadium had to be from April to October. When they were on the road, little activity could be planned for the site, since any major event might damage the playing field. Football games were in the works for the months of for October and November. That left the winter months, when no activities were likely. For this reason, Kennedy believed the manager for the Public Auditorium could take on the additional duties of stadium manager. Under his premise, the stadium job was really part-time, and the city would save some funds by having one man handle both positions.

The debate continued over the next two weeks. At the end of the month, Kennedy learned that the council finance committee had listed the salary for stadium manager at a range of $6,000 to $10,000. The lower figure was to be paid during construction, while the higher amount would kick in when the stadium opened. Kennedy reacted sharply, noting that council members were paid $6,000. Why did this job warrant the same pay? Committee members asserted that the figures were arbitrary and could have been stated at one dollar. Kennedy answered back, "Then make it a dollar!" The arguments back and forth were highly partisan, with the Republicans in the clear majority. Regardless of their salient points, the Democrats lacked the numbers to block the appointment.

On December 10, the *Cleveland Plain Dealer* ran an editorial denouncing the nomination of George Bender as stadium manager, saying, "The office of stadium manager ought to be thoroughly divorced from political consideration. It will not be if Mr. Bender gets the position. It is a big job which should be filled with no thought of party politics." A few days earlier, City Manager Morgan had gone before the city council to deny that any politics were involved in his decision. Folks who were following the situation had to suspect that this was a political favor, though. Certainly, this practice was nothing new, but an important job was about to be handed out to a person without the proper expertise. The new stadium was of huge importance to the city of Cleveland. The job needed to be handled by a true professional, not by a political hack.

The minority in the council kept on fighting to the end. Councilman Emil Robechek introduced an ordinance to reduce the salary of the Public Auditorium manager from $10,000 to $6,000. This move, if accepted, would mean there was no justification for paying the stadium manager anything above the $6,000. Robechek told the council, "I've felt there are too many people in the city government getting fancy salaries while there are too many jobless laborers unable to get $4.80 a day." He suggested that, if there was such a strong need for a stadium manager, he should have been appointed the previous May. At the present time, events were already being booked for 1931, and football for 1932. Apparently, there was no urgent need for a manager. Clearly this was a last-ditch effort by Robechek to stop Bender's appointment, or at least to limit his pay. Regrettably, logic and common sense did not apply here. On December 18, the city council voted 18–6 in favor of George Bender for stadium manager. The salary reduction failed to win any support. With eight months remaining on the construction timetable, the new man in charge had a lot on his plate. One could only hope Mr. Bender stayed out of trouble.

It did not take long for Bender to be the center of controversy. The civic leaders scored a major coup by securing arrangements for a heavyweight title fight between the champion Max Schmeling and challenger William "Young" Stribling. The date for the contest was set for July 3, 1931. If construction stayed on schedule, this fight would be the grand kickoff for sporting events. In doing the math for gate receipts, it was determined that a crowd of twenty-five to thirty thousand needed to attend in order to break even. Bender took it upon himself to lure the big-money men to Cleveland, writing letters to likely people guaranteeing choice seats. The letter read, in part, "If you will address me personally I will see to it that you will get just what you want," and was signed off with, "Fond Regards." One of the letters was received by a gentleman who did not know Bender personally and forwarded the correspondence to a Cleveland city official. He wrote on the message, "Bad Business." The letter was handed to Daniel Morgan, who could not have been pleased with the contents.

In late May, the Schirmer Company received a special contract to install the boxing ring and seats for the fight. The construction people insisted that no unauthorized workers or engineers enter the new work area unless approved by Schirmer. The city agreed that the site would be off limits. By mid-June the seats were installed and the ring area was near completion. A day later the construction crew entered the site and discovered that the freshly painted seats were scuffed up and damaged. An investigation revealed that George Bender had authorized a meeting of the several thousand ushers at ringside. This action was in clear violation of the construction agreement. Most of the seats had to be repainted and some damage repaired, to the tune of $1,500 above cost. All this because of one man's carelessness.

Later, a Cleveland company bid for the rights to install the fire extinguishers in and around the stadium concourse. They met with the city engineer and fire chief to discuss their plans. The company was assured that a decision would be reached in a week. In spite of this, the gentlemen soon discovered that George Bender had already given the contract to a rival firm. According to the losing business, their rival did not manufacture fire extinguishers that functioned below freezing temperatures. They would be useless at football games and any winter events. Bender was guilty, at least, of not doing his homework when he awarded the contract without the knowledge of the city engineer or fire chief.

Before the debut of the stadium on July 2, 1931, the *Cleveland Press* reported that the actual cost of the stadium was nearing $3 million. Various factors had pushed the original estimate up by $500,000. The Schirmer Company needed an additional $15,000 to speed up the work. They had fallen almost two months behind in pouring concrete. The lighting system was $120,000 over budget, too, due to a decision to add flood lighting for possible night activities. Another cost issue arose when the builders realized that lighting only the locker rooms and a few dark passageways would not be feasible. Lighting for all stairways in the stadium was therefore added, at additional cost. Meanwhile, the two pedestrian bridges leading to the lakefront had major cost overruns. All these factors contributed to a 20 percent increase in the overall cost estimate. Andrew Meyer and his lawyers were already proved to be correct: the stadium could not be built for $2.5 million.

The opening of the new stadium was planned to be an event of far-reaching proportions. City officials believed a crowd of approximately 75,000 would be attending the gala affair. The mostly free admission (with box seats going for a quarter) seemed likely to assure a substantial crowd. Yet, only 8,000 people came to see the completed stadium. There was a multitude of speakers, including all the significant politicians. A plane flew overhead and dropped a large flower arrangement on the field. Bands played while a chorus of a thousand singers entertained. The huge number of empty seats, though, was a disappointment to the all the people involved in bringing the stadium from an idea on paper to a state-of-the-art facility. They had to be swallowing hard at the nonsupport of the citizens of Cleveland. A bad omen indeed.

Roger Peckinpaugh (*left*) and Billy Evans (*right*), December 1927, plotting the 1928 season. *Author's collection.*

Willis Hudlin at League Park, c. 1935. *Author's collection.*

Eddie Morgan publicity photo, c. 1930. *Author's collection.*

Dick Porter, c. 1928. "Twitchy Dick" spent eight years in the
International League before the Indians could pry him loose.
Author's collection.

Mel Harder, 1928. Harder was a four-time All-Star and Cleveland's best pitcher of the early 1930s. *Author's collection.*

Jonah Goldman, November 1927. Goldman was a star halfback at
Syracuse University and one of the first Jewish ballplayers for the
Cleveland Indians. *Author's collection.*

Wes Ferrell, c. 1930. *National Baseball Hall of Fame Library, Cooperstown, New York.*

Oral Hildebrand, c. 1933. Hildebrand was an American League All-Star in 1933, when he won sixteen games and threw six shutouts.
Author's collection.

Earl Averill inside League Park, c. 1933. *Author's collection.*

Hal Trosky, c. 1936. *National Baseball Hall of Fame Library, Cooperstown, New York.*

Glenn Myatt (*left*) and Willie Kamm (*right*) shortly after their 1935 banishment by manager Walter Johnson. Fans and sportswriters were aghast at Johnson's decision. *Author's collection.*

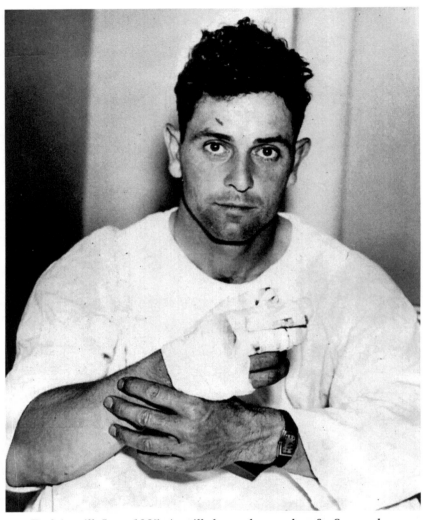

Earl Averill, June 1935. Averill shows the results of a firecracker accident that sidelined him for several weeks. Note the abrasion over the right eye. *Author's collection.*

Opening Day at Municipal Stadium, July 31, 1932. *The Cleveland Press Collection, Michael Schwartz Library, Cleveland State University.*

Alva Bradley (*left*) and Walter Johnson (*right*), August 1935.
The Indians owner believed he had the ideal manager in
Walter Johnson. After two years and a number of missteps,
Johnson was gone. *Author's collection.*

Joe Vosmik, c. 1935. A product of the Cleveland sandlots, the "Blond Viking" had a banner year in 1935, leading the American League in hits, doubles, and triples. He missed the batting title by one point.
Author's collection.

Johnny Allen, an outstanding pitcher with a bad temper. In 1936, Allen tore up a Boston hotel after a tough loss. *Author's collection.*

William Feller (*left*) and Bob Feller (*right*), October 1936.
The Fellers are in a pensive mood after Bob's spectacular debut
for the Indians. *Author's collection.*

Bruce Campbell relaxing, April 1935. Just days later, he would be stricken with meningitis. *Author's collection.*

Chapter 6

A HOMEGROWN STAR

While the United States plunged deeper into a serious depression, the Major League winter meetings took place as usual. There was still no concern displayed for the future of professional baseball. Even with high unemployment creeping into the fan base, the baseball men were in a jovial mood. The owners' attitude was summed up by Pittsburgh's longtime boss Barney Dreyfuss. In an interview with reporter James Kilgallen, Dreyfuss cheerily stated, "Give me a good tight pennant race and baseball business will be fine in 1931. I am not worried at all about this talk of economic depression." *Baseball Magazine* strongly believed that the game was safe from any diminishing gate receipts. The publication wrote that the sport was a place where a man went to escape his troubles. Even the out-of-work fan could scrape together a dollar to buy a seat and a hot dog. Or so they thought. The editors stated that attendance for 1930 was excellent and baseball would not suffer the same fate as the failing industries, specifically automobiles and railroads.

For their part, the Indians were not hesitant to spend money for players. Billy Evans doled out $105,000 to obtain four pitching prospects. He proudly told reporters that his club was the youngest in the American League, his players averaging only twenty-six. He had a good ball club with all kinds of possibilities, though maybe not pennant winners yet.

During the course of the winter meetings, Evans spread the word that three of his players were on the trading block. Lew Fonseca, the oft-injured former batting champ, was one, Bibb Falk another, and, at the old age of thirty-two, Joe Sewell. Evans wanted pitching help in return, or possibly an infielder. Rumors circulated that the Indians were prepared to give Sewell his unconditional release, making him a free agent. The team believed his legs were gone and he no longer had the range to play in the majors. From the 1913 season through 1928, Cleveland only had two men at the shortstop position. The late Ray Chapman held the job until his heartbreaking death in August 1920. Sewell was rushed to the big leagues to fill the gaping hole at shortstop, and the young man from Alabama proved to be an excellent player. He flourished through the 1920s, batting well over .300 and playing above-average defense. His minute number of strikeouts was legendary. He once told *Baseball Magazine* that, if he wanted, he could go an entire season without striking out. Sewell firmly believed he could see the ball hit the bat and, based on his infrequency of strikeouts, nobody argued with him.

On January 21, 1931, the Indians released Sewell. All the teams in the American League passed on the $7,500 waiver price. Sewell was earning a salary near $15,000 and the clubs that were interested did not want to pay anything close to that. They waited several days for waivers to clear, then the bidding frenzy started. In less than a week, Joe Sewell was the third baseman for the New York Yankees. His salary likely took a significant cut, but the chance to play in another World Series had to be appealing enough.

Contracts for the 1931 season were mailed and once again Wes Ferrell was an unhappy customer. The newspapers believed Ferrell made $10,000 the previous year. He apparently wanted to double that amount, lifting him above the salaries of Lefty Grove and George Earnshaw. It was speculated that the Indians offered their star pitcher a 50 percent raise, but Wes wanted considerably more. Joining Ferrell in the holdout club were Earl Averill, Johnny Hodapp, Eddie Morgan, and possibly Dick Porter. The club had received no communication from Porter and assumed he was after more cash.

The most exasperating holdout was Eddie Morgan. After a remarkable year, Morgan told friends he was going to retire from baseball and join the family business. His father owned a company that manufactured boxes. Soon the newspapers discovered that Mr. Morgan had decided to close his company and put himself out to pasture. Friends of Eddie assured reporters their pal would never retire because he loved the game too much. They even said that, if necessary, he would play for free due to his undying affection for baseball. Morgan was something of a free spirit dating back to his playing days at Tulane University. The night before a key game with Georgia Tech, the coaches worried that Morgan would break curfew by staying out most of the evening. They came up with a plan to lock him in his hotel room at 9:00 p.m. The scheme apparently worked and the coaches relaxed. One of them stayed in the lobby just in case, but by 1:00 a.m. all seemed in order. The coach walked across the lobby, only to spot Morgan walking through the front door. He had been to a typical fraternity party where there was dancing, women, and a lot of fun. How did he get out? Simple: he climbed out a window and then dashed down the fire escape. Morgan promised the coach all would be fine by game time. Sure enough, he swatted three base hits to lead his team.

The Indians front office had pretty fair knowledge that during the season Eddie was out cavorting while his teammates were sleeping. The label given him was that of a playboy. When Lew Fonseca fractured his arm, his replacement seemingly abandoned the good life and concentrated on baseball. The result was an eye-opening performance that the team did not expect. Now they had serious concerns about Morgan's threat to give up the game.

Surprisingly, most of the holdouts folded early. Dick Porter had been busy with his sausage business and was far behind with his mail. He had no problems with his contract, which had the biggest raise of all the Cleveland players. A big sigh of relief came on February 24 when Wes Ferrell announced he would sign. Wes spent the winter golfing and playing basketball. In an old-timers' game at Guilford College, Wes poured in twenty-three points, more than half of the team's output. Earl Averill put down the fishing rod and hunting rifle and reported to New Orleans. He now had an official nickname, the "Earl of Snohomish." Johnny Hodapp and Luke Sewell reported, leaving only Eddie Morgan as the one player out of camp. The Indians received word that Eddie had recently married and was on his honeymoon somewhere in Mexico. He still maintained that he was retired from baseball. The drama continued until March 18, when Morgan walked into training camp announcing his un-retirement. Billy Evans and Roger Peckinpaugh celebrated by spending the evening in Baton Rouge with Louisiana governor Huey Long.

During the Bradley regime, the Indians front office had gotten rather cozy with the popular Long. Through the governor's efforts, Cleveland's spring training headquarters were reserved for the Hotel Roosevelt. In 1928, when Bradley's ownership became public, Long sent one of his agents to Cleveland to ensure that the Indians would continue to train in New Orleans and stay at the elegant hotel. Favorable rates were offered to seal the deal.

A few years later Billy Evans began making noise about a new venue for spring training, possibly a city in California. Soon, a March dinner meeting took place with Governor Long, Bradley, John Sherwin, Evans, and Roger Peckinpaugh. The result of the conference was that Huey Long became a stockholder in the Cleveland Indians and Bradley along with Sherwin became honorary colonels on the governor's staff. All talk about a move to California ceased. New Orleans was notable as a favored playground for the wealthy. It stands to reason that Bradley and his fellow stockholders had been previously acquainted with Governor Long, at least on a social basis. The relationship in the 1930s became more entangled when Long bought into the ball club. The governor was on his way to a seat in the Senate, and, later, a bid for the presidency of the United States. His wide public appeal and unorthodox methods likely caused some apprehension among Bradley and his partners.

While the millionaires toasted one another and with Eddie Morgan temporarily absent, the young Cleveland recruits worked doubly hard to make an impression. After a few days of camp, a particular newcomer began driving home runs at a frequent clip. One of the shots nearly hit the four-hundred-foot sign in dead-center field. In a rare gesture, the fans at Heinemann Park stood up and applauded. The young man drawing the attention was Joe Vosmik.

The son of Joseph and Anna Vosmik was born in Cleveland on April 4, 1910. The father came to the United States from Eastern Europe when he was five years old. As an adult he worked in the stockroom of Reliance Electric, married Anna, and bought a house on Cleveland's southeast side at Broadway and 65th Street. Vosmik was raised there along with five sisters and a brother. In an interview given when Vosmik was a member of the Indians, he related a story about his first baseball experience. He had just turned three when he noticed a baseball bat owned by a neighbor. He grabbed hold of the bat and tried to drag it to his home. The neighbor boy seized the stick, which made the toddler scream and cry. He carried on to such an extent that Mrs. Vosmik gave one of the girls a dime to run to the neighborhood drugstore and purchase a bat for her brother. Vosmik was delighted with this new toy that started him on his quest to be a Major League ballplayer.

Vosmik remembered playing catch in the street before he was old enough to start school. In elementary school, his first and only subject was baseball. Around fourth grade, Vosmik began skipping class and finding his way to League Park. He snuck into the grounds to watch the games, but most of the time the ushers spotted him and tossed him right out to the sidewalk. On one occasion a truant officer nabbed him and brought Vosmik back to this teacher. She picked up a wooden yardstick and smacked the young man several times on his shins. The thrashing kept Vosmik in school for a time. Be that as it may, once the bruises healed he ducked class and raced down 65th Street to League Park.

In his teen years, Vosmik attended East Tech High School. He was shocked to find out there was no junior or varsity baseball team. Instead of playing ball he ditched school and went to games at League Park. Once again a truant officer caught him and hauled him off to the principal's office. According to the apprehended youth, the principal said to him, "Joe Vosmik, you will never amount to anything and you'll probably wind up in jail or in some lowly position in life." Apparently the educator scoffed when the guilty party explained that he was going to be a ballplayer.

At age fifteen Vosmik was starting to grow into a frame that would eventually be six feet tall and about 185 pounds. He had a big upper body with strong shoulders and arms. Before school let out for the summer, a local coach asked him to try out for a team in the Cleveland Amateur Baseball Association. Vosmik looked good in the trial and won a place on the Ruggles Jewelry team, a Class E club. He played first base and did a large share of the pitching. In two years he advanced to Class A, where he joined the Rotbart Jewelers team. His manager convinced Vosmik to give up pitching and exclusively play the outfield. He struggled a bit at the new position, but his first-class speed and strong throwing arm compensated for the lack of experience. At one point the young outfielder got his nerve up and cornered former Indians great Tris Speaker. He peppered Spoke with questions and received some helpful advice on how to play the outfield.

On Sunday, August 26, 1928, the CABA held a baseball tournament at League Park. The idea originated from Commissioner Max Rosenblum, who wanted to showcase his elite players and raise additional money for the league. Earlier in the year Rosenblum met with Alva Bradley and Billy Evans. The purpose was to create the tournament at League Park and have the Indians officials select two Class A players for spring training. The chosen ones would accompany the Cleveland club to New Orleans. If they showed some skill a contract would be in the offing.

Cleveland amateur baseball had a number of accomplished ballplayers who attracted crowds of 5,000 or more for each game. When Sunday the 26th rolled around, over 10,000 fans paid their way into League Park. It was a festive day, with a band playing and music from the popular Five Foot Harmony Quartet. Bradley, Evans, Rosenblum, and several Cleveland sportswriters were in the stands to select the top players. First up was a championship game followed by an All-Star contest. The level of play was so competitive that four players were asked to attend spring training. One of the top picks was Joe Vosmik.

A colorful tale concerning Vosmik emerged from the afternoon. Supposedly, the Indians officials were having difficulty choosing the fourth and final prospect. Billy Evans turned to his wife and asked her to pick somebody on the field. Almost immediately she pointed her finger toward Vosmik and said, "I'll take that blond Viking!" There was no question he was a handsome guy, with blue eyes and straight blond hair. That notwithstanding, the blond Viking was the leading hitter in Class A and well known to every baseball fan in the bleachers. His name and his exploits on the diamond were in all the Cleveland newspapers. It stands to reason that the story was not true, but for years the yarn appeared in various publications where Joe was featured.

The following spring, eighteen-year-old Joe Vosmik reported to New Orleans. The Indians gave him a quick look, then assigned him to their Frederick, Maryland, club to play in the Class D League for the summer. Though far away from home, he blossomed at Cleveland's lowest affiliate, batting .381 with thirty-nine doubles, twenty-four triples, and thirteen home runs. He received plenty of attention there, so much that Billy Evans left Cleveland to see Joe play. With the general manager in the stands Vosmik let the pressure get to him by striking out four straight times. After the game he cringed when Evans came by to talk. It turned out to be an upbeat conference, with Evans reassuring Joe that quite a few ballplayers tensed up when they knew the boss was watching. Next year a promotion to Terre Haute was being planned. Evans left Frederick believing, in spite of the strikeouts, that he had himself a top-flight prospect.

As early as May 1930, Ed Bang was authoring a piece about the hot-hitting outfielder now playing for Terre Haute. In his column he quoted Evans as saying Joe Vosmik was a sure thing for the Indians. There were a number of good prospects in the Cleveland organization, but Evans believed Joe was the best to surface since he became general manager in 1928. Being a native Clevelander and a sandlot star gave him all the more appeal. Evans described Joe as having a great swing with good power to all fields. He could handle any pitch, fast or slow, and could tear around the bases with the best of them. When Evans paid a call to Terre Haute the results were entirely different than they'd been in Frederick. A relaxed Vosmik stroked three line-drive hits in a row. Throughout the summer he flirted with batting .400. He missed by a couple of hits, finishing with an average of .397, thirteen home runs, and 116 RBIs. As a reward the Indians brought Joe to Cleveland when the Three-I League ended its season.

It was September 13 when Joe made his debut against the Philadelphia Athletics. Of course, Lefty Grove was on the mound, whistling fastballs past the Cleveland hitters. Manager Peckinpaugh called on Vosmik to pinch hit. He was startled at the velocity of Grove's pitches, but managed to ground out to second base in a 9–2 loss. A week later he started in center field, replacing Earl Averill. Joe delivered a single and a double, driving in two of the Indians' three runs. As far as the local sportswriters were concerned, a star was born. The "Blond Viking" had made an auspicious debut.

In spring training of 1931, Joe was the talk of the camp. Day after day he excelled, pushing old vet Charlie Jamieson to the sidelines. Vosmik was in left field for a March exhibition game against the New Orleans Pelicans. He got five straight hits, leaving spectators and players shaking their heads. Billy Evans was ecstatic about his outfield of Porter, Averill, and Vosmik. If everything went as planned, he might just have the best outfield in the American League. Certainly, Babe Ruth and Al Simmons were in a class by themselves, but in total the three Cleveland outfielders could match their three counterparts on any given team.

When the Indians came home to start the season, most of the fans in town wanted to know every detail about the new left fielder. Sportswriters planted themselves at the Vosmik home, talking to Mom and Dad as well as Joe's five sisters and one brother. They brought photographers along to snap pictures of the family. Joe was asked a large variety of questions, including what he liked to eat for dinner. Chicken with dumplings and mashed potatoes was his favorite, but he avoided any kind of dessert when he played baseball. Mrs. Vosmik told the *Cleveland News* she'd been against her son becoming a ballplayer, but now that he was with the Indians she'd become a fan. The *News* reported taking phone calls from people who wanted to know when Joe was playing, and where was this League Park? The city of Cleveland was about to go wild for the new prodigy.

A near-record crowd for Opening Day at League Park saw the Indians edge the White Sox, 5–4. Over 26,000 fans were in the seats and on the field. Major League Baseball had a banner day for attendance, with 250,000 taking in the eight opening games, the largest number of fans ever recorded in Opening Day tallies. Yankee Stadium had 70,000 fans walk through the turnstiles, while the Chicago Cubs at Wrigley Field hosted 46,000. For the moment, *Baseball Magazine* was correct in its assertion that baseball would be unaffected by the hard economic times.

In Cleveland, Wes Ferrell gave up three runs early but held Chicago in check for the rest of the game. Cleveland trailed 4–3 going into the bottom of the eighth, but a single by Ferrell tied the game. Earl Averill singled with the bases loaded to win it. The fans were treated to a new public address system approved by Alva Bradley. The age of the megaphone announcer was officially over at League Park.

Although the Cleveland fans were pleased with the victory, they did not get the opportunity to see Joe Vosmik play. Manager Peckinpaugh believed the crowd and family members would spook Joe and affect his play. The next day, in front of a much smaller crowd, Vosmik started in left field and collected two hits in five trips to the plate. The Indians lost, despite a home run and double from Earl Averill. In game three, Joe had an excellent day, with three hits, including two doubles and two RBIs. Clint Brown threw a six-hit shutout in a 7–0 win. On April 18, the Indians pasted the White Sox, 11–2. The fans attending witnessed the rookie left fielder having a perfect day, with five hits in five at bats: three doubles and a triple along with an ordinary single. The triple was a moonshot to the base of the center-field wall. In three games, Joe had delivered ten hits in just fourteen at bats. The Cleveland papers were filled with stories about their hometown guy. The national news services picked up on the reports as well. Baseball fans from California to Massachusetts were reading features about a twenty-one-year-old who was rivaling the exploits of Ty Cobb and Joe Jackson.

After a day off, the Detroit Tigers came to town. Waite Hoyt, the ex-Yankee great, was doing the pitching for the visitors. In the bottom of the second inning the fans let out a tremendous ovation when Joe Vosmik stepped to the plate. Hoyt had been pitching successfully in the American League for fourteen seasons and had seen the young phenoms come and go. His first pitch was a high, hard one right around the ears. Vosmik hit the dirt and slowly got to his feet. The next pitch was over the plate and Vosmik ripped the ball to deep-left center for a triple. The crowd and sportswriters dropped their jaws while the rookie streaked around the bases. Pitchers were throwing him every pitch in their arsenals, yet they could not get him out. Now, after a beanball just missed his head, Joe had got up, dusted himself off, and laced a triple. This was Frank Merriwell come to life. Surely no ballplayer could be this outstanding. For the moment, it was all good in Cleveland. Vosmik created so much excitement that, after the Detroit series, attendance stood at 70,000 and it was still April.

Though Vosmik was the main attraction, other Indians players were off to hot starts. Earl Averill was hitting shots off the right-field wall, while Johnny Hodapp and Eddie Morgan were heating up as well. On April 29, Wes Ferrell outdid everybody by throwing a no-hitter against the St. Louis Browns. He walked three batters while striking out eight in the 9–0 victory. It was the first Major League no-hitter since Carl Hubbell of the New York Giants threw one in May 1929. The last no-hitter at League Park went all the way back to October 1908, when Addie Joss threw his perfect game to beat the White Sox, 1–0. Ferrell had his good stuff from the onset and throttled the Browns over the entire nine innings. The only play of interest occurred in the eighth inning when Wes's brother Rick hit a hard ground ball between third base and short. Johnny Burnett could not get a glove on the ball, but new short-stop Bill Hunnifield did and made the long throw to first. The toss was wide, pulling Lew Fonseca off the bag an instant before Rick Ferrell arrived. The official scorer did not hesitate and gave Hunnifield an error on the play. For the day, this was the third and last miscue by the Cleveland shortstop. The revolving door with Hunnifield, Goldman, and Burnett at shortstop would continue throughout the season.

On the offensive side, Cleveland leading hitter for the day was none other than Wes Ferrell. In the fourth inning with a man aboard, Wes hit a two-run homer. In the seventh, Earl Averill stroked his third homer of the year, another two-run shot. With two men on base in the eighth inning, Ferrell delivered again, this time a double for two more runs. A single brought him home with the ninth and final run. The Indians pitcher was still only twenty-three, but he already had two twenty-game seasons and had established himself as one of the best-hitting pitchers in either league. With the efforts of Vosmik and Ferrell, the Indians raced to a 9–3 record. They appeared to be on their way to an excellent season.

Before Cleveland fans were able to buy their World Series tickets, though, the team bus got a flat tire. From May 7 through May 21, the Indians dropped twelve games in a row. The skid began with a loss to St. Louis, then three to Boston and two to Washington, followed by a four-game sweep by Philadelphia. The Athletics out-scored Cleveland 41–22, including a 15–10 loss where Al Simmons and Jimmy Foxx both launched three-run homers. The streak continued with two more losses to the Yankees before the Indians scored another victory. Along with the losing streak, Joe Vosmik would gradually come back to earth. His batting average dropped to the .300s, where it stayed for the remainder of the year. However, even though he would not eclipse such Cleveland greats as Napoleon Lajoie or Joe Jackson, Vosmik's best days were still ahead of him. Being a hometown guy, the Indians fans had their hero, the kid from 65th Avenue. His presence in a uniform with a block *C* on his chest brought great excitement to League Park. Wes Ferrell and Earl Averill were fan favorites, but they were not from the streets on the south side of town. Joe was a Clevelander in all respects, some-one the fans would always cheer their hearts out for.

The balance of the season saw the Indians struggle to stay above .500. During the month of May, Billy Evans traded Lew Fonseca to the White Sox in exchange for slick-fielding third baseman Willie Kamm. The thinking here was that, with Fonseca out of the picture, Eddie Morgan could play first base regularly for years to come. The veteran Kamm gave them an average hitter but an excellent glove at third base. Evans claimed he was canvassing the market for a shortstop, but hoped Burnett or Jonah Goldman might step up and take the job permanently.

Near the end of June the Indians walloped the Red Sox in a doubleheader. The combined score was 23–0. In game two Willis Hudlin allowed a single in the second inning and that was it. The ground ball just eluded Johnny Burnett and Hudlin settled for a one-hit shutout. Earl Averill swatted seven hits in ten at bats to pace the attack. It seemed the Indians were gaining momentum, but that was not the case. Instead they watched Philadelphia win a staggering 107 games, well ahead of the second-place Yankees. Washington claimed third place with a surprising ninety-two wins.

In order to finish the year above .500, the Indians swept Detroit in a four-game series. Before the final game, the Indians and Tigers set up a six-event challenge to entertain themselves and the handful of fans at League Park. One of the trials involved picking up a fungo bat and seeing who could slam the baseball the farthest distance. Joe Vosmik tossed the baseball a few feet in the air, then hammered it 417 feet. Several Tigers and Indians tried to match the distance but nobody came close. According to the unofficial fungo statistics of the era, the only player to hit the ball farther was the Sultan of Swat himself, Babe Ruth. One of the best events was the test of accurate throwing for catchers. A barrel was placed on its side just over second base. Cleveland's backup catcher Glenn Myatt fired one from behind the plate and clipped the rim of the obstacle. The Tigers managed to win the other events, with Roy Johnson heaving a baseball 390 feet and another Detroit player running the hundred-yard dash in a speedy 10.5 seconds and circling the bases in less than fifteen seconds.

With the 1931 season complete, Alva Bradley took a hard look at the attendance figures. He had put a strong team on the field, but the numbers at the box office were disappointing. For the year, the Indians drew 483,027 customers, averaging 6,233 per game. The American League average total attendance across all eight teams was 485,027. For comparison, the 1930 season at League Park had a figure of 528,657, or an average of 6,886 fans per game, representing a drop in Cleveland attendance of 45,630. The American League average plummeted by 100,000, while the National League had similar numbers, a startling revelation. The owners had to acknowledge that the depression had invaded Major League Baseball.

The winter meetings of 1931 were not as merry as in previous years. The cavalier attitude that had been a theme of the last meeting did not reappear. The fan who was out of work failed to show up at the ballpark and spend his last dollar on his favorite team. *Baseball Magazine* published an editorial using the theme of "Retrenchment." It was time to mull things over and develop a new strategy for the game. The easiest solution was to put the onus on the players and cut their salaries. The magazine emphasized that Babe Ruth had a salary of $80,000 and estimated Rogers Hornsby to be making $40,000, Cubs slugger Hack Wilson $35,000, and Al Simmons thirty grand. The writers believed the average player earned somewhere between $7,000 and $8,000. The payroll for sixteen teams was $3 million. The New York Yankees owned the highest payroll in both leagues.

Colonel Jacob Ruppert, the boss of the Yankees, told the magazine, "Baseball cannot afford any such salaries." Talking specifically about his star outfielder, Ruppert said emphatically, "Baseball will never again pay a ballplayer a salary of $80,000." The general consensus was to slash player salaries across the board by 10 percent. Whether or not the ballplayers would cooperate remained to be seen. Their careers could end on a moment's notice. A broken leg, an elbow injury to a pitcher, and all that they had worked for was gone in an instant.

Articles made use of the fact that workers in the auto industry and manufacturing were taking pay cuts to keep their jobs. That was expected, but the difference remained that an industrial or corporate worker might have the same job for thirty years. A ballplayer had to start a second career when he reached his mid-thirties. There were no guarantees that a coaching or manager job awaited those who retired. Surely, a number of players went to the minor leagues to keep earning a salary, but sooner or later the inevitable unconditional release came their way. Ballplayers needed to earn the most money possible in a short time span. It remained to be seen if any of the owners sympathized with that.

The decline in attendance signaled that owners were losing money at the gate. *Baseball Magazine* asserted that in 1931 each club was down several hundred thousand dollars. Balance sheets were not public knowledge, and the hard numbers were not about to be revealed. Teams such as the Athletics and St. Louis Browns claimed attendance at some games was actually below a thousand fans. *Baseball Magazine* issued the cry, "Now is the time for all good men to come to the aid of their party." Was this for all baseball personnel or just the ballplayers? It was not a time for scapegoats, but that appeared to be the action soon to take place.

When the winter meetings concluded, the owners issued a joint statement to the press. It read, "Resolved, that by reason of prevailing conditions and decreased attendance at our games, it becomes necessary that the general operating expenses, including the salary cost of the ball players of the clubs in both leagues be substantially reduced." There were no specifics announced concerning the amount of the cuts. Still, the 10 percent idea was likely the standard set.

It was possible to interpret this as the owners taking an opportunity to radically improve their bottom lines. Since few people outside of the owners' inner circle knew the true financials, the door was open for all kinds of devious schemes. With the depression in full force, there might be a case or two where an individual team owner could use the overall economic times to stick it to the players. Who or what was there to stop an owner from gouging players to increase profits? An owner might need to cut salaries 10 percent to make certain he would finish in the black, but why stop at ten? Why not go to twenty or thirty and force players to accept salaries from years past? There were no safeguards to stop this from happening. The history of professional baseball is filled with examples of owners tightening the screws on the hapless players. The reserve clause was the most predominant method, followed by attempts to stop the players from creating unions. The trust factor was not on the owners' side.

Billy Evans announced that the salary cuts for the Indians would be about 8 percent. A chunk of this was accomplished by reducing the salaries of Charlie Jamieson and Bibb Falk. As longtime veterans, both were at high-end salaries for part-time play. Neither man objected to the cuts. A few further reductions for borderline players, and Evans easily reached his goal. Players including Wes Ferrell, Earl Averill, and Joe Vosmik were not affected by the cutbacks. In fact, Ferrell got a significant raise for winning twenty games three years in a row.

Baseball fans, at least in Cleveland, were on the side of the players. A gentleman wrote a letter to the *Plain Dealer* criticizing the owners, saying, "I haven't noticed that the club owners are reducing admission prices. They've got a lot of nerve to ask the players to shoulder the whole burden of the depression. Other commodities have been cut, why not baseball tickets?" In the owners' defense American League president Will Harridge reminded fans that ticket prices had been the same since the last decade, while the price of admission for boxing and basketball rose dramatically. Harridge maintained that the excess profits in baseball went mainly to the players. Now the owners were simply trying to bring those salaries back in line.

The early returns in the salary wars were somewhat favorable to the team owners. The newspapers reported the New York Giants attempted to reduce Bill Terry's salary by 40 percent. The first baseman was one of the elite players in either league. In the 1931 season Terry batted .349 with 213 hits and 20 triples, the best in all of baseball. The year before, Terry had batted an incredible .401. He was earning $22,000 and the Giants offered him $13,000. Other National League stars including Mel Ott and Babe Herman received contracts far below what they expected. It remained to be seen how all this was going to sort itself out.

In the midst of all the cutbacks came the news that Alva Bradley had purchased the Toledo Mud Hens of the American Association. Bradley cited the need to have complete control over at least one minor-league franchise. In that manner, the front office could keep a close watch on the players and hire their own manager to consult with. The logistics of Toledo were excellent. Billy Evans and Bradley could visit on a moment's notice and still keep in touch with the home office. Bradley was able to buy the franchise for a drastically reduced price, as the team was in receivership. The old owners were unable to make payroll and had to give the club to its creditors. Earlier, the Indians had removed themselves from the Frederick and Terre Haute clubs, but feared the idea of assigning talent to minor-league teams they had no affiliation with. That prompted Bradley to second-guess himself and buy the bankrupt Mud Hens.

The Indians' plan of making only small salary cuts worked well. Most of the contracts mailed came back with signatures on them, and there were no indications of holdouts. Now Bradley and his staff concentrated on negotiating with the city of Cleveland for a favorable lease agreement. The front office submitted its lease demands in the fall. The agreement called for the same $50,000 payment plus an additional 15 percent on attendance above 725,000. Another stipulation called for the team to handle all the field maintenance at its expense. However, the lease was currently sitting in limbo while the city council refused to act. The November elections had on the ballot a measure for voters to choose whether or not to keep the city manager position. A no vote would mean the removal of Daniel Morgan from office and a general election in February to elect a mayor. The incumbents in the city council wanted to see the election results before approving any major legislation, including a stadium lease. In addition, council members believed the lease needed to provide more revenue for the city.

The voters of Cleveland proved they were fed up with city managers, voting to revert back to a mayoral system. Harold Burton, the city law director, was appointed interim mayor until the February 16th special election. The lease agreement would likely be delayed until at least February or March, when the new mayor was to be inaugurated.

On December 4, Alva Bradley and his chief groundskeeper, Frank Van Dellen, went to visit the stadium. They examined the baseball field and discovered that the pitching mound was too high. Further investigation revealed that the first and third base positions were not at proper height, either. This required a major renovation that would take two to three months. Fingers were pointed in all directions, but Van Dellen insisted he was not consulted on the various phases of the infield construction. One of the parties would have to grudgingly shell out the money for repairs. The faulty infield set back the date for any baseball to be played until June or July. Now there were problems outside of the lease.

In all fairness to the city of Cleveland, the last person in the world you would want to negotiate a lease with was Alva Bradley. This man was the largest holder of real estate in northeast Ohio, and probably all of the Midwest. He earned his living negotiating leases for buildings, residential homes, apartments, and just about anything with a roof over it. He had been around the block many times and was not going to put his name on a document unless it was favorable to him. He had already dealt with William Hopkins and Daniel Morgan. Now the unnerving task fell to interim mayor Harold Burton, who had about three months to cut a deal. There was no conceivable way Bradley could lose.

Two weeks later the city submitted a revised lease to the Indians. This one had rental fees based on a sliding scale. If the team drew well at the new stadium, rental fees would be raised. Conversely, poor attendance meant lower rental fees. The Indians' board of directors met to discuss the terms of the agreement, and after some tweaks they agreed to submit a bid to the city council for use of the stadium. The rules stated that the council had to approve bids for any use of public property over a set amount. The stadium fell into this category. Once approved, the lease could be negotiated by the parties involved.

The bid itself was a formality, but the terms of lease met strong opposition. Bradley and his partners refused to budge on the $50,000 minimum payment. They did offer to pay an extra 10 percent on attendance between 675,000 and 825,000, and upped the ante to 15 percent on attendance figures from 825,000 to one million. A clause stated that the team would reimburse the city twenty-five cents for every free pass distributed and redeemed at the gate. Realistically, with thousands of Clevelanders out of work, the chances that the Indians could draw 675,000 or better were quite slim. The likely scenario was that the Indians would pay $50,000 for seventy-seven home dates. Members of the council were in an ugly mood over the latest proposal. They were certain the city was getting fleeced. The bond money had been raised, costs escalated by half a million dollars, and construction hurried to have the stadium playable for a good part of the 1931 season. For all this, the city was going to realize a yearly payment of $50,000, far below what they expected.

In addition to the standoff with the Indians, stadium manager George Bender had a number of events to book at his facility. There were twenty boxing and wrestling matches, college football, the Negro League was interested in bringing games there, and of course there was high school and sandlot baseball. Due to the elephant in the room (Indians baseball), Bender could not schedule anything from April through September until he knew the outcome.

After a thorough review of the latest lease, the city council refused to take any action, tabling the issue until the new mayor assumed office in late February. With the problem regarding the infield height adjustments and the stalemate on the lease, League Park remained the only place to stage a professional ball game. In 1928, voters had gone to the polls and showed they were in favor of a modern new stadium. Now, four years later, there was a state-of-the-art facility that had no major tenants. The new mayor had an almost impossible task to get a baseball team in the stadium.

The special election was held in February and the Cleveland voters chose Ray T. Miller for mayor. Miller was a Democrat and city prosecutor since 1928. His election signaled the end, at least for now, of the Republicans' hold on the city. Within a day, resignations gathered on the mayor elect's desk, including that of George Bender. The stadium manager's controversial tenure ended with a whimper, not a bang. In a month the city would file a lawsuit against Bender to retrieve certain papers that had disappeared from his stadium office.

As the new mayor, Miller had plenty of issues to deal with. He understood the importance of getting a workable lease for the Indians. In April he was back at the table, trying to succeed where others had failed. He made progress with Bradley, but another new issue came into play: the Indians wanted a forty-year lease while the city believed twenty-five years was more appropriate. After much debate, Mayor Miller strongly advised the council that forty years was the best they could get. Bradley had insisted that twenty-five years was too short for him to make a commitment. Miller had to be aware of Bradley's resolve and the fact that baseball season was approaching. The idea of an empty stadium for 1932 was unacceptable.

Meanwhile, there was baseball to play, even if it did not take place at the new stadium. In early April the Indians left New Orleans for a short series of exhibition games. The team stopped in Alabama for a game against the Birmingham Barons. Earl Averill had a spectacular day as Cleveland trounced the Southern Association boys, 18–1. On his initial at bat Averill smacked a bases-loaded home run, then added a triple and a double for a total of eight RBIs. The Indians center fielder was rapidly becoming one of the elite players in the game. For the 1931 season he had placed third in home runs, RBIs, and total bases. His 209 hits were only two behind the leader, the Yankees' Lou Gehrig. The New York duo of Ruth and Gehrig, plus the Athletics' Foxx and Simmons, were the only players to have an edge on Averill. For most of his career, Earl would have the misfortune to play in their shadows, although as far as Cleveland fans were concerned, the best player in the American League was their own center fielder, the "Earl of Snohomish."

Before the home season began, there was a big announcement regarding the radio broadcasts: exclusive rights were awarded to station WHK. Unfortunately, this put an end to Tom Manning and his long association with the Indians. He had been the first and only radio voice for the team and had handled the megaphone duties at League Park in previous years. Manning had a contract with NBC, though, which prohibited him from leaving WTAM and staying behind the microphone.

There was a very small pool of experienced sports announcers to choose from. WHK decided to go in another direction and hire former Indian Jack Graney. The ex-ballplayer had been a popular guy in Cleveland for many years. He started in 1910 with the Cleveland Naps and became the regular left fielder for nearly a decade. After his playing days, Graney stayed in Cleveland and did some coaching of sandlot teams. He knew League Park inside and out and likely kept up with the players, both current and past. The one unknown dynamic was his ability to broadcast. The bosses at WHK took a risk in hiring Graney, but his name factor already scored them a lot of points. The station and their announcer were scheduled to debut at the Indians–White Sox series on April 28.

On April 20, the Indians opened the home schedule against Detroit. Ray T. Miller threw out the first pitch, which landed in the dirt several feet in front of home plate. It was a less than perfect appearance for the mayor, the first Democrat to have the ceremonial pitch honors in sixteen years. The maintenance crew had once more spruced up the old park, hanging red, white, and blue banners from the upper deck. The advertising billboards in left field all got a fresh coat of bright paint. The fans were some 23,000 strong: all the permanent seats were taken and hundreds of ticket requests were unable to be filled. This had to make an impact on Bradley and Evans, knowing that a lease agreement at the new stadium could have accommodated all of the requests.

Clint Brown started the game for Cleveland, opposing old friend George Uhle of the Tigers. The contest developed into a pitchers' battle with neither team able to generate any offense. The Indians managed to score in the bottom of the second when Joe Vosmik, after a loud ovation, singled to left. He went to third on Willie Kamm's base hit. Uhle got the next two hitters, but Clint Brown surprised the crowd by lashing a single to score Vosmik. The game was tied 1–1 going into the Tigers half of the eighth inning. Roy Johnson doubled off the right field wall. With two men gone, center fielder John Stone lifted a foul pop behind catcher Glenn

Myatt. Myatt raced back to the grandstand, but tripped on a folding wooden chair left behind from the pregame ceremonies and dropped the ball, allowing Stone another chance. This time, the Detroit hitter lined a double to right field. Uhle held on for the final two innings as the Indians dropped the home opener, 2–1.

A few days later, Billy Evans announced a trade with Chicago. Johnny Hodapp and part-time outfielder Bob Seeds went to the White Sox in exchange for second baseman Bill Cissell. Evans was unhappy with Hodapp's deteriorating batting average and thought Cissell could be an upgrade. The players in Chicago had nicknamed Cissell the "$123,000 Beauty," due to the enormous amount of money paid to Portland for the second baseman. In 1927, the White Sox front office doled out $75,000 cash for Bill, in addition to four minor-league players worth $48,000. He never lived up to the hype, but played a better-than-average second base and had some pop in his bat. Cissell was still twenty-eight years old, which sort of fit into Evan's youth movement. The Cleveland infield now had Eddie Morgan at first, Bill Cissell at second, Johnny Burnett, the latest hope, at shortstop, and Willie Kamm holding down third. Evans believed he had a stable infield to go with an outfield of Vosmik, Averill, and Porter.

When Chicago arrived in town, Jack Graney was set to begin his play-by-play career. He received mostly passing grades from fellow members of the media. They noted his vast knowledge of the game, his ability to call balls and strikes, and, most important, his flair for the dramatic. Graney would improve with each broadcast and establish himself as one of the best in the business.

While Graney was broadcasting his first game, engineers at WHK picked up another broadcast of the ball game. It came from station WJAY and sounded mysteriously close to Graney's description. What made it even more puzzling was the fact that WHK had the only broadcasting equipment at League Park. Yet the voice on WJAY was giving accurate descriptions similar to Graney's. The engineers believed they were being hacked by the rival station. To prove it, Graney was asked to call three straight balls no matter what happened at home plate. Sure enough, the voice on WJAY called three straight balls as well. Adding weight to their conclusion, one of the players had a slight ankle injury but Graney thought he had hurt his eye. WJAY reported an eye injury as well. The next day, the executives at WHK accused WJAY of monitoring the live broadcasts and rebroadcasting them just seconds later. They threatened to take the matter to the Federal Radio Commission if the broadcasts did not cease. Apparently, WJAY had had their fun, and the issue disappeared.

The Indians radio broadcasts were sponsored by the Weideman Company, one of the largest wholesale grocery businesses in the country. The company had been in Cleveland since the last century and figured to increase its profile through the radio. During the course of the broadcasts a contest was announced that promised fabulous baseball prizes to those who took part. The grand prize was a trip to the 1932 World Series, round-trip rail fare, meals, and hotel included. The second prizes were seven Philco "Baby Grand" radios (to listen to the series, of course), and the third prizes were an assortment of fifty autographed baseballs signed by Jack Graney and various ballplayers. To win, an entrant needed to purchase Saegertown Beverages soda pop, including ginger ale, club soda, lime rickey, and root beer. Each bottle cap was to be mailed to the Weideman Company, and entrants sending in the most bottle caps would win the contest. The World Series winner would be accompanied to the games by the Weideman-sponsored announcer, Jack Graney. The contest drove people by the thousands to Cleveland-area grocery stores to pick up the product. Radio advertising and baseball were just beginning to start a long and healthy partnership.

Before the month ended, the Indians moved on to St. Louis and beat the Browns, 7–1, topping off a three-game sweep. Wes Ferrell went the distance, scattering five hits over the nine innings. Earl Averill slammed his third home run of the year, a two-run shot to deep left field. Joe Vosmik hit a double off the center-field wall, which sportswriters noted was one of the longest hits ever seen at Sportsman's Park. Fred Schulte, the Browns center fielder, made no attempt to catch the ball, but turned his back to the infield and waited for the ball to bounce to him. He quickly threw to second, keeping the fleet Vosmik from advancing further. The display of batting power from the Indians outfielders was something to behold.

The 1932 Indians were well on their way to a much-improved season. The pitching staff, with Ferrell, Harder, Hudlin, and

Brown, was starting to bring a degree of consistency to the rotation. Ferrell had his eyes on a fourth straight twenty-win season, while Harder and Brown were trying to establish themselves as full-time starters. Waiting in the background was Oral Hildebrand, another promising young pitcher. It was a long season, but the early results were quite promising for both the team and the fans. Whether they played at League Park or Cleveland Stadium, one thing was certain: this team was going to win their share of ball games.

As the Indians were sweeping the Browns, Mayor Miller sent a letter, or more of a plea, to Alva Bradley. It read, in part, "The city would like very much to see the Cleveland Indians occupy the stadium. We feel that it would be beneficial to the ball club. It would draw more fans and attendance because it is within walking distance of all downtown buildings." Miller ended the letter with a bit of desperation, writing, "Before you close the door to negotiations I wish you would give this thing further consideration because I know that people in Cleveland feel that the stadium was built for the Cleveland Baseball Club."

The letter had a positive effect on Bradley. The owner advised the newspapers that if the city was ready to do serious business, he would schedule the time to meet and discuss a solution. He said, "Let the city get together with itself first. I'm willing to match my time with the time of anyone from the city who can speak for the city."

Bradley got his point across, that he was willing to talk but only if there was a genuine offer on the table. He had no interest in meeting to discuss nickel-and-dime issues. For him to come back and negotiate there had to be a legitimate offer from the mayor and the city council. In the middle of the exchange between Miller and Bradley, the new stadium manager, E. E. Adams, revealed that a group of Clevelanders had approached him about buying a National League franchise and transferring it to Cleveland. The gentlemen convinced Adams they could get the vote of the National and American League owners and move right into the stadium. The possible franchises mentioned were Pittsburgh, Philadelphia, and St. Louis. This sudden announcement may have been a ploy to get Bradley moving, yet the fact was that without the Cleveland owners' consent the move could not be made. At any rate, Bradley agreed to meet with Mayor Miller the first week of May.

The conference was held at the mayor's office, with only Miller, Bradley, and Joseph Hostetler, the team secretary and attorney. They did not reach any type of agreement, but scheduled further talks on May 4. The next afternoon, the three gentlemen talked for several hours, then adjourned to attend the Indians game at League Park. Though nothing concrete was accomplished, it became clear that the mayor and Indians officials were establishing a rapport. Two weeks later a tentative agreement was reached. Smaller but important issues, including who would get the concessions and who would pay for after-game cleanup, were settled. Under the terms of the lease, the Indians would keep all revenues from concessions. In return, the club consented to handle all expenses for the cleanup necessary after each home game. For the remainder of the 1932 season, sixty-five days of stadium use were allocated for baseball, including off days when the team needed to practice. Bradley requested that the abbreviated days begin on July 26 when the Indians returned for a long home stand. The terms for a complete season gave the Indians eighty-four days for games and practice, running from April 1 through October 15. The schedule included an extra week for a possible World Series appearance. The city retained the option to schedule up to three events during the baseball season, but anything planned had to be on a day other than Sunday or a holiday.

One crucial point allowed Alva Bradley to terminate the lease before the 1934 season. If for some reason the stadium collapsed or the attendance numbers were unsatisfactory, the team could walk away and return to League Park. If the club committed to stay after the 1934 season, they were in for the long haul, meaning until 1957, or twenty-five years from the original signing date. A stipulation was added to allow the ball club to negotiate a new lease after completion of the 1946 season. They would retain that right until 1949. If no action was taken by the club by then, negotiations could not begin until the expiration of the lease in 1957.

The amount of revenue for the city remained unchanged, with the minimum total rent staying at $50,000. As Bradley demanded, a percentage of additional revenue would be paid to the city if and when the attendance reached 675,000. The city gained awfully little from the agreement, but on the other hand Mayor Miller had broken the impasse and cleared the way for Major League Baseball to be played at Cleveland Stadium. The only remaining obstacle in his path were the firebrands on the city council.

A week later, the city agreed to bear all the expenses in repairing the infield. That project involved digging up the entire area and adjusting the height of the bases and the pitcher's mound. For good measure, the city decided to resod the outfield as well. All of this activity proved that the mayor was on top of the situation and performing as the voters expected he might. Surely a battle with the council was only days away, but the mayor had shown a good deal of leadership.

The debate at the city council began on May 26. In a touch of irony, one of the council members was none other than former city manager William Hopkins. The first order of business was to grill Hopkins on the assertion that the stadium was built solely for the Cleveland Indians. All the promotion and publicity back in 1928 was believed to be a smoke screen to divert attention from the actual purpose of the facility. The promise of civic events, pageants, opera, and even the circus was all baloney. Hopkins fervently denied the accusations despite the heavy cross-examination from his colleagues.

Another area of major concern was the Indians taking all the concession revenue. One councilman argued that the team would recoup their rental fees solely from the concession money. He declared that several concessionaires in the city, given the chance, might fork over $50,000 just to obtain the rights to sell food and souvenirs. The debate continued for most of the session, removing any chance of a quick vote.

Just two days later, the council met again to argue the merits of the lease. A large amount of grandstanding occurred from the members, who wanted to remind all concerned that the stadium was a civic enterprise. It was not built for the convenience of the Cleveland Indians. One council member believed baseball was not even needed. A few large-revenue events and numerous activities might be all that was needed for the community to benefit. Joseph Hostetler weighed in, warning the council it was treading on thin ice: "If the council makes up its mind to use the stadium for all kinds of things without regard to income, we [the ball club] cannot afford to keep up the arena. It is an impossible task."

Council president John D. Marshall claimed the lease was a monopoly and the Indians had veto power to stop almost any events other than baseball. In effect, this was true. Still, the stadium could not function without a monster tenant such as a Major League team. Marshall was arguing after the fact, anyway. A baseball field had already been laid out and a crew was working long hours to get the infield in playable shape. Who was kidding who? The anti-Indians faction knew that hotels and restaurants were in position to gain more revenue and downtown traffic stood to increase. It was all about the money. Baseball was coming to downtown, and the city council had to know it. The naiveté of the council was appalling and quite unconvincing.

Joseph Hostetler quietly listened while certain members of the city council demonstrated their commitment to community affairs. He remained silent while talk of pageants, concerts, and Boy Scout conventions was bandied about. Finally, he rose to his feet and addressed the council one more time, saying, "If you make up your minds that the financial end doesn't count I would say that you should fire the stadium manager, open the gates and let anyone use it." He was right on point.

Alva Bradley mulled over the situation in an effort to placate the members of the council who were delaying the lease approval. In between meeting with his legal counsel, he attended the May 30 doubleheader pitting the Indians against the White Sox. It turned out to be a Memorial Day extravaganza. The afternoon developed into a wild affair, with near fights on the field and umpire-baiting from the Chicago players. In game two, veteran umpire George Moriarty was behind the plate. A former ballplayer who had spent years with the Detroit Tigers, this umpire was a tough cookie. Throughout his playing days, he enjoyed a reputation for throwing a punch or two.

Accounts of the game had Moriarty jawing back and forth with the White Sox bench. The visitors were upset with some questionable calls. In the bottom of the ninth the Sox led 11–8. A single by Wes Ferrell scored one run, then with one out Earl Averill blasted a triple to center field, tying the game at eleven. Chicago manager Lew Fonseca had his pitcher walk Joe Vosmik and Eddie Morgan to load the bases and set up the possibility of a ground-ball double play. Luke Sewell, a slow runner, tapped a slow roller. The force was made at second, but Eddie Morgan came flying in and knocked Jackie Hayes over to prevent the relay to first. Averill scored the winning run for an Indians 12–11 victory.

The White Sox players were angry enough, but when they walked up the players' runway, who was standing there but tough guy George Moriarty. After a few threats, pitcher Milt Gaston stepped forward and the fight was on. The umpire threw a right to Gaston's jaw, breaking his hand in the process. With Gaston lying prone on the runway, all hell broke loose. Catchers Charlie Berry and Frank Grube, burly fellows and ex-football players, joined the struggle along with Fonseca. Alva Bradley was on his way to visit the Indians clubhouse when he came upon the battle. He saw Moriarty on the ground being pummeled and kicked by the White Sox catchers and manager. A few of the Cleveland players heard the commotion and raced down the runway to break up the brawl. Bradley escorted Moriarty to the owner's car for a trip to Cleveland Clinic. There he received X-rays for the hand and treatment for the cuts and bruises.

A report went to Will Harridge, who announced an immediate trip to Cleveland for a hearing. Tommy Connolly, umpire in chief for the American League, boarded a train, as did the Chicago White Sox executives. Rules stated that any player striking an umpire was subject to a ninety-day suspension and a fine. Since both Berry and Grube were catchers, the possibility existed that the White Sox would have to quickly find backstop help or put a reserve outfielder or infielder behind the plate.

The hearing took place the following morning at the Hotel Cleveland. President Harridge told all in attendance that he had never experienced such a thing in his twenty-seven years of service. An umpire fighting four players was unheard of. Lew Fonseca testified that Moriarty had been verbally abusing his players ever since the beginning of the season. He claimed umpires normally used a separate exit to reach their dressing room, not the player's runway. He further swore that the ex-ballplayer challenged the four of them to a fight. Fonseca argued that it was Moriarty who provoked the fight, not the players. Alva Bradley testified, but for some reason Harridge did not call the Indians players who stopped the scuffle. The previous day they had told reporters that a group of them tried to hustle the umpire out of danger. In spite of their efforts, Moriarty said, "Don't hurry me boys, I'm not afraid of what those fellows will do." Harridge had a signed statement from the umpire explaining his side of the confrontation.

Harridge reviewed the testimony and in essence found George Moriarty guilty of inciting the riot. Milt Gaston received a ten-day suspension, Fonseca a $500 fine, while Berry and Grube were fined $250. Harridge issued a severe rebuke to the umpire and accused him of neglect of duty. Based on the testimony, Harridge thought Moriarty should have thrown Fonseca and Berry out of the second game. Had they been sitting in the visitor's locker room the fight likely would not have taken place. Harridge explained to reporters that the ninety-day suspension would only apply if an appeal were filed in the office of Commissioner Landis and subsequently lost. Nobody wanted to pursue that route, and the matter was closed. The newspapers had a field day with Moriarty, claiming surprise that he only challenged four players and not the entire team. For his part, the defeated umpire quietly slipped out of town. This was a rare case of the American League siding with the players and not the umpire. The verdict really said, "It was your fault for getting your rear end kicked."

With the brawl incident behind him, Alva Bradley and his legal team agreed on a compromise to present to the city council. One new provision would allow the city to terminate the Indians' lease after the 1934 season. In effect, the Cleveland front office was offering a two-year trial. If after two baseball seasons the city was unhappy with the arrangement, the lease could be broken. Still in place was the Indians' escape clause allowing it to leave before the start of the 1934 season.

Another stipulation added to the proposal gave the ball club the right to collect from the city 50 percent of the maintenance costs projected at League Park. This requirement would be valid during the two-year trial. In this manner the old ballpark would be kept in ready condition in the event the Indians returned. Joseph Hostetler informed the council that Bradley and his partners had pumped a million dollars into the club. In four years of ownership the team had lost approximately $240,000. They were not in a position to pay the full costs to keep League Park in Major League shape while they played elsewhere. The club estimated maintenance to be between $8,000 and $20,000.

This gesture from the Indians seemed to melt a good deal of the resistance. The anti-baseball faction warmed to the idea of the opportunity to remove their tenant after the 1934 season. On all fronts, an agreement with the city council inched closer to reality. On June 21, with the Indians' proposed debut at the stadium about a month away, council president Marshall still had some nitpicking to do. He favored the two-year trial, but wanted the council to have the sole control of renewing or canceling the baseball lease. He proposed to eliminate the mayor's veto power from consideration. This resolution probably violated the city charter, but Marshall feared the mayor would automatically veto a lease termination. His anxieties were fueled by an increase in the council to thirty members by 1934. If the council voted to terminate the lease and Mayor Miller exercised his veto power, Marshall worried that he would not be able to raise the two-thirds majority needed to override the veto. If that was not enough, he brought up the lack of availability of Sunday and holiday dates for civic events. An exasperated Joseph Hostetler, speaking for Bradley, said, "If we have to pass up Sundays and holidays you'll have no tenant!"

Regardless of all the last-minute posturing, on June 23 the lease agreement came to a vote. After calling the roll, the result was fifteen votes yes, nine no. The lease was approved, but lacked the two-thirds majority vote to qualify as an emergency act. Had there been seventeen yes votes, the lease could have been activated immediately. The Indians were forced to file another formal bid that would not be heard until July 18, the next scheduled council meeting. The bid would have to be approved, but a two-week waiting period was part of the procedure. This pushed the Indians' occupancy date back to August 2, meaning several more games would remain at League Park.

One of the nay votes belonged to William Hopkins; yes, the same former city manager who had worked day and night to get the stadium off the ground. One could make the case that his reasons in casting the negative vote were personal. He no longer controlled the action, and the lease he drew up three years before had been completely reworked. Some petty jealousy may have clouded his judgment in compelling the ball club to further delay their stadium schedule.

Mayor Miller left town to attend the Democratic National Convention in Chicago. Alva Bradley's legal counsel Joseph Hostetler did the same. For roughly one week the matter of the lease went ignored. Sometime after the mayor returned, a tad of skullduggery was in the making. The pro-Indians Democrats got together and decided to revise the agreement one more time, removing the clause stating that the city had the right to cancel the lease agreement after the 1934 season. The formal reason given was the concern over paying half of the League Park maintenance costs. With the original clause and the two-year trial, the city would lose anywhere from $16,000 to $40,000. There was legitimate concern in the council, as a block of the Republican members did not want to pay any maintenance costs at League Park. They would have their way, but now the Indians were in complete control. Even if the city council wanted to throw the ball club out of the stadium, they no longer had the power to do so. Before the change was introduced, Mayor Miller and his Democratic allies made certain the votes were there to pull off the mischief. The plot met with angry opposition, but the mayor had his sixteen votes, and all obstacles to playing baseball at the stadium were permanently removed.

To salvage a start date of July 31, Bradley and his lawyers needed to sign a temporary lease. This agreement ran until August 2, when the actual twenty-five-year lease kicked in. The mayor had the authority to draw up the temporary lease and get Bradley to sign. The lease was signed on July 30 at home plate, with the signatories sitting around a small wooden table. Alva Bradley and Joseph Hostetler sat on one side, with Mayor Miller and E. E. Adams on the other. After a few pleasantries, the fountain pens were brought out and the marathon three-and-one-half-year struggle came to an end. Photographers asked the group to take off their hats for a picture. Alva Bradley smiled and said, "Boys I'd take off my shirt, that's how glad I am to be here!" Everybody shook hands. It was time to play ball.

Chapter 7

GRAND NEW STADIUM

G oing into the month of July, the Indians had a mediocre record of thirty-seven wins against thirty-two defeats. The day before, manager Peckinpaugh had read the riot act to his ballplayers in an effort to shake them out of their lethargy. The team was fifth in the American League standings, twelve games behind the Yankees. The tactic worked, as the club showed signs of life in a 7–4 win over Detroit. Wes Ferrell charged the home-plate umpire on a disputed check swing. The rest of the infield came dashing in and argued the call to back up their pitcher. Later, Joe Vosmik walked and came all the way around on a double. The Indians' third-base coaches usually played it safe, but Vosmik never looked for a stop sign when rounding third and speeding his way home.

Peckinpaugh was pleased at the fight exhibited by his troops. The tongue-lashing seemed to have a lasting effect, continuing throughout the entire month of July. Of the thirty-one games played, Cleveland took twenty-one. They were peaking at the right time, particularly when they were about to enter a brand new $3 million stadium. The Indians needed to be playing great baseball to attract fans at the new facility.

The depression still hung over the city and country like a black cloud. In Cleveland alone there was over a 20 percent reduction in the workforce while wages and salaries had dropped nearly thirty.

There were few jobs being created and thousands who needed relief. *Baseball Magazine* tried to put a positive spin on the hard times, counseling fans that baseball was an escape from the bill collectors, a place to leave your troubled thoughts behind. Considering that most unemployed folks had no idea where their next dollar was coming from, buying a ticket to a ball game was not high on the list. There existed a core of fans who still held their jobs and had money to spend, but attendance was a foremost concern for the owners in both leagues.

Even with dwindling crowds and the steady loss of revenue, ballplayers and owners tried to help the less fortunate. A charity organization in Cleveland ran a campaign to acquire sporting equipment for the benefit of the unemployed. The idea was to collect as much money and equipment as possible to arrange for free usage of balls, bats, gloves, tennis racquets, horseshoes, chess sets, and checkerboards. The items would be available at various parks in the metro Cleveland area, and unemployed men and women could visit any of the parks and borrow what they needed. Alva Bradley donated two boxes of baseballs and Babe Ruth signed two bats, one of which he supposedly used to hit a homer at League Park. Lou Gehrig donated a signed bat, as did local star Earl Averill. The bats were used to raise money for equipment. It was a small gesture, yet still showed a certain amount of compassion.

On July 9 the Indians ended a five-game series at Washington. They narrowly missed a sweep as the Senators managed to salvage the last game on Saturday. The club boarded a train for Cleveland to start another five-game battle, this time with Philadelphia. These were away games, but the first landed on Sunday, meaning they would have to play game one at League Park due to the Philadelphia ordinance already mentioned. After the contest, the teams would have to travel back to Philadelphia for a Monday doubleheader and two single games on Tuesday and Wednesday. To say this was grueling is an understatement.

The two teams arrived in Cleveland to play one of the most remarkable games in Major League history. In eighteen innings, the Athletics defeated Cleveland, 18–17. A number of records were set, including shortstop Johnny Burnett stroking nine hits in eleven at bats. (According to the *Cleveland News* the old record was set in

1892 by Wilbert Robinson of the Baltimore Orioles. In that game against the St. Louis club, Robinson recorded seven hits in seven at bats.) The Indians totaled thirty-three hits, the most in a game since 1901, when the New York Giants got thirty-one. The Athletics had a mere twenty-five hits, but the combined total of fifty-eight topped a 1922 high set by the Philadelphia Phillies and Chicago Cubs. The Indians left an astounding twenty-four men on base and, incredibly, neither team used a pinch hitter.

There were no further records broken, though Jimmy Foxx blasted three home runs, a double and two singles for eight RBIs. His teammate Al Simmons had five singles and scored four runs. On the Indians' side, aside from Burnett, Earl Averill launched a home run and four singles and Eddie Morgan had two doubles and three singles. The only players who did not hit well were both team catchers. The Athletics receivers went zero for nine, while Glenn Myatt had one hit in seven at bats. The 10,000 fans in attendance got their money's worth and then some. The game would last over four hours and did not end until 7:00 p.m.

Connie Mack was worried about his pitchers for the five-game series, which led him to start nondescript hurler Lew Krausse. Cleveland scored three times in the first inning, prompting Mack to change pitchers. Eddie Rommel took the mound in the bottom of the second and pitched the remaining seventeen innings. The veteran allowed a whopping fourteen runs and twenty-nine hits. Apparently, Mack made his mind up early to use only two pitchers and stuck with the plan. Cleveland started Clint Brown, who survived until the seventh when the Athletics scored seven times. Roger Peckinpaugh brought in Willis Hudlin, who walked the next two batters to load the bases. Sensing disaster, Peck called for Wes Ferrell to relieve Hudlin. After a few warm-up tosses, Ferrell gave up a bases-clearing double to Jimmy Dykes. Jimmy Foxx homered for the second time before Ferrell retired the side. Philadelphia now led, 13–8.

Fans shook their heads in disgust and booed Peckinpaugh for his selection of pitchers. They quieted down quickly when the Indians came fighting back to score six mind-boggling runs and regain the lead, 14–13. Johnny Burnett started the inning with his fifth hit of the game. Averill followed with a single, then Joe Vosmik and Eddie Morgan both doubled to account for three runs. Glenn Myatt walked and Bill Cissell attempted a sacrifice bunt. The ball popped in the air and, rather than catch it, Rommel let it drop to start a double play. The intention was good but his throw was wild and Morgan came around to score. Willie Kamm, part of the Chicago connection, sacrificed and Dick Porter singled in the fifth and sixth runs.

Neither team scored in the eighth inning, leaving Philadelphia one last chance to pull out the win. Ferrell got the first two batters, bringing up Jimmy Dykes for one last opportunity. The Cleveland fans held their breath when Dykes hit an easy roller to first. Eddie Morgan moved in and somehow let the ball sneak through his legs for a crucial error. It was such a routine play that the Indians outfielders started to jog toward the dugout when the ball left the bat. Dick Porter had to stop in his tracks and retrieve the baseball, holding Dykes at first. Ferrell seemed to unravel here, walking Al Simmons. Jimmy Foxx was next and he took advantage by lining a double to left field. Vosmik fielded the ball and threw to second, thinking Simmons would hold at third base. Al took off and beat the relay home to put Philadelphia ahead, 15–14.

Now the Cleveland fans began to march toward the exits. They soon paused when Willie Kamm opened the inning with a double. Wes Ferrell, usually a good hitter, flied out. Porter went out, but Johnny Burnett put the fans back in their seats with a single to score Kamm. Averill singled, leaving runners on the corners. On the first pitch he stole second base without a throw. Joe Vosmik went the opposite way, lining a sinking drive to right field. Mule Haas raced in and caught the ball off his shoe tops, turning a somersault in the process. The inning was over, but the Indians had tied the game.

The Indians threatened in the eleventh inning when Dick Porter walked and Burnett doubled off the right-field wall. Porter stopped at third instead of trying to make a dash to the plate. Eddie Rommel steadied himself and got out of the inning. In the bottom of the twelfth, Morgan doubled. Bill Cissell singled to left field, but Morgan hesitated while rounding third, then tried to dash home. A strong throw caught him at the plate.

Three more innings went by without any heart-stopping action. Several fans yelled for popcorn, but there were no vendors left in the park. Apparently, all the food was gone and the concessions were closed. In the top of the sixteenth, the Athletics came to life when Jimmy Dykes singled. Al Simmons forced him at second, then Jimmy Foxx homered deep into the left-field bleachers. Once again the fans headed for the exits, but scurried back after Dick Porter doubled and Burnett singled, his ninth and final hit of the game. Averill lofted a sacrifice fly to close the gap to one run. The Cleveland crowd was astonished when Vosmik and Morgan singled to tie the score at 17–17. Incredibly, the game was going to eighteen innings.

At the top of the frame, with Jimmy Foxx on first, shortstop Eric McNair singled to left field. The ball took a weird hop and bounced over Vosmik's head. Foxx came all the way around to make the score 18–17. Did the Indians have another miracle left? No, they did not, and the incredible four-hour back-and-forth struggle went to the Athletics. Both teams barely had time to shower, then board their train back to Philadelphia.

This game would be remembered by players and fans for many years. Alva Bradley claimed it was the most amazing game he had ever witnessed as the Cleveland owner. The newspapers devoted several pages of summaries in the morning editions. The coverage might have been slightly more run-of-the-mill if Eddie Morgan had fielded the easy ground ball in the ninth. His error led to nine extra innings of baseball and several new entries in the record books. It is a wonder his teammates let him on the train to Philadelphia.

One would think that the four remaining games in Philadelphia would turn out to be pitcher's duels. The hitters should have been worn out by the eighteen-inning game and the all-night train travel. On Monday, July 11, the Indians and Athletics played a doubleheader with a combined score of Cleveland 21, Philadelphia 15. The Indians took both of the slugfests with timely hitting and slightly better pitching. In the first game, Cleveland pitcher Jack Russell lurched through eight-plus innings in a 9–8 win. This was no surprise, being that Russell, recently acquired from the Red Sox, had lost thirty games over his last two seasons. Despite allowing eighteen hits, he left the game a winner. Connie Mack called on Lew Krausse to pitch the ninth inning in relief of Rube Walberg. Connie was probably hoping the Indians had forgot about Krausse from the day before. Earl Averill greeted the relief pitcher with a home run that proved to be the game winner.

The second game had Mel Harder facing Roy Mahaffey. The young Cleveland hurler turned in the best pitching performance (if one could call it that) of the series to date, winning 12–7. Harder went the distance, allowing seventeen hits, while Mahaffey was charged with all twelve runs in seven innings of work. Dick Porter and Averill did most of the damage, accounting for eight hits between them. Averill blasted two more home runs, giving him a total of four in the last three games. Johnny Burnett came back to planet Earth, only picking up two hits in the doubleheader.

The Indians won the last two games by scores of 7–6 and 7–5. In the first win they pounded Lefty Grove for another eighteen hits. The final game went extra innings again, but this time only ten. Averill clubbed his fifth home run of the series and the Athletics' Al Simmons belted two, each of them off rookie Oral Hildebrand. Regardless, the Cleveland pitcher could rightly claim the best pitching performance of the five contests. He struck out five to win his fourth game of the year. The complete score for all the games was Cleveland 52, Philadelphia 44. Johnny Burnett finished with fourteen hits in the series. Each game was a thriller, with both teams scoring runs at a furious pace. Any fan who had to take a bathroom break no doubt missed a significant part of the action.

When the Cleveland club left town to finish the Philadelphia series, their record stood at forty-three wins versus thirty-six losses. On July 24, they concluded the road trip in Chicago and headed back home with an improved mark of fifty-four victories against thirty-nine defeats. The boys had moved all the way up to second place. It had taken Billy Evans four years, but now the Indians were a formidable ball club. Their outfield of Porter, Averill, and Vosmik continued to be as good as or better than any other team's in baseball. The three were thought of so highly that Cleveland team trainer Lefty Weisman named his second son Jed, as in Joe, Earl, and Dick. The pitching behind Wes Ferrell had much promise, with Mel Harder and Clint Brown beginning to display Major League ability. The players were surely ready to start a new era at Cleveland Municipal Stadium.

The Indians were back at the ranch to open a long home stand, beginning with the Yankees. The teams would square off at League Park, then the Athletics were set to arrive for one last game at the old grounds. The next day, they would take on Cleveland at the new facility. Nostalgia was the theme of the day as fans remembered the forty-one seasons at 66th and Lexington. The historic park had seen many of the great stars from the nineteenth and twentieth centuries including Cy Young, Ty Cobb, Walter Johnson, Joe Jackson, and George Sisler. A spectacular World Series had taken place in 1920. The fans had witnessed a perfect game and several no-hitters, and even watched Indians pitcher Ray Caldwell get struck by lightning. Now the days were just about over when young boys could sneak into the park for free or climb trees to catch partial views of the playing field.

The *Cleveland News* ran a story about baseball's mightiest sluggers coming to town, saying, "Cleveland fans are fortunate to say the least for during the next week they will be privileged to look at five of the six outstanding sluggers in baseball. And when we say sluggers we mean just that, nothing else but." The newspaper added to the hype of the stadium by getting baseball fans excited about Ruth, Gehrig, Foxx, Simmons, and Averill. The last-minute wrangling by the city council meant the Yankees had to miss playing downtown, but who better than the pennant-winning Athletics to christen the new playing grounds? Each day, the three Cleveland papers ran stories to generate increased attention for the July 31 grand opening.

As the day grew closer, stories were printed about the big names planning to attend. The commissioner of baseball, the fun-loving Judge Landis, was on the register, along with American and National League presidents Will Harridge and John Heydler. The governor of Ohio, George White, received an invitation. Alva Bradley predicted a crowd of 60,000 or better. Billy Evans commented that the stadium premiere would undoubtedly attract the largest advance sale of tickets in Cleveland baseball history. In fact, the downtown and League Park ticket offices were flooded with fans who wanted seats for the game. Extra people were hired to man the windows to meet the demand. The grounds crew stationed themselves at Municipal Stadium to add more sod and soil for an immaculate playing field.

Baseball fans in a three-hundred-mile radius had already purchased $2,500 worth of tickets. The front office reported six hundred mail-order requests in one day amounting to $10,000 in cash. There were baseball fans planning to attend from Indiana, Pennsylvania, and New York. Estimates showed 25,000 fans were coming from outside of the city. Bradley was certain a record for a single game was about to be set in Cleveland.

A civic organizations committee had the task of sponsoring the game-day festivities inside and outside of the stadium. The groups participating included the Chamber of Commerce, Rotary Club, Cleveland Automobile Club, the American Legion, the Knights of Columbus, and the Cuyahoga County Bar Association. Each organization sent a similar message to its members: "Buy tickets!" In addition to filling the park, the groups were buying decorations and hiring bands to perform. The National Air Races held every September in Cleveland agreed to have a number of airplanes for a fly-by during the game. Earlier in the week several planes flew over downtown, dropping sets of tickets to the lucky folks who found them on the sidewalks.

The *Cleveland News* reported that the stadium infield had an excess of clay to it, creating the hardest infield in the league. Infielders were warned to take notice. The hot July weather had browned the outfield grass to an extent, but the stadium manager, Mr. Adams, assured both teams their outfielders would have no problems with any unusual bounces. The grounds crew was on standby just in case. The city had taken one of its three dates to schedule a Monday night fight featuring a local boy, outstanding heavyweight Johnny Risko. Promises were made to the Indians that all seats would be in foul territory and the stands. The ring was to be placed just outside of first base. Nothing was going to interfere with the grandest of openings.

The Yankees came to town for the last hurrah at League Park. Babe Ruth had a minor leg injury that kept him out of the July 27 doubleheader. Without the "Bambino" in the lineup the Indians swept both games, 2–1 and 12–10. Oral Hildebrand won his fifth game impressively, scattering four hits over nine innings. Joe Vosmik had two hits including a home run to lead the Cleveland attack. Game two had little pitching from either team. Mel Harder could not get out of the first inning and Jack Russell came on to allow six runs in one and a third innings. Roger Peckinpaugh brought in Willis Hudlin, who went the final seven innings allowing only two runs. The next two games were split, the Yankees winning 10–1 and dropping the last game 4–3. In the first game the Babe came off the bench to detonate two home runs and drive in seven, while Charlie "Red" Ruffing held the Indians to one run: Earl Averill's twenty-fourth homer. The Yankees' final appearance at League Park featured a colossal home run by Ruth that cleared the houses on Lexington Avenue. The ninth-inning blast closed the gap to one run, but Cleveland held on to win.

The Indians had taken three out of four from the mighty Yankees. They had everything going for them entering the July 30 last game at League Park. Cleveland held a half-game lead over the Athletics for second place with a chance to extend it further. Now was the time to enter the new stadium on a winning note. They failed to do so, getting knocked around by Philadelphia, 7–2. Only 5,000 people watched the game, including super-fan Dick Davis, who had seen every home contest dating back to 1891. The ball game ended on an appropriate note of futility when Eddie Morgan struck out with the bases full. A fan stood on the Indians dugout and played taps. All the Indians, Athletics, and umpires gathered on the field and took off their caps while the trumpet sounded. It was a solemn moment, seemingly the last Major League gathering at the park.

Even with the disappointing loss, all attention turned to Sunday. The Cleveland Railway Company announced plans to reroute four of their streetcar lines to give fans better access to the stadium. The west-side cars had a new route north via West 3rd to a thousand feet from the stadium. Fans from six different west-side stops had the option to arrive downtown, then transfer to the West 3rd route. The east-side Payne and Wade Park cars normally brought folks to League Park. For the downtown opener they were rerouted west on Superior to downtown to Ontario Street off Public Square, then north to Lakeside, a short walk to the stadium. Additional service was made available from East 14th Street and East 9th to allow room for automobiles to weave in and out of the streetcar lines.

The day's entertainment included comedy and music. Al Schacht and Nick Altrock, the official clowns of Major League Baseball, were scheduled to entertain before and during the game. They were both former players and currently base coaches with the Washington Senators. The duo had created a comedy act that they performed at baseball games to rave reviews. Senators owner Clark Griffith loaned the comics out for the occasion. Other plans included ceremonial flag raising, rousing music, and parades. The main parade was scheduled to march down Euclid Avenue, led by the fifty-piece Jimmy Johnson band. Governor White had the honor of throwing out the first pitch to Mayor Ray Miller. Commissioner Landis agreed to stand behind Miller and call the pitch. Estimates of 60,000 fans were being raised to the 70,000 range. The victories over New York and the Indians' temporary rise to second place had amplified the excitement and produced an outbreak of last-minute ticket buying. Several different movie companies were in town to set up cameras to film all the celebrating and parts of the ball game. Later the film was to be placed at movie theaters around the country.

Ticket sales continued to move along at a brisk pace. Special sections needed to be set aside for the bankers of the Cleveland Trust Company and employees of the Goodrich Tire & Rubber Company. The Chamber of Commerce and Rotary Club bought hordes of seats and requested additional special seating. The Al Sirat Grotto, the Masonic "gentlemen of fraternity and good cheer," were bringing members from Sandusky, Akron, and several other cities. Their large numbers got them a reserved section as well. Estimates for out of town attendance passed the 25,000 mark. The travelers were using cars, trains, and a number booked flights to the Cleveland airport. At least for a day, Cleveland was the best location in the nation.

The railroad companies took advantage of a huge opportunity to make money. The Nickel Plate Railroad had trains running from cities west of Cleveland such as Lima, Findlay, Fostoria, and Lorain. Fares ranged from seventy-five cents to $1.75. The round-trip excursions departed as early as 4:00 a.m. and left Cleveland at 6:00 p.m. The New York Central and Big Four Railroads were covering Detroit, Buffalo, and Erie, Pennsylvania, as well as eastern Ohio and the central part of the state. Several trains were leaving from Cincinnati, Columbus, and Dayton.

The grand opening of the stadium would not be complete without a special box reserved for former Cleveland baseball players living in the area. Players mentioned to have invitations were current scout Bill Bradley, WHK baseball announcer Jack Graney, Larry Lajoie, former manager Lee Fohl, Terry Turner, Elmer Flick, Bill Wamby, Earl Moore, Tris Speaker, and a host of other favorites. A special invite went to all-time pitching great Cy Young. The *Cleveland News* printed all the ballplayers' home addresses in hopes that neighbors would knock on doors and remind the ex-players to attend.

Alva Bradley planned a pregame luncheon at the stadium for two hundred guests from Cleveland and out of town. During the week, Bradley spoke at the regular meeting of the Rotary Club. The last time he had addressed the group was in 1928 when he lobbied for the building of the stadium. The Cleveland owner seemed to have everything in order for a spectacular debut at his new place to play ball.

Stadium manager Adams handed out temporary parking rights to the Hanna Parking Company. The rate for Sunday was twenty-five cents per space. All day Saturday, a crew of 175 to two hundred men worked to clean up the dirt and level the parking area. One could only guess how much dust was going to be stirred up by the huge amount of autos. There were no estimates offered on how many cars could be squeezed in the areas east and west of the stadium. From day one, it had been a major concern how automobiles would be able to get in and out of the parking zones without snarling the regular downtown traffic. City officials were probably lighting candles in hopes that the situation would take care of itself.

As late as Saturday morning, cigar stores away from the city were telephoning for more tickets to be sent. A store in Akron called for 2,000 more, while a Youngstown store sold their allotment of 500 and requested extra. With all the ticket requests still coming in, team officials were now expecting well over 70,000 people to pack the stadium.

The Saturday newspapers were filled with testimonials and plaudits for Alva Bradley, Billy Evans, and the Indians players. One local official wrote, "Billy Evans has made good three times—as umpire, newspaper writer and now as baseball general manager. Alva Bradley is a game guy. He has bought talent as Evans found it and paid no attention to the world wide stomach ache [the depression]. When they open at the stadium the Indians will break the world record for baseball attendance."

Bradley and Evans had done close to miracles during the world wide headache, but they had a long way to go to consistently fill up a gigantic new stadium. A large majority of people who bought tickets for Sunday were very wealthy men, leaders of industry. They did not speak for the common man, out of work and scuffling to put food on the family table. Few took note of the attendance figure of 5,000 for the final game at League Park. The Indians had already acknowledged that they were operating in the red. Certainly, the 70,000-plus would give a considerable boost to the 1932 attendance figures, but the question remained whether healthy attendance at the stadium was possible in the shadow of what would come to be called the Great Depression. Bradley and Evans hoped so. The city hoped so. So did Major League Baseball.

In his last column before the opening of the stadium, Ed Bang wrote a moving farewell to League Park. Bang, who had seen more games there than any other Cleveland sportswriter, said, "Everything is in readiness to shift the big tent of Cleveland's major league baseball circus to the lake front stadium tomorrow. After today splendid old League Park will remain desolate as far as American League activity is concerned. It is difficult to abruptly sever connections once and for all with a place that carries as many stirring associations as League Park." A chapter was ending, a new one beginning.

That evening, WHK Radio hosted a pep rally for the big event on Sunday. The studio had room for 450 fans as well as the entire Cleveland team. Jack Graney interviewed most of the players, while the revved-up fans cheered and raised broadcast levels to a dangerous high. When the live program ended, the Indians players patiently signed baseballs, bats, and gloves for the adults and children. Thousands of listeners were at home, glued to the radio to hear all about their favorite ballplayers. The promotion campaign ended on a high note.

Sunday morning came and the weather forecast called for temperatures near eighty degrees with a slight chance of rain. With everything at stake only a monsoon could get the game postponed. At 11:00 a.m. the ticket windows opened to extensive lines of people waiting for a chance to see the game. There was a short supply of reserved seats left, but thousands of general admissions seats remained. Fortunately for the ticket buyers, several of the office staff were holdovers from the 1920 pennant race and were able to keep up with the rush. Walter McNichols, the longtime business manager, hurried back and forth to handle any problems at the windows. Edna Jamieson, who had supervised all the ticket orders for the Cleveland-Brooklyn World Series, took care of numerous angry fans looking to purchase better seats. Miss Jamieson had been with the club since she left high school in 1913. Edna was held in such high esteem that she received a fair share of the champion's take in 1920. Her calm demeanor and quick thinking prevented any riots from erupting at the box office.

As game time approached, the lines extended further and further out. One of the ticket takers kept making runs to the vault to break out new blocks of tickets. As each minute passed, the possibility of a sellout became more and more likely. The office people glanced at the standing-room-only signs, wondering if they were going to be removed from the shelves and placed outside.

Once the fans were able to purchase their tickets, they had 476 ushers throughout the stadium to assist with seating. This compared with 220 at the smaller League Park. The ushers were essential, as none of the ticket buyers had any familiarity with the seat locations. Few people could find their seats without help.

A few minutes after twelve o'clock, the parade began down 21st and Euclid Avenue. Thousands of fans got in line behind Jimmy Johnson's band and clumsily marched toward the stadium. Many others had gathered downtown for some late breakfast and shopping. When they heard the band strike up, they dashed to the parade and joined in. Alva Bradley opened the stadium offices and ushered in his guests for the catered buffet. Mayor Miller and his wife were one of the first to arrive, along with Governor White and his daughter. Commissioner Landis entered with his two accomplices, Will Harridge and John Heydler. Billy Evans made a brief appearance, as he had been writing his introductions for the ex-ballplayers all morning. The politicians and stockholders checked in and had a wonderful time schmoozing with one another.

Among the box-seat holders arriving at the stadium was Charles Otis. Through his efforts as chairman of the citizen's committee the 1928 bond issue passed allowing for the facility to be built. For the day, a truce was arranged between the city Republican and Democratic leaders. They sat together in their box seats talking only baseball. Former city manager Daniel Morgan took his seat along with one-time acting mayor Harold Burton. Thomas Shibe, the owner of the Athletics, joined the group, as did Mrs. Ernest Barnard, the wife of the late American League president. All present were in line for a most entertaining afternoon.

Another group of box-seat holders approached the stadium via their elaborate yacht. They had left the dock at Rocky River, cruising east on Lake Erie. The skipper of the boat carefully nosed the yacht up to the government pier and tied off there. The party walked the short distance to the stadium entrance, avoiding all the dust stirred up by the approaching automobiles.

Within a short time, the speakers on the stadium scoreboard crackled with noise. Jack Graney, the announcer, welcomed the boisterous crowd to the inaugural baseball game at Cleveland Municipal Stadium. Governor White and Mayor Miller were introduced to take part in the pregame ceremonies. As the governor walked toward the pitching mound, he said to Wes Ferrell, "I'm in rotten shape. Please pray for me!" Next came the former ballplayers, each greeted with tremendous ovations. There they were, Cy Young and Chief Zimmer of the Cleveland Spiders, Bradley, Turner, and Moore of the beloved Cleveland Naps. The great Lajoie received the loudest ovation of any of the former stars. The boys of the 1920 World Champions were the last to take a bow. Out walked Bill Wamby, the architect of the only unassisted triple play ever seen in a World Series. Elmer Smith, the man who socked the first bases-loaded home run in World Series history. And there was Tris Speaker, the player-manager of the great 1920 team. If the fans were not energized now, they would never be.

The newspaper photographers and newsreel cameras worked overtime to record all of the ceremony. They followed the old ballplayers as they waved to the giant crowd and took their seats.

Governor White picked up the shiny new baseball and threw a weak ground ball to Mayor Miller. The field announcer introduced the grand old man of baseball, Connie Mack. He stood awkwardly in front of the microphone and revealed to the enthusiastic crowd that a new attendance record for Major League Baseball had been reached. The exact numbers were not available yet, but even so it was safe to guess that nearly 80,000 people were in the stands.

The mandatory giant wreath of flowers was presented by the Cleveland Fire Department. While the firemen slowly carried the gigantic display, the silver blimp of the Goodyear Tire & Rubber Company flew silently overhead. A moment later, four Ohio National Guard biplanes streaked across the sky, signaling the playing of "The Star-Spangled Banner." A most dazzling pregame ceremony came to a graceful end.

The ball game itself was anything but anticlimactic. Lefty Grove was on the mound for Philadelphia and Mel Harder, a surprise choice, was pitching for Cleveland. Part of the reason for selecting Harder was that Wes Ferrell had pitched on the 28th. Starting the ace of the staff on only two days' rest would mean using a tired hurler. Harder, still only twenty-two, had been coming on strong over the course of the season and owned a record of eleven wins against nine losses. Manager Peckinpaugh had enough confidence in Harder to give him the start in front of the largest crowd ever assembled for a Cleveland baseball game.

At ten minutes past three, Max Bishop led off for the Athletics with a single, the initial base hit at the stadium. Harder had his curveball working and pitched out of the inning without any further trouble. Lefty Grove walked to the mound seeking his sixteenth win of the year. His fastball exploded by the Indians hitters from the outset. Later, players of both clubs complained that the ten thousand fans in the bleachers with their white shirts and straw hats created a serious glare which obscured the batter's view. The sun came in from the southwest, reflecting off the bleacher people and blinding the hitters trying to find the baseball. Nevertheless, Grove was delivering bullets to the Cleveland lineup which had little to do with the sun.

In the third inning the Indians mounted the first rally of the game. Bill Cissell led off with a base hit. Willie Kamm laid down a sacrifice bunt, advancing Cissell to second base. Pitcher Harder grounded out to second, allowing Cissell to move to third. Dick Porter came to the plate but could not produce a base hit, stranding the runner. In the Athletics' half of the fifth, Harder got the immense crowd on their feet by striking out Mickey Cochrane, Al Simmons, and Jimmy Foxx. For the day, Harder fanned seven of the very tough Philadelphia batters.

The Indians had their best chance to score in the bottom of the seventh inning. Earl Averill led off with a single. Joe Vosmik bunted and raced to first, just beating the throw. Eddie Morgan tried to move the runners over, however Grove came charging off the mound, fielded the bunt, and whistled a throw to third to catch Averill. Luke Sewell fanned, bringing up Bill Cissell. The crowd screamed when the second baseman lined one of Grove's fastballs down the right-field line, but at the last second the ball curved foul. The next pitch was grounded to Bishop to end the inning.

Throughout the game, sportswriters made trips to the huge wooden bar that seated thirty-five people. One could only order a harmless soft drink, but the writers envisioned a day in the not too distant future when Prohibition ceased and the beer and whiskey would flow. For now they settled for the free Cokes and lemonade courtesy of Billy Evans. While the writers beat a constant path to the bar, Commissioner Landis stayed put, intently following the action in his box seat. He had a black cigar clamped between his teeth, leaning forward with both arms on the railing in front of him. On either side of Landis sat Will Harridge and John Heydler. The absolute ruler of the game was in his customary position, complete with his ever-present scowl.

Philadelphia broke the scoreless tie in the top of the eighth inning when a single, a sacrifice, and another base hit scored the only run of the day. The baseball debut at Cleveland Stadium ended with a 1–0 loss. Regardless of the loss, Mel Harder pitched a remarkable game, limiting the hard-hitting Athletics to just four singles and a double. As well as he pitched, Lefty Grove was never better, allowing only four singles to Burnett, Averill, Vosmik, and Cissell. The record-smashing crowd saw an excellent game at a state-of-the-art facility. The views from the seats were better than League Park and had more legroom for those hefty gentlemen that needed it. The modern scoreboard listed everything electronically, including balls, strikes, outs, and the player's numbers. The only negative to the opener was the final score.

With the last out of the game another key test began. How in the world were approximately eighty thousand people going to get out of the place? The best guess had somewhere around twenty-five thousand cars parked, one thousand taxis, and several hundred buses in the area. When fans reached their cars, they were shocked to see their vehicles covered in a thick brown dust. Windshields and side windows needed to be cleaned before any attempt at driving. A gentleman who had driven all the way up from Texas claimed he had never seen so much of the brown stuff before, and that included his home state. Many people had to search around until they recognized their car.

To start off the traffic jam, thirty buses along with taxis parked four deep were sitting outside the west exit. The crowd poured out at once, stopping any movement other than foot traffic. The forty policemen on traffic duty counted fifteen minutes before any vehicles moved. Soon all the motor traffic blocked East 9th Street and West 3rd. The police did all they could, but parking lots away from the stadium began to empty, creating an even bigger mess. The buses and cabs kept returning to the stadium for more pickups, stopping traffic in both directions. Folks would have to wait over an hour to exit the downtown streets.

The official attendance for the day was 80,284. That figure broke down to 76,970 paid attendance, 3,005 passes, and the several hundred employees of the Indians. This number was 241 more than the previous high on September 9, 1928, at Yankee Stadium. Those 80,043 New Yorkers were attending a doubleheader, which gave the Cleveland record a bit more prestige.

Though the batters had problems with the glare from the bleachers, they had other issues to deal with. In the many years at League Park, right-handed hitters learned to go the opposite way and aim for the short wall in right field, only 290 feet in distance. There was no wall and screen at the stadium, meaning the righties had little advantage by hitting to right, which was now 320 feet deep. They needed to pull the ball to left field. That fence was the same 320 feet away, or 30 feet further than the high right-field wall at the old grounds. It would take time to adjust.

Another factor was the large space to cover in the outfield. The center-field fence was nearly 470 feet deep, while the power alleys were well over 400. Outfielders, especially the men in center field, had to be conscious of balls going over their head for extra bases. Corner outfielders, especially those with heavy legs, had much more ground to cover in the stadium. Back at League Park, with the wall only 290 feet away, outfielders could easily patrol right field. Now anybody brave enough to play the outfield had to be ready for a track meet.

The next afternoon, the Indians and Athletics played game two at the stadium. There were no bands playing or biplanes buzzing overhead, just a game of baseball. The results were just about identical, Philadelphia winning again, 1–0. Wes Ferrell matched pitches with Rube Walberg for eight innings. In the top of the ninth Mickey Cochrane singled, went to second on a sacrifice, and scored on Eric McNair's base hit. The players still complained about the white shirts in the center-field bleachers. After the game the Cleveland front office announced that ropes were being put up in areas of the bleachers. This barred fans from sitting where the sun reflected back to home plate. Going forward, the players were assured that all they would see when they stepped in the batter's box was the pitcher and the empty green seats.

The opening home stand at Cleveland Stadium went reasonably well for the Indians. The losses to Philadelphia dropped them further in third place. Still, a four-game sweep of the lowly Red Sox, a split with Washington, then three out of four wins over Detroit kept them in contention. On August 6, Wes Ferrell pitched against Boston. He gave up a ground-ball single to Dale Alexander in the fourth inning, and that was the only hit he allowed in the 3–0 win. Five days later Wes pitched his second shutout in a row, blanking Detroit 3–0. The Tigers managed seven hits but never seriously threatened to score.

After a week at the stadium, not a single home run had been hit. In the downtown office area there was word of pools taking bets to see who would hit the first four-bagger. The honor fell to an unlikely hero, Johnny Burnett, to get the job done. On August 7, in the first game of a doubleheader with Washington, Burnett lifted a fly ball that just reached the lower portion of the right-field seats.

Burnett called for the baseball and once again Clay Folger and his security staff converged on the home-run ball. A seventeen-year-old boy had the souvenir but gladly exchanged it for an autographed Indians team ball. Earl Averill connected in game two, this time driving the ball deep into the right-field section.

There were nearly 22,000 fans at the Cleveland-Washington doubleheader. Yet, overall attendance at the stadium was spotty, with crowds of 3,000 to 5,000 at the early contests. The 1933 season would give a much better idea of the type of attendance the club might expect. Nevertheless, the Indians played exceptional baseball on their new grounds. The home runs were not flying out on a regular basis, but the big hitters were racking up a significant number of triples. Averill, Vosmik, and Morgan took advantage of the wide-open pastures to drive the baseball between the outfielders and leg it around to third. The Cleveland outfielders learned quickly how to position themselves correctly when opposing hitters came to bat. Averill had the most difficult task, trying to cover the huge amount of territory in center field. With his speed and strong throwing arm he handled the assignment well.

When the home stand ended, the Indians traveled to Philadelphia to play four games. They lost them all, just about ruining any opportunity for second place. The road trip moved on through the east, eventually stopping in Boston. On August 30, Wes Ferrell was on the mound against a team he had beaten many times in his four seasons. Marv Olson led off the bottom of the first with a single. Marty McManus singled, the next hitter went out, but base hits by Dale Alexander and Smead Jolley brought in the first two runs. After a base on balls, manager Peckinpaugh walked slowly onto the field and signaled for Jack Russell to enter the game. Ferrell completely lost his temper, taking off his hat and stomping the ground. The *Plain Dealer* described his antics as that of "a child deprived of a piece of candy." Peck asked for the ball, but Ferrell refused to give it up. Still in a rage, he gripped the baseball and ignored his manager for several minutes. His teammates stared in disbelief as the furious pitcher openly defied his boss. After what seemed to be an eternity, Ferrell gave up the ball and stormed into the visitor's dugout. According to several witnesses a heated exchanged took place on the bench between manager and player. Ferrell said one too many things and wound up with a ten-day suspension without pay. The papers guessed the suspension cost the irate Ferrell somewhere around $1,500.

Within twenty-four hours rumors swirled that, depending on who was talking, either Peckinpaugh or Ferrell was on the way out of Cleveland. There existed a theory that trouble had been brewing between the two since early in the season. Ferrell was once being interviewed by a reporter and was asked who the best manager in the American League was. Wes, probably not thinking it through, said Joe McCarthy. This answer may have angered Peckinpaugh and at least several of the Indians players. More gossip had the team trading Ferrell to the Yankees for pitcher Vernon "Lefty" Gomez. Other tales had Connie Mack sending George Earnshaw or Rube Walberg to Cleveland in exchange for the suspended pitcher.

Most newspaper writers gave the players and managers a ton of leeway when it came to verbal exchanges, fights, and off-color behavior in the clubhouse. This unwritten rule went back a long way to protect baseball people from unwanted publicity. The writers always traveled with teams, usually turning a blind eye when it came to something controversial. In this case, the ugly incident happened right on the pitcher's mound in full view of the spectators, umpires, vendors, anybody at Fenway Park. The sportswriters had a free pass here. News of the episode was going to be spread whether they wrote about it or not, so the writers chose to print the story and not hold back.

Ed Bang in his "Between You and Me" column took the opportunity to unload on the suspended pitcher. He wrote, "First of all, Ferrell should have been jacked up long before this for acting like a spoiled child. Had he been put in his place the first or second time he pulled the prima donna stuff, the present situation never would have come to pass. Before anybody realized it, the Indians star pitcher had developed into one of the most temperamental players in the history of the game."

There were choice words for Peckinpaugh as well. Bang thought the manager should know when and if any of his pitchers had a sore arm and take steps accordingly. The previous year Ferrell was sent to several doctors for checkups and treatment for his right arm. It would not have hurt to keep a constant watch and make certain the arm was fine for the 1932 season. Maybe Ferrell had arm trouble. The team had a large investment in their star pitcher and should have been more attentive.

The rumors concerning Peckinpaugh were all about the manager being fired. Since he had accepted the job in 1927, Peck had received a one-year contract each July for the following season. He had not received one yet for 1933. Some of the partners were unhappy that their venture had not won any pennants in their five years of ownership. Chuck Bradley, the more impatient of the two brothers, wanted a change. Apparently he was not alone in his demands. The Ferrell incident only put more heat on Peck. True enough, the best the Indians had done was a third-place finish in 1930. The ownership had indeed spent a huge amount of money to build a contending team and expected a larger return on their investment. Now they had a new stadium and the partners wanted results.

Roger Peckinpaugh was not a screamer or the rah-rah type as a manager. He let the players do their jobs, which most appreciated. Was this Indians team of championship caliber? Hardly. Their pitching staff had one twenty-game winner and a mixture of young talent with several journeymen. This staff could not match pitches with New York or Philadelphia. There was no shame in that, as most teams in both leagues could not either. The Yankees and Athletics traded off winning over one hundred games season after season. One or the other usually captured the World Series as well. To blame Peckinpaugh for not overtaking these two teams was quite foolish. More talent was needed before the Indians could steal away first place.

For his part, Alva Bradley was on vacation when news of the confrontation reached him. He assured the press that he supported Peck wholeheartedly in the debacle with Ferrell. He guaranteed the suspension and fine would stand. He did tell reporters that any decision on the manager would not take place until after the season. Bradley did not plan to return to Cleveland until after Labor Day and appeared to be in no hurry to address the situation. The fans wanted somebody's blood now. Nonetheless, they would have to wait.

Ferrell claimed he was unaware of the punishment until he arrived back in Cleveland. A telegram from Peckinpaugh had spelled

No Money, No Beer, No Pennants

out the details. Ferrell should have stayed quiet, but he unwisely agreed to speak with reporters. He told the *Cleveland News*, "There's nothing I can do or say. It is in the club's power to suspend me if they want to. I don't think I deserved anything like that." He went on to say that he had been pitching with a sore arm for the last two seasons. About all the trade rumors, Ferrell said, "I'm satisfied with the Cleveland club and want to stay but if I'm traded I don't care where they send me."

The *Cleveland News* then contacted Peck for a response. As expected, the harassed manager had much to say. He stated, "The same thing has happened a half dozen times before. Ferrell didn't seem to be bearing down, maybe his arm is sore, we never know, and they were hitting him." It was interesting that Peck claimed he was not sure if his pitcher had a sore arm or not. Ed Bang had recently written about this and the manager inadvertently confirmed what the sports editor was questioning. As far as the clash on the mound, the manager had this to say, "Then when I waved him out, he stormed around in the box, acted childish, and when he sat down at the other end of the bench he made some remarks referring to me. I thought it over and decided to suspend him."

Ferrell had already won his twenty games when the suspension hit. Many of his wins were against the lower-division clubs including Boston, St. Louis, and Chicago. He had not fared well against New York and Philadelphia, the teams he needed to beat. For that and his favorable comments about Joe McCarthy, the Cleveland fans were quite upset. Wes really needed to stop talking and try to let everything quiet down. The more he spoke out, the deeper the hole he climbed into.

Before long, several of the Indians players weighed in on the situation. Speaking anonymously, one player said, "If Peck hadn't said something like that he would have lost the respect of the team. Ferrell won sixteen games by July 4th and he has won only four since then. Some of the boys were wondering if he really was trying to win, although it's hard to figure out why he wouldn't want to win." The players queried were united in saying Ferrell had it coming. Supposedly, several of the players spoke to Ferrell before the start of the Boston game. They asked Wes how he felt and wanted him to bear down so they could finish the road trip on a winning note. Allegedly the pitcher assured his teammates that his arm felt pretty good and he would try his best. Whether or not either of those assertions were true, the Indians ended up having an embarrassing loss.

Still smarting from the incident and all the rumors, Peck had more to say. He told the *Cleveland News*, "I didn't talk to the players to know they didn't like Ferrell's actions. I could sense it from their attitude. They certainly were disappointed and puzzled Tuesday. When Wes began lobbing the ball up in the first inning, the rest of the team got disgusted and played that way."

One of the juiciest rumors around was that Tris Speaker had been seen hanging around the ball club for the past few weeks. Speculation persisted that Tris had his eye on getting his old job back with the Indians. In 1927, the gossip had Spoke and a partner buying the team. Now that a possible change in managers was in the offing, there was Speaker, patting players on the back and making himself visible. The plot thickened.

Faced with all the bad publicity, Ferrell thought he had to speak out again. This time he said he was okay with the suspension and offered no further protest. Though somewhat contrite, he wanted fans and media to know that, despite a sore arm, he had more wins than any other Cleveland pitcher. He reminded folks he was always willing to do relief pitching. A case in point was his eleven innings in the wild 18–17 loss to Philadelphia, when he'd had only one day's rest. Wes answered charges that he was not effective against the eastern clubs by saying it was only a coincidence. If he had stopped there much of the controversy might have died down. Instead, he decided to take another shot at manager Peckinpaugh, saying, "Sure I was mad and cussed. Taking me out like that made me look bad. Peck saw his chance to get me down and took it." That was enough criticism, but Ferrell had more venom to let go. He stated, "I've always thought that Peck was a fine fellow personally but as a manager, well I certainly don't care to pitch for him anymore."

Once the comments went to print, the reporters flocked to Peck for his response. The manager took the high road, trying to calm everything down. He told the writers that every club has a player that does not like the manager, and that is fine as long as he plays ball. He gave an example of the late Miller Huggins, when Peck was the shortstop for the Yankees. At that time a number of his teammates wanted Huggins to quit in the worst way. "Hug" stood his ground and the revolt died away. Peck assured reporters that as long as Ferrell gave the effort on the mound that was enough for him.

Alva Bradley had stayed out of the escalating dilemma, but after reading the papers he called Wes in his office for a conference. He explained in his polite manner just who the boss was and how a player should handle himself on and off the field. The chat seemed to work and Ferrell agreed to mind his manners the remainder of the season. Wes did win three more starts to finish the season with twenty-three victories, his fourth straight year of winning twenty games or more.

Connie Mack arrived in Cleveland to speak before the Rotary Club. With five hundred people in the audience Mack came to the defense of his fellow manager. Mack told the group, "It has been my experience that a baseball club impatient to shift authority is a club that doesn't get very far. When Peckinpaugh took over the management there were three outstanding teams in the American League, New York, Washington, and Philadelphia. Peck has added Cleveland to that list. It seems to me it would be a mistake to change managers at this time." In what was viewed as a swipe at Wes Ferrell, Mack remarked, "No player is greater than the club or the manager."

Whether or not members of the Indians board of directors were in the audience is not known, but the rebellion cooled and Peck got a contract for the 1933 season. The agreement called for a significant reduction in salary. This action was not a warning for the manager, but in keeping with the Major League policy of slashing the payroll until the economy turned around. The owners decided to meet in New York the day before the World Series to possibly map out further reductions. The ballplayers were going to have to brace themselves for another cut in pay.

Chapter 8

THE BIG TRAIN COMES TO TOWN

The Indians finished the 1932 campaign in fourth place with a record of eighty-seven wins and sixty-five losses. It was their best performance in the Bradley regime, but still nowhere near first place. To win a pennant in the American League a team needed to win over a hundred games. Billy Evans still had a lot of preparation to do in finding another fourteen or fifteen wins to climb over the Yankees, Athletics, and now the Washington Senators. It looked to be an especially busy winter.

With the baseball season complete, the city of Cleveland had the fall months to stage events at the stadium. The officials were more than eager to get the grounds ready for football. Through the efforts of several influential alumni, the mighty Fighting Irish were scheduled to play Navy on November 19. The Notre Dame squad was the reigning powerhouse in college football, guaranteed to pack any stadium they played in. Ever since the first day of construction, well-known men in town had schemed to bring Notre Dame to Cleveland Stadium. They had a major stumbling block in convincing the school's athletic department to break a commitment in their 1932 schedule. Initially the local leaders wrote to Knute Rockne and urged him to play a home game in Cleveland. The legendary coach was skeptical about attendance and the amount of gate receipts. He ruled out 1931 but left the door open for the future. Tragically, in March of that same year, Rockne died in a horrific plane crash. After a reasonable amount of time the negotiations continued, with a plan targeting the 1932 Navy–Notre Dame game scheduled to be played in Baltimore. The Cleveland contingent argued that the seating capacity in the new stadium could hold more fans and offer a larger return in gate receipts. The proposal was faultless, convincing both colleges to change their slate of games and play in Cleveland.

The days leading up to game time were taken up with frenzied activities. Both teams were scheduled to arrive on Friday before noon. The Rotary Club arranged a luncheon featuring both coaches, Heartley "Hunk" Anderson of Notre Dame and Edgar "Rip" Miller of Navy. The Notre Dame band was to play live on WGAR Radio. On Saturday night at 9:00 a banquet was scheduled at the Hotel Statler to honor the Fighting Irish players. Again, WGAR set up their remote microphones for a live broadcast. Navy may have felt a touch slighted, but the heavy Notre Dame alumni base in northeast Ohio was calling the shots. At least the Midshipmen were in for a big payday.

On Saturday morning the temperature hovered around the thirty-seven-degree mark. The football fans arrived with Indian blankets, sheepskins, and cushions. Tickets were selling briskly, with some folks buying blocks of ten seats at a time. By the 2:00 p.m. start time the crowd was approaching 70,000. Mayor Miller, a graduate of Notre Dame, welcomed the teams to Cleveland. Charles Otis, always involved in major affairs, presented the Notre Dame players with an Irish terrier named Brick. The game was on, and turned into another hard-fought victory for the Irish, the final score 12–0. Navy played a great game on defense, keeping their rugged opponent out of the end zone for most of the four quarters. The players slogged through the muddy field, destroying what was left of the baseball outfield.

The game was a financial success for all parties involved. The gate totaled $150,000, of which the city received 10 percent, or $15,000. The remainder was split between the two schools. Note Dame, as the home team, received all the concession money. The cold, hungry spectators ate all the hot dogs and drank most of the coffee by halftime. Both coaches assured city officials that the facilities were first class and a return date was very possible.

To close the fall football schedule, the high school city championship was scheduled for Saturday, November 26. Cathedral Latin and Collinwood were to meet to determine the best high school team in the city. The game was sponsored by the *Plain Dealer* charities to benefit people in need for the Christmas holiday, all the proceeds going to the charity fund to purchase gift baskets for thousands of families. Most of the leading companies of Cleveland bought blocks of tickets to help the gate. All told there were 25,000 tickets sold that yielded between $5,000 and $6,000 for the families still reeling from the depression. Latin defeated Collinwood for top honors in the city. That ended the first year of activity at Cleveland Stadium. It was far too early for any type of assessment, although it was safe to say, as went the Cleveland Indians, so did the stadium.

While the mud turned to a freezing mess, the Cleveland front office attended the winter baseball meetings. The theme was similar to 1931, with salary cuts and various ideas to stop the hemorrhaging of money. *Baseball Magazine* editorialized that "Great corporations drastically reduced expenditures, writing off billions of dollars. Major League baseball needs to cut further." The publication quoted economists who believed prices had retreated to the levels of twenty years before. At that time, the average ballplayer was earning about $5,000 per year. Now the salaries were nearly double that of the early teens. Once again the players were about to take a huge hit.

The magazine had to acknowledge that the unemployed man was not going to baseball games anymore to get away from his troubles. The depression had fully arrived in the national pastime, with attendance figures taking a sizable whack. The New York Yankees were said to be the only team earning a profit. The Chicago Cubs seemed to be healthy, with attendance figures of 974,688, an average of 17,000 per game. The Indians had a figure of 468,953, down about 15,000 from 1931. It is important to note that the Opening Day attendance at the stadium totaled nearly 80,000. When that number is backed out of the overall attendance, the amount comes to 388,000. In 1933, there was little or no chance of any other single game drawing that kind of crowd. Other teams had horrific figures to report. The St. Louis Browns drew a paltry 112,558 for an average of 1,500 per game. The Boston Red Sox left most of Fenway Park empty with 182,150, or 2,366 each game. Rumors persisted that the Cincinnati Reds were just about broke and the Red Sox were not far behind. The owners were not worried about the Browns, due to Phil Ball's willingness to put his own money in the franchise. Ball was said to be one of the richest owners and happily funded his team whenever necessary.

The owners had a difficult problem to solve in a very poor economy. The depression showed no signs of weakening, at least in the near future. The baseball men could not sit back and wait for a miracle. Instead, they were united in cutting the player salaries to make up the deficits. To save more money, decisions were announced to invite fewer rookies to camp. Those who were invited could expect to room at the cheapest hotels. Spring training was cut by a couple of weeks, and squad limits were discussed, with teams keeping twenty-three players instead of twenty-five. Everything was on the table, including meal money and train travel. *Baseball Magazine* claimed the average club spent anywhere from $30,000 to $50,000 on spring training. Those costs needed to be trimmed, even if it meant the regular players staying in crummy hotels and wearing dirty uniforms. Even if clubs adopted all these measures, there was no guarantee regarding the bottom line.

Connie Mack did not wait to see how things worked out. As part owner of the Athletics he had a personal stake in earning a profit. In one gigantic move he sold Al Simmons, Jimmy Dykes, and Mule Hass to the White Sox for a reported $80,000. This mass sale of key players would probably take Philadelphia out of contention, but Mack wanted to save his investment above all else. He would stay afloat through all the hard times by dismantling his ball club.

After the meetings, Judge Landis announced he was taking a voluntary pay cut of $25,000. This was a symbolic move to show the public that baseball was doing its part to help the economy. Whether the owners and their front office staffs were doing the same was not announced. It remained to be seen if the men at the top had any intention of following Commissioner Landis's lead. Only time and attendance receipts would tell the tale.

The slashing of salaries began with the mailing of the 1933 contracts. Most of the players saw cuts of anywhere from 10 to 20 percent. Mel Harder, winner of fifteen games and a newlywed, did not receive a cut. Joe Vosmik got a slight raise. The remainder of the team had to grin and bear it. The largest cut to any of the players went to the angriest pitcher in baseball, Wes Ferrell. For the 1932 season Wes had earned $18,000, the highest of all the Indians players. Even though he won twenty-three games, the new contract called for a reduction of $6,000, or nearly 35 percent. Based on previous years, Billy Evans and Cleveland fans expected a long, drawn-out holdout. They were right on the money, so to speak. Ferrell did not sign until March 18. The final deal called for a base salary of $12,000, plus a $2,000 bonus for winning twenty games and another $1,000 if he won twenty-five. With incentives reached, he could earn $15,000. Billy Evans organized the bonus plan to counter Ferrell's demand of a $15,000 salary. If he pitched well, the $15K was his.

Spring training began on March 1, a trifle later than usual. There were a few new faces in camp, one a big first baseman who could drive the baseball to the next county. This was Harold "Hal" Trosky from the small town of Norway, Iowa, about seventeen miles southwest of Cedar Rapids. Hal was born on November 11, 1912, the son of John and Mary Trojovsky. The family of two boys and two girls grew up on a spacious farm where Dad, an old ballplayer himself, grew tobacco and took care of a herd of dairy cows. The blond, blue-eyed Hal played baseball, but started out as a hard-throwing pitcher. He took part in amateur ball around town, sometimes hiking to county fairs to play in games there.

As a seventeen-year-old, Hal knew very little about Major League Baseball. He, like everybody else, had heard about Babe Ruth, but that was the extent of his knowledge of professional baseball. Hal later summed up his reasons for playing the game, saying, "When I was a kid baseball was a game that you played because it was more fun than anything else you could do." One day in the fall of 1930, Hal turned on the family radio. He turned the dial to find a station and discovered a live broadcast of the World Series. He sat down and heard the announcer mention Simmons, Foxx, Bing Miller, and others. The names stuck while Hal followed the exciting action.

A short time later, a letter came from the Danville club of the Three-I League. They wanted Trosky to report in the spring for a tryout. Hal and his father were not sure what to make of the invitation.

They had questions, but nobody to pose them to. Hal remembered the World Series broadcast and the play-by-play man mentioning that Bing Miller lived in Vinton, Iowa. Dad gave son the car for the thirty-mile ride to Vinton. Hal found Miller's house and luckily the Athletics outfielder answered the door. The two men talked for a while, with Miller advising Hal not to answer Danville just yet. Bing was leaving for Philadelphia in a few days. He promised to speak with Connie Mack on Hal's behalf.

Thrilled by the news, Hal drove home to Norway to tell his father. He burst into the kitchen to find the elder Trosky, a distant cousin, and a man he did not recognize. The unknown party was Cleveland scout Cy Slapnicka. For quite some time the cousin had been pestering Slapnicka about his great ball-playing relative in Norway. Either from curiosity or to get the cousin to shut up, the scout had agreed to see Hal.

The four men gabbed about baseball for several enjoyable hours. Hal and his dad liked what Slapnicka had to say. Soon, a contract from the Cleveland Indians appeared on the kitchen table for Hal to sign. His father shrugged and said that all his son did was play baseball, anyway. Slapnicka had no way of knowing he had just struck the jackpot. The Indians super-scout fell in love with the size of the six-foot-two Trosky and envisioned him as a power hitter rather than a pitcher. His assumption would be dead on.

Days after the visit, Hal received a large envelope from the Philadelphia Athletics. The contents included a contract sent by Connie Mack. A somewhat embarrassed Trosky returned the envelope with a note explaining he had already signed with Cleveland. The next week, a letter arrived from Mr. Mack wishing him the best of luck. A few years later, Mack probably crumpled his scorecard when he saw the Indians' new first baseman and how he could hit.

Now a member of the Cleveland organization, Hal was sent to Cedar Rapids in the Mississippi Valley League to learn the outfield. He played well enough there to start a second season in Burlington, now a Cleveland affiliate in the league. The home runs started to fly, allowing a midseason promotion to Quincy of the Three-I League. Trosky ended the 1932 season with a combined nineteen homers and a batting average of .322. The Indians were happy with the progress, assigning him to Toledo for the next summer. After some discussion, Hal got an invite to New Orleans where manager Peckinpaugh got a fair idea of what he had. Despite a barrage of home runs throughout training camp, Peck determined that Hal, now twenty, needed to spend the season at Toledo to fine-tune his game. While playing for the Mud Hens, Trosky, at the advice of manager Steve O'Neill, switched to first base. The old Indians catcher could not help but notice the player's long arms and long reach, perfect for a Major League first baseman. O'Neill taught Trosky how to shift when taking throws at the bag and how to play the hitters, especially the lefties. Hal proved to be a student of the game, learning the new position in a relatively short time. Throughout the summer the Mud Hens' new first baseman socked home runs at a regular clip, ending the summer with thirty-three long ones and a .323 average. The Major Leagues beckoned.

Another youngster to catch the eye of Peckinpaugh was third baseman Arvel Odell Hale. A product of the Deep South, Hale was born in Hosston, Louisiana, on August 10, 1909. The village in the northwest part of the state was and is home to about three hundred people. It may have been tough to get enough bodies together for a ball game, but Odell played every chance he got. In later years he would say baseball was the only ambition he had. After an outstanding showing in high school, Hale signed to play for Alexandria in the Cotton State League. Depending on which account one reads, Odell blasted seven or eight home runs in his first few games. A teammate, flabbergasted by the barrage of home runs, supposedly blurted out, "When that guy hits he is really bad news!" The name stuck, and from that point on Arvel Odell became "Bad News" Hale.

In 1930, Bad News signed to play with Decatur in the Three-I League. For some reason it seemed that any prospective Cleveland player wound up in the Three-I. Hale played second base, shortstop, and third base while keeping his average over .300. His next stop was at New Orleans, where the Indians would see him extensively while in spring training. Billy Evans saw enough of Hale and signed him for the 1932 season. Hale spent the year at Toledo, batting .333 with 206 hits and over one hundred RBIs and runs scored.

In the off-seasons, Hale spent time in El Dorado, Arkansas, loading railroad tank cars. Though only about 170 pounds, he developed

No Money, No Beer, No Pennants

great strength, able to drive baseballs far over the outfield fences. While in El Dorado he visited a local drugstore and was smitten by a young woman behind the counter. Bad News ordered several chocolate phosphates and stared at the clerk, hoping she would notice him. Nothing happened, but he returned several days later with a friend, who introduced Hale to Mabel June Rainwater. They started dating, but Hale did not like going to clubs or dancing. Instead, they often went swimming at the community pool. Months later, in the middle of the pool, he proposed. Certainly not the most romantic spot, yet Mabel said yes and the couple was married before Hale joined the Indians. The new Mrs. Hale called her husband "Sammy," his off-the-field nickname.

Throughout spring training of 1933, Hale played outstanding ball, but had Willie Kamm still in front of him. As well as Bad News played, the Indians were satisfied with Kamm at third base. Nevertheless, he made the ball club and came north with the team. Before long a spot would open up and Hale grabbed it.

Billy Evans and manager Peckinpaugh had to be pleased with their time in New Orleans. They had found a great prospect in Hal Trosky, promoted Bad News Hale to the big-league roster, and took a long look at a new catcher. His name was Frank Pytlak from Buffalo, New York. Every sportswriter who filed a story from New Orleans had one word for the catching hopeful: peppery. At a shade under five foot seven and weighing 160 pounds, Pytlak was a ball of energy. He was born on July 30, 1909, leaving him just shy of his twenty-fourth birthday. As expected, at Masten High School he played baseball and basketball and ran track. When he had extra time, he learned to box and fought as an amateur. A local boxing promoter who knew Frank saw him play baseball. In 1928, the gentleman recommended Pytlak to the Buffalo Bisons of the International League. At the time, Frank pitched as well as filling in behind the plate. He left for the tryout only taking the catcher's mitt, which turned out to be a wise idea. The Buffalo manager was not looking for any more pitchers but gave Frank a chance to catch. He barely played a few games in Buffalo before being farmed out to Hagerstown in the Blue Ridge League.

During his short stint with the Bisons, Frank experienced the thrill of his life. The Philadelphia Athletics stopped in Buffalo for an exhibition game. Ty Cobb was in the lineup for the A's and reached first base in the opening inning. Frank got his adrenalin pumping, in the event the aging Cobb might try to steal. The pitcher delivered and Cobb raced for second base. Pytlak threw a rope to second and caught Cobb by a wide margin. For the rest of his playing days, that would be his fondest memory.

In 1930, Pytlak found himself in the Central League playing for the Erie Sailors. One of the pitchers on the club was Robert Kline, who later played for the Boston Red Sox. Kline was six foot three, and fans had a big laugh when Pytlak walked to the mound for a conference. The two were likened to the popular comic strip, *Mutt and Jeff.* Though being of small stature, Frank was a tough customer behind home plate. While in high school he earned money by working in the stockyards. His boxing skills and work experience helped him to block the plate with the best of them. Throughout his career he took on much larger players and stopped them cold while trying to score.

A promotion back to Buffalo gave Pytlak a much higher profile. He caught over seventy games and batted a respectable .300. The Indians came calling and bought his contract. He played sparingly in 1932, finishing the season in Toledo. The 1933 spring training gave him an opportunity to show how polished his skills were. Cleveland was planning to start Roy Spencer, recently acquired in a trade for Luke Sewell. Spencer, a reliable catcher, was in his mid-thirties and coming off an injury. Glenn Myatt was still around and Peck liked him as the backup catcher. Pytlak was not concerned with the two veterans ahead of him. He did everything well, including run like a deer, which most catchers could not do. Peck did not plan to take three receivers north to Cleveland, but Pytlak forced his hand. Soon he would be the best catcher on the squad.

Though he had been raised in a fairly big city, Frank was about as naive as they come. Early in his days with the Indians, the team stopped in New York for a series with the Yankees. Pytlak was rooming with Willie Kamm, who realized the catcher was easy pickings for a good practical joke. The club was staying at the New Yorker Hotel, where they had rooms on the thirty-third floor. Kamm explained to Pytlak that there was a ten-cent charge if one rode the elevator above the eighth floor. Worried that he would run out of money, Frank took the elevator to the eighth floor, got off and walked all the way up to his floor. He did this for several days, until manager Peckinpaugh found out what was going on. Peck told Pytlak a deal had been cut with the hotel to allow the Indians to ride the elevator for free.

On another trip to New York, Kamm advised his roommate about the large number of gangsters who patrolled the city streets and hotels. Kamm explained that everybody on the club kicked in five dollars and paid off the gangsters for protection. If one did not pay, the bad guys might show up in your room and tear it apart. Pytlak happily gave Kamm the five dollars and went about his business, knowing the gangsters would leave him alone. Kamm always had a nice dinner or two in New York City.

With several young untested players on board, declining attendance, and a country in a serious depression, Bradley and Evans were still optimistic about the season ahead. Their hopes were lifted by a pitching staff that appeared to be solid. They had the hitters in Averill, Porter, and Vosmik. They did have their sixth different shortstop in as many years in Bill Knickerbocker, yet this one had the potential to stick around a while. Add all this in with a full season at the new stadium, and the result was rampant excitement in the Cleveland front office.

In a questionable attempt to lure more fans to the stadium, Bradley canceled live radio play-by-play. He allowed WHK and announcer Jack Graney to recreate the games after play was finished. The idea was that a number of fans could not wait until the evening for game results and would find their way to the stadium and pay for a ticket. Bradley had believed from the outset that live radio hurt attendance, but went along with it until 1933. The American League allowed owners to make their own decisions regarding broadcasts, freeing Bradley to cancel his. Billy Evans gave the okay to WHK to set up a microphone in the clubhouse and interview players after the game. It was a small compromise, but at least something for the fans.

The 1933 campaign opened on April 12 in Detroit. Clint Brown got the start and pitched thirteen strong innings as the Indians were victorious, 4–1. Brown and the Tigers' Tommy Bridges were locked up in a pitcher's duel that lasted twelve innings. In the top of the thirteenth, Averill flied out, then Bill Cissell doubled. Joe Vosmik popped out, but Eddie Morgan drew a base on balls. Singles by Willie Kamm, new guy Roy Spencer, and Clint Brown added three runs, and that's how it ended. Attendance for the day was 19,000. When added to the other four opening games, total attendance had already reached an impressive 100,000. The Cubs and Cardinals drew 25,000 as did Pittsburgh and Cincinnati. On the lower end of the scale, the St. Louis Browns had only 4,500 at Sportsman's Park. In spite of the encouraging overall numbers, there was still reason for concern. What would attendance be after Opening Day?

The Indians stayed on the road, traveling to St. Louis for three games. On April 16, Wes Ferrell took the mound for his first start of the season. His annual holdout had left him behind the other pitchers. When he reported to spring training his teammates noticed how thin and tired-looking Wes appeared to be. He told his friends on the club he was on a liquid diet, recommended to clear up the on-and-off shoulder problems he had experienced. A dentist pulled several of his teeth on the theory that the bad incisors had spread toxins to his shoulder. With all the medical help, Ferrell believed he was free of any arm problems. Ferrell got off to a great start, holding the Browns to one run over six innings. His hitting was in midseason form with a double and a single and two RBIs. In the bottom of the seventh Ferrell tried a curveball and grabbed his right shoulder in obvious pain. He tried to shake it off, but could not continue, leaving the mound with a 6–1 lead.

Cleveland won easily, but Wes left for the hotel to meet with the Browns' team doctor. After a thorough examination, the physician gave Wes good news. The pain was caused by adhesions breaking which had been holding his shoulder back. According to the doctor he now had complete movement, which meant his arm problems were apt to disappear. After some rest Ferrell would pitch again and find out if the Browns doctor knew what he was talking about.

When the three-game series ended, the Indians boarded a train for home and the long-awaited opener at Cleveland Stadium. A downpour on the 19th postponed the game for twenty-four hours. The grounds crew worked furiously, attempting to clear the water with sponges and brooms. Several temporary drainage ditches were excavated to keep the infield clear. To everyone's relief, the skies lightened somewhat on the 20th. Fans with the vantage point looked downtown to find the American flag hoisted high over the Terminal Tower: the game was on! Evans and Bradley were quite eager to see what kind of a crowd flowed into the stadium. Each year they turned down ticket requests at the League Park openers. Now in a park three times as large, they no longer needed to close the ticket windows. The weather cooperated, with temperatures near sixty degrees, exceedingly warm for a Cleveland opener.

Despite the moderate temperature, Cleveland fans got their initial exposure to the winds off Lake Erie. The strong breeze came from the north, entering the grounds through the open end of the outfield bleachers. The builders and planners of the stadium did not take into account the close proximity to the lakeshore. The gusts swirled around the stadium, enough to make the fans shiver. Usually the winds stayed in full force until mid-May, at which time the football blankets were no longer necessary.

The Indians emerged from the clubhouse with spotless new home uniforms. They had red numbers on the back of their jerseys with a red block *C* over the chest. The pants had red stripes down the side, along with black socks and more red stripes. Their caps were black with a red button on the top. Some of the fans remarked that they mistook the players for the Chicago Cubs.

By game time the crowd was counted at 25,000. This had to be a letdown for Alva Bradley and his general manager. The number of fans was close to a new record for Opening Day, but far short of what the front office was expecting. One could list several probable reasons for the moderate turnout, including weather, the new location, or lack of a car or other transportation. The one cause the front office had to acknowledge, though, was that there were still thousands of folks unemployed who did not have money for baseball games. Even those with steady jobs were watching their savings carefully. The stock market crash had happened four years ago, but its effects still lingered over the local area and most of the country. Cleveland, as an industrial city, continued to deal with a mounting number of relief claims. Slowdowns in steel manufacturing and auto assembly showed no signs of a recovery. One auto plant completely shut down and converted to a brewing facility. The owners gambled that Prohibition would end soon, and they could get a jump on the other beer manufactures.

There were few jobs being created to lift the economy. New president Franklin D. Roosevelt had an ambitious plan to put people back to work. The New Deal promised a wide variety of programs designed to help those out of a job. Eventually people would build roads and bridges and facilities in the national parks. The effects would not be felt for several years, though, keeping people on relief and walking the pavement for any type of work.

Cleveland, behind the steady pitching of Clint Brown, won the opener, 3–1. The concessions did not run out of peanuts, hot dogs, or soda pop. There were no severe traffic jams leaving the park for home. Bradley had to be wondering where in the world the minimum $50,000 rental fee was going to be coming from. Crowds of 4,000 or 5,000 were not going to be enough to meet expenses. Something had to give.

One unforeseen problem that occurred was a prolonged slump by the Indians hitters. As of April 28, Earl Averill was batting .140, while Joe Vosmik was right behind, hitting an anemic .130. With the exception of new players Bill Knickerbocker and Frank Pytlak, nobody else seemed to hit at Cleveland Stadium. It stands to reason there would be a period of adjustment from League Park, but the returning players had already had time in 1932 to fine-tune their batting styles. There were numerous fly balls that would have been homers at League Park, but at the larger stadium were simply long outs. Sportswriters agreed the players' issues were mostly psychological. They reasoned that, when Averill drove a high-fly ball short of the 320-foot sign, he immediately thought that it would have been a home run at the old park. He and the other hitters were frustrated and were in the process of convincing themselves that it was not possible to hit at the stadium. The newer guys had little or no experience at the old ball yard, so the change did not bother them.

Manager Peckinpaugh tried to keep things positive, but he had to be conscious of the developing problem. Only the fine pitching of Brown, Hildebrand, and Harder was keeping the record respectable. In the first twenty-eight games of the season, the Cleveland pitchers had allowed only twenty-eight runs and carried a minimal ERA of 2.15. The pressure was on the Indians' hitters to produce.

A week later, an exasperated Bradley made appointments at the Cleveland Clinic for both Averill and Vosmik. Each had extensive

NO MONEY, NO BEER, NO PENNANTS

eye exams to determine if either one needed glasses. A few weeks earlier, Vosmik had a bout with the flu, and doctors believed his eyes were weakened some. Other than that, both ballplayers received clean bills of health from the clinic and returned to action.

Early May proved to be a very lively time at the stadium. The Yankees were in town for a doubleheader, which promised to draw the biggest turnout of the season. The Indians' superb pitching had kept them near the top of the standings, so a sweep of both games would put the team in first place. When the first pitch was thrown, a terrific crowd of 55,000 was in their seats to watch the clubs battle. Earl Averill proved his eyes were just fine, collecting eight hits in the two games. Try as they might, though, the Indians could do no better than a split, keeping them in second place.

The next day a female member of the city council introduced a resolution calling for the return of Ladies Day at the ballpark. The council suspended the rules and voted to reestablish the free day at the stadium. Mayor Miller approved and Alva Bradley agreed to hold the first of several on Friday, May 11. The most recent Ladies Day in Cleveland dated back to 1928. At that time the new regime of Bradley and Evans probably did not favor the idea of a free admission day for women. After all, the ladies now had the right to vote, what more could they want? Both Bradley and Evans had a strong preference for paying customers in the undersized confines of League Park. On the other hand, Cleveland Stadium had seventy-eight thousand seats. There was no danger of the ladies taking up a majority of the room. Besides, they might buy scorecards, a few hot dogs, and popcorn while cheering for the home team against Philadelphia.

The total attendance for the game was 22,000, of whom 14,000 were women. They were mostly seated behind the visitor's dugout and filled up the entire section. Norma Hendricks, a reporter for the *Plain Dealer*, was among the women attending and filed the story. She wrote, "We exulted, suffered, and finally died with every individual player on the team and until the fatal ninth we had ourselves one very swell time." Reporter Hendricks added that the ladies overwhelmingly went for the Blond Viking, Joe Vosmik, as their favorite player. She ended the piece with a strong assertion that women made natural professional baseball fans, writing, "All in all we made it pretty plain that the idea that women aren't interested in baseball is just so much froth."

Cleveland led 3–2 going into the ninth, but the A's rallied and pulled out the victory 7–3. Jimmy Foxx led off the inning with a single. Mickey Cochrane walked, then Pinky Higgins bunted down the third-base line. Willie Kamm fielded the ball, saw that the only play was to first, and fired a strike to the bag. Johnny Burnett was slow to cover and missed the throw. Foxx scored and Cochrane went to third, Higgins going all the way to second. That play opened the floodgates and the game was over.

The losses began to pile up, dropping the team further in the standings. In late May the club was in New York and was surprised by a visit from Alva and Chuck Bradley. The players soon realized that this visit did not appear to be a social one. Alva was blunt in saying that the boys had better start playing ball or Peck would be fired. He believed they had the talent to win, but if things continued as they were, a change in managers was coming. For his part, Peck took the news in stride, telling reporters, "I am a good soldier. I have been treated very fairly by Mr. Bradley and his associates. If the Indians can't win with me at the helm I certainly would not hold my employers to blame for making a change."

Bradley was particularly irate at center fielder Earl Averill, who he thought was playing listlessly and carelessly in the outfield. The owner expected considerably more from one of the highest-paid players on the team. Bradley revealed that he had not cut Averill's salary for 1933, believing his star player would have another banner season.

The fact of the matter was that nobody on the team was hitting. Bradley in previous years had kept his distance from clubhouse meetings. It seemed that the prospect of losing more money, along with lackadaisical play from his team, became too much for the usually even-tempered Bradley. A change appeared to be coming and the manager was in jeopardy. Unless the Indians went on a hot streak, surely a new field boss would be replacing Peck. When Bradley left the clubhouse he tried to put a positive spin on the meeting. He told reporters, "There is no dissension among them. To a man they are behind Peck and have pledged themselves to give him 100 percent effort in every game."

That was a great sentiment, but the only thing that mattered were victories, and a lot of them.

During the Bradleys' trip to New York, an exciting story came out of Chicago. The city was hosting the World's Fair and wanted to add a baseball theme to it. Arch Ward, the sports editor for the *Chicago Tribune*, suggested a July All-Star Game between the American and National Leagues. The fans would vote for the players and the league presidents select the managers, coaches, and umpires. For years baseball publications had listed All-Star teams for each league, but never was there any serious thought of an actual game. Now, under the auspice of a grand World's Fair, why not show off baseball's greatest stars?

Commissioner Landis sanctioned the game and agreed that proceeds should be donated to the Association of Professional Ball Players of America. This organization doled out funds to retired ballplayers that were in dire straits. In a time when baseball pensions did not exist and the American economy was at a standstill, the older retirees needed a fair amount of help. Arch Ward expected a large crowd for the game at Comiskey Park, which would translate into a big donation to the APBPA.

Over one hundred newspapers across the country were designated to receive the votes through June 25. A tentative date of July 6 was set for the All-Star matchup. Fans were asked to cast ballots for three pitchers, two catchers, six infielders, and four outfielders. Early returns had, from the Indians, Earl Averill among the leading outfielders along with pitchers Wes Ferrell and Oral Hildebrand. At the top for the American League were Ruth, Gehrig, Simmons, Gehringer, and the Senators' Joe Cronin. The National League had as leading vote-getters Johnny "Pepper" Martin, Chuck Klein, Bill Terry, Paul Waner, and Carl Hubbell. The fan vote turned out to be a mix of the best players and the most popular. In the local view, Averill was in the midst of his worst season, while Ferrell pitched sparingly with his cranky shoulder. Their votes were based on previous years, with a likely dose of ballot stuffing in northeast Ohio.

The unexpected votes for Oral Hildebrand showed some thoughtful consideration from fans in all different cities. As of the middle of June, "Hildy" owned a record of nine wins versus three losses. Four of his wins were shutouts, including a sparkling one-hitter over St. Louis and a two-hitter against Detroit. The product of Indiana had come out of nowhere, spending just one year at Butler College before moving on to Indianapolis of the American Association. Billy Evans spotted him there in 1930 and sent three players and cash to Indianapolis for the young hurler. Hildy had all the pitches, reminding Evans of a younger Wes Ferrell.

In his first full season with Cleveland, Hildebrand won eight games while showing all sorts of potential. In 1933 he wowed the American League by throwing shutouts as if they were commonplace. The result was his last name on thousands of All-Star ballots. Of all the pitchers in the American League, only Lefty Gomez, Lefty Grove, and Wes Ferrell had more votes.

Meanwhile, back in Cleveland, the death watch continued for Roger Peckinpaugh. Each day fans opened their morning papers to see if Peck was still managing. Once again the names of Willie Kamm, Tris Speaker, Steve O'Neill, and even John McGraw were mentioned as possible successors. The ball club did little to help their boss, struggling to put together anything resembling a winning streak. As of June 8, a loss to St. Louis left the club barely treading water at 26–25. The next day, Alva Bradley decided to make the change. After five and a half years as manager of the Cleveland Indians, Peck was fired.

Although the move did not shock anyone, the fans all around Cleveland were buzzing with the news. Bradley released a statement to the local media regarding his actions, stating, "It is with great regret that the board of directors of the Cleveland Baseball Company find it necessary to change managers at this time. For five years every effort has been made to build a winning team in Cleveland. Roger Peckinpaugh has worked hard and has done everything in his power to make a winner." The next part of the statement stunned just about everybody who was paying attention: "We have given very careful thought to his successor and have decided to employ Walter Johnson. His experience both as a player and manager should be most helpful." Bradley ended his announcement with words that followed him throughout his tenure as owner of the Indians, offering his soon to become famous line, "The owners of a ball club can hire a manager, but the public fires him." An insightful statement, however it proved that the front office paid attention to the fans who ultimately bought the tickets.

In all the rumors and speculation about a new manager, the name of Walter Johnson had never come up. Bradley added that the hiring of Johnson was his personal choice and that Billy Evans had traveled to Washington to pose the offer. This move contradicted Bradley's philosophy of only hiring Cleveland boys for management positions. Apparently, the owner had changed his way of thinking.

Everybody who knew something about baseball was familiar with Walter Johnson. An American League pitcher for twenty-one seasons, the "Big Train" had no peers. His career statistics were in the stratosphere. As a pitcher for the Washington Senators he won an incredible 414 games, second only to Cy Young. For ten straight seasons he won twenty games or more, with a high of thirty-six in 1913. With his sizzling fastball he led the league in strikeouts on twelve different occasions. His resume as the most dominant pitcher in baseball history undoubtedly made an impression on Bradley. Still, Johnson had other qualifications that mattered. He had managed the Senators from 1929 to 1932 and in that time guided Washington to one second-place finish and two third places. After the 1932 season, Clark Griffith, the team owner, raised a few eyebrows by firing Johnson. Apparently, the manager wanted to take a more aggressive approach with his players and Griffith shot down the idea. The two could not reach a compromise and the fairly successful manager was let go.

Johnson did many interviews after he accepted the Cleveland job, during which he fielded numerous questions about milestones in his remarkable career. One remark he made gave reporters and fans alike quite a start. Throughout his career, he claimed, at no time did he ever have a sore arm. Johnson stressed that he knew his limitations well and never had occasion to overexert himself. He claimed he could still throw the "smoke ball," even at age forty-six, but his legs were no longer in baseball shape. The interesting side to Walter's comments was, how would he deal with sore-armed pitchers on his new club? He had to know that Wes Ferrell had a chronic condition that kept him on the bench for long periods. Could he effectively deal with his pitching staff when complaints of sore elbows and shoulders came up? It would not take long to find out.

Roger Peckinpaugh handled his firing without sounding off to the press. The day after he got the news, Peck dug out his golf clubs and played eighteen holes. Most of the criticism he endured said he had been too easygoing with the players. The *Cleveland News* called him a "go along manager." The paper believed that, as a former player, he sided with his guys rather than the front office. The writer claimed Peck looked the other way when players reported to spring training ten or fifteen pounds overweight. The inference was that the team needed more discipline than they had been getting.

The belief in the Cleveland front office was that Johnson did have the toughness in him. The papers agreed on this. An editorial in the *Cleveland Press* stated, "There has been an impression that Johnson like Peckinpaugh might be too easygoing as a manager. It is the opinion of others that this is not the fact. They believe it was interference with Johnson by the owner of the Washington club that produced that impression. There will be no such interference here, we are told. That is sound policy."

Before cleaning out his office, Peckinpaugh assured his former players that the new manager was a good fellow and asked them to give him a chance. Johnson and Peck were onetime teammates at Washington and had remained good friends. This led to a smooth transition and a clean slate for Johnson to inherit.

Plans called for Johnson to arrive on Sunday, June 11, to officially begin his duties. A proclamation was drawn up to make Sunday "Walter Johnson Day." Mayor Miller assembled a group of fifty prominent Clevelanders to greet the new manager at the train station. Photographers shot pictures of Johnson as he hopped off the arriving train. A new period in Cleveland baseball had begun.

Sunday came with sweltering temperatures reaching ninety-three degrees. Manager Johnson was asked to celebrate the afternoon by throwing out the first pitch. He still had the smoke but not the accuracy, throwing two wide ones before creasing the plate. The Indians were not exactly on fire against the Browns, scoring the game's only run in the bottom of the tenth inning. Joe Vosmik singled, then came around to score on a single by Oral Hildebrand.

Mel Harder pitched the first nine shutout innings, then gave way to the near All-Star Hildebrand in the tenth. The team had a day off on Monday but Johnson ordered the hitters to show up at the stadium and take batting practice. He could see they needed it.

The fortunes of the Cleveland Indians did not immediately change under Walter Johnson. For the remainder of June the team posted a record of eight wins and eleven losses. Particularly galling were home stands against the Athletics and Senators. Out of nine ball games the club managed to lose seven, including six in a row. The hitting remained abysmal, though Earl Averill gradually began to hit, raising his average to nearly .300.

Frank Pytlak continued to rap the baseball, causing reporters to question him on his secret to good batting habits. The answer was, a plate of his mother's old-fashioned sauerkraut. While playing for Buffalo, Pytlak found himself in a deep slump. He went home after a particular game and sat at the family table for dinner. He was not a big fan of sauerkraut, but, being hungry, he ate a plateful. The next day he drilled several base hits and convinced himself that it was the food that broke the slump. From that day on, at least during the regular season, a plate of sauerkraut was mandatory. Apparently the rest of the players were not interested in adopting Pytlak's dinner preference.

The chief reason the Indians were winning at all revolved around the pitching staff. In two-thirds of the team's victories, the pitchers had allowed one run or less. They had thrown seven shutouts and posted eight games allowing no more than three runs. Any kind of hitting might have significantly boosted the win total. To really accent the point, Cleveland pitchers had won six games with their bats. Timely hits by Harder, Hildebrand, Ferrell, and Hudlin were responsible for squeezing out the additional wins.

Even though he was stroking the baseball, Ferrell's shoulder kept on interfering with his pitching. He could not take his regular turn, and when he did throw his pitches simply were not there. On June 18 Ferrell was on the mound against the Detroit Tigers. For a change the shoulder pain was bearable. He locked up in a pitcher's battle with the always durable Tommy Bridges. In the bottom of the third inning, Wes came to bat with no score and the bases empty. Bridges delivered and Ferrell launched a monster shot into the upper deck in left field. Fans were startled at the tremendous blast, for sure the longest home run at Cleveland Stadium to date. Billy Evans immediately ordered a measurement to determine the distance. Several of the office staff got out the yardsticks and concluded that the baseball had traveled an incredible 450 feet, a prodigious blow at any park. The fact that the batter was not Ruth or Foxx or Averill, but a pitcher with a sore shoulder, added to the grandeur of the moment. Whether or not Ferrell ever overcame his arm problems, his legacy as a Cleveland Indian was secured.

On June 25 the All-Star balloting closed. More than five hundred thousand dedicated fans had cast their votes. The Indians were represented by Earl Averill, Wes Ferrell, and Oral Hildebrand. The Yankees placed no less than six players on the squad: Babe Ruth and Lou Gehrig led the way, along with Tony Lazzeri, Lefty Gomez, catcher Bill Dickey, and outfielder Ben Chapman. Between them, the Indians and Yankees represented half of the American League squad. On the National League side, the St. Louis Cardinals had four starters in pitcher Bill Hallahan, catcher Jimmie Wilson, third baseman Pepper Martin, and Frankie Frisch at second base. Connie Mack was named manager for the Americans. John McGraw agreed to come out of retirement and manage the Nationals. Both NBC and CBS announced plans to broadcast the game live.

The days leading up to the game were filled with discussion on which team had the better talent. Both teams had power, with Ruth, Foxx, and Gehrig for the American League against Bill Terry, Chuck Klein, and Chick Hafey for the Senior Circuit. The pitchers were outstanding, with names including Lefty Grove, Carl Hubbell, Lon Warneke, and the already mentioned Gomez.

July 6 came around with 49,000 enthusiastic fans packing Comiskey Park. The World's Fair had to take a distant second billing for a day. The highlight of the game happened in the bottom of the third inning with, Charlie Gehringer on base for the American League. That brought to the plate none other than Babe Ruth. Everybody in the stadium anticipated what might come next. Bill Hallahan sent a pitch over the plate and Babe belted a long drive into the seats for the first home run in an official Major League All-Star Game. The Nationals answered with a home run by Frankie

Frisch, but a sixth-inning base hit by Earl Averill sealed the 4–2 win for the American League.

With the huge crowd at Comiskey Park, over $40,000 was collected for the Association of Professional Ball Players. Thousands more fans had listened on the radio, and talk began to stir about making the game an annual event. Ed Bang wrote a column urging the Cleveland city leaders to begin lobbying for an All-Star Game at the lakefront stadium. He reasoned that if nearly 80,000 fans attended the first game downtown, why not 80,000 more for an All-Star Game? He bragged that the city had the best facility in professional baseball, along with a central location for teams and fans to travel to. Bang would not be the only cheerleader for Cleveland, and soon the city would be giving serious consideration to making a bid to host the game.

Before the goodwill of the All-Star Game wore off, Walter Johnson found himself at the center of controversy. Just one month into his tenure, word leaked that several of his pitchers were unhappy with his managerial style. On July 12, Oral Hildebrand lasted less than one inning in Philadelphia before Johnson replaced him. Later, Hildebrand claimed he'd had a sore arm and was in need of a few days' rest. It seemed the manager coerced his pitcher into taking his turn even though his arm was hurting. At least one other pitcher had arm problems, but Johnson did not allow any time off. The next day, Johnson denied he had forced Hildy to pitch with a lame arm. That quieted the tension for a few weeks.

The fireworks exploded on July 31 in St. Louis. The game featured plenty of hitting and very little pitching. With the Browns threatening in the bottom of the seventh, Johnson called on Hildebrand to pitch in relief. The result was one base hit and three walks in a third of an inning. Johnson came out of the Indians dugout and waved for a new pitcher. Hildy lost his cool, smashing the resin bag into the ground. As he walked away, Johnson yelled to him, "That will cost you one hundred dollars!" The pitcher fired back, "You can take all my money, but you can't take my arm!" At that point Johnson allegedly yelled to Hildebrand that he was indefinitely suspended and to leave the clubhouse right away.

Reporters sensed a juicy story and followed the suspended pitcher. Still angry, Hildebrand spoke when he should have kept silent. He said, "I don't want to pitch for Walter Johnson any more, but if I have to I'll take it and like it. But I'm not quitting baseball. I'll be pitching when Johnson is back digging ditches!" Hildebrand went home to Indianapolis, then wired Billy Evans that he wanted to meet to give his side of the story. The next day he traveled to Cleveland to sit down with the general manager. Before entering the team offices Hildy had more to say. The reporters could not jot down the words fast enough. He remarked, "I'll finish out the season, but next year if Johnson is here, I don't want to be. I'll ask to be traded to some other club." He then went to see Evans while sportswriters waited outside the office for more colorful quotes. Evans firmly told his pitcher that the argument was between him and Johnson. It was up to Hildebrand to swallow hard and make peace. The front office would stay out of the dispute. Evans added that his pitcher had no chance at any time of being traded or sold.

Hildebrand had few options but to apologize and rejoin the team. He mentioned to reporters that he had spoken with his teammates before he left for Indianapolis. He told them his arm had gotten sore right before Johnson replaced Roger Peckinpaugh. The arm hurt off and on, but he took his regular turn. He had spoken to Johnson about getting a couple of days' rest, but the manager only allowed him one. Hildebrand said, "He didn't seem to care whether I was ruining my arm or not. I don't think that's the way to run a team. Johnson is a nagger and there are plenty of other boys complaining on the quiet." With nothing more to protest about, Hildy then quietly apologized to his manager and all was forgiven. At least on the surface.

Less than two months after Walter Johnson became the Indians manager there had been a major dispute with a player. It had taken five years before Peckinpaugh and Ferrell went at it. What was happening here? Johnson may have wanted to assert his authority, and Hildebrand gave him the opening to do so. The new manager laid down the law for all his players to see. Going forward, there was a new sheriff in town. The players had to adjust or find somewhere else to play ball.

Dan Daniel of the *New York Telegraph*, one of the most respected sportswriters in baseball, wrote a column about the incident. He believed there was more trouble brewing in Cleveland. Daniel wrote,

"The fining and suspension of Oral Hildebrand one of the younger pitching geniuses of the American League by Walter Johnson came as no surprise to those in the know. Before 'Big Barny' becomes established firmly as manager of the Indians he may be forced to take similar action with one or two of his other players." Daniel believed a number of Hildebrand's teammates were still angry at the change in managers, and went out of their way to let the front office know it. Who these players were went unnamed, but Daniel was certain that Johnson had some bumps in the road ahead. How he handled the problems would dictate Johnson's tenure in Cleveland.

As Walter Johnson tried to plot his course, other complications surfaced in the Cleveland Baseball Company. Billy Evans did an interview for the *Saturday Evening Post* in which he explained the financial issues most teams were facing. Evans maintained that total attendance of a million was necessary for his club to break even. That figure included at home and on the road, though the general manager stated that home attendance had to be at least 500,000 to stay afloat. Evans broke down the expenses for his organization, with a total budget of $535,000. Player and coaching salaries were the largest piece of the overhead, totaling $250,000. Next were salaries and expenses for scouts and the office staff at $50,000. Other areas that cost the team included park upkeep and labor costs of $30,000, the telephone system at $2,500, and even new baseballs for the season at $7,500.

Evans did not include the rental fee of $50,000 for one summer at Cleveland Stadium. It remained to be determined if home attendance would reach the desired number of 500,000. Sunday games were drawing well and the 55,000 at the early-May Yankees doubleheader certainly helped. In spite of this, weekday attendance lagged behind. In one instance 6,000 fans showed up for a game, nearly 4,000 of whom were schoolchildren with complimentary passes. Alva Bradley and his partners added generous sums to the till, but even they were beginning to have second thoughts about contributions. These gentlemen were far above any suffering from the depression, but they were beginning to take a hard look at the bottom line. The $50,000 stadium rental fee loomed larger each day.

The Indians finished the 1933 season by losing thirteen of their last twenty games. Their record of seventy-five wins against seventy-six losses was the worst showing since 1928. Manager Johnson spent most of the month tinkering with new lineups. Fans took notice of a new left fielder taking the place of an injured Joe Vosmik. Wes Ferrell had moved to the outfield on a semi-regular basis. He pitched his last game on September 8, allowing seven runs on eleven hits while staggering through six innings. On the other hand, Wes added a two-run homer, his seventh of the year. By placing Ferrell in left field, the Indians let the rest of the American League know that they had given up on Wes as a pitcher. He was now getting an audition to determine if he could reinvent himself as an outfielder.

On September 11, Hal Trosky received his call-up from Toledo. He went hitless in his debut, but soon demonstrated to fans why the Indians were taking a look. On September 18, Trosky hit his first home run in a 9–0 win over the Red Sox. It happened in the top of the first inning with two runners on board. Oral Hildebrand allowed only two harmless singles in recording his league-best sixth shutout. Left fielder Wes Ferrell had three hits for the day, proving he could still pound the baseball on a regular basis. It was his defense that needed a lot of work, and with Joe Vosmik retuning next year the odds of Wes sticking with the Indians were greatly diminished.

After the season ended, Evans and Johnson sat down to evaluate each player on the team. The first player to go was Bill Cissell, who Johnson believed was of no use to the club. Rumors surfaced that Cissell had gone to a late-night party or two and Johnson wanted him out of Cleveland as soon as possible. Evans announced that only a small portion of the squad was not available in trade talks. New players Pytlak and Hale were staying, as was Joe Vosmik. On the pitching staff, Mel Harder was untouchable, along with the now contrite Oral Hildebrand. Even Earl Averill was for a time on the trading block, but was later pulled from consideration. The winter meetings in December looked to be busy for Cleveland.

Alva Bradley remained active in the months following the baseball season. In October he announced his support for the re-election of Democrat mayor Ray Miller. This move puzzled fellow Clevelanders, who knew Bradley to be a staunch Republican. In 1928 he donated $5,000 to the Republican war chest and later gave

$250 to Daniel Morgan's campaign for city manager. When Bradley came out for Miller, he resigned his position as a member of the Republican executive committee. Bradley advised his somewhat confused friends that he was a "Republican at heart," though he felt the need to support the Democratic mayor. Folks wondered if there was something more to the unexpected move.

On October 8, the *Cleveland News* broke the shocking story that the Indians were terminating their lease agreement with the city of Cleveland and returning to League Park. The official date of the move was said to be November 1. Bradley refused to affirm or deny the story, but an inside source spilled the beans to the *News* reporter. The paper alluded to heavy losses sustained during the ongoing depression. The increased costs of playing at Cleveland Stadium had pushed Bradley and his board of directors to exercise their out clause.

Estimates were given that the ball club had lost approximately $200,000 in just one year at the stadium. In addition to the financial loss, Bradley had been the target of opponents to the reelection of Mayor Miller. They had accused the Indians owner of political horse trading in his negotiations with Miller to carve out the lease. The mayor claimed he'd known nothing of Bradley's decision to void the lease. There was talk of a counterproposal to reduce the ball club's rental fee, but an informal poll of city council members indicated that support was lacking.

The newspaper asserted that the most important reason for the move back to League Park centered on attendance. The 1932 partial season began with the July 31 crowd of nearly 80,000, which gave the club a huge shot in the arm. For the thirty-two games played from July through September, the Indians paid the city a prorated $23,000. The 1933 attendance was a disaster, with a total of 387,936 or an average of just over 5,000 fans per game. Ladies Day had been a terrific success, but the free admissions did not help the team raise the revenue needed. Billy Evans had earlier said the team required 500,000 fans through the home turnstiles to break even. Based on the reported attendance, they were 113,000 customers short.

Another reason for the team voiding the lease was the playing field itself. Fans did not care for being so far away from the playing field. They had a fine view of the diamond but could not get used to sitting a good distance from the action. Many of the players were already on record as stating that the outfield was too difficult to cover. The lack of hitting spoke for itself. No doubt the team was looking forward to a return to League Park and the inviting short right-field wall.

The big loser in the lease cancellation had to be Mayor Miller. He inherited the project but made it the signature accomplishment of his administration. He fought the battles with the city council while spending long hours negotiating terms with Alva Bradley. He'd managed to get support for the final version of the lease, allowing for the city to make upwards of the $50,000 rental fee, based on anticipated attendance. The mayor did not factor in the severe economic effects of the depression, which kept fans from spending their precious dollars. Unemployment in Cleveland showed no signs of lessening. There simply was not any easy way to lure people to the stadium other than letting them in for nothing. Now the mayor would have to focus on bringing the circus to town, and pageants of all types, to garner any revenue from the so-called white elephant.

The *Cleveland News* printed up ballots in the sports section for fans to decide whether the stadium or League Park was a better fit for the Indians. Early returns had the stadium out front, but with several days to think about it voters began to support League Park. The initial returns were Stadium 116, League Park 96. Comments ranged from "The stadium is much more convenient" to "It's much more intimate and interesting to see a game at League Park." One comment neatly said, "The stadium is too big for baseball and the parking facilities atrocious."

In all the give-and-take regarding the stadium, it appeared the city officials had overreached from the outset. Surely, in 1928 they had had no inkling of the stock market crash just a year away. They could not have foreseen the massive depression that crippled the United States economy for years to come. Despite many of the Major League owners' belief that baseball was immune to a financial catastrophe, the grand old game was not spared. Disposable income melted away, and with it went a large sampling of the ticket-buying public.

In the midst of all this turmoil, the city of Cleveland went ahead and built the supersized facility on the lake. City Manager Daniel Morgan gave some thought to lessening the size and lowering the seating capacity, but did not make an aggressive push to do so. Possibly a stadium that seated fifty-five to sixty thousand would have had a better chance to survive in such desperate times. A smaller facility would have meant lower construction costs as well as maintenance. The Indians might have been able to make a go of it with a smaller staff and a lower rental fee. Nevertheless, the city was not to be denied, and the huge structure went ahead as planned. As the saying goes, you reap what you sow. Here was a classic example.

Chapter 9

RETURN TO 66TH AND LEXINGTON

With the stadium lease no longer a hindrance, Alva Bradley began the task of turning his baseball club into a money-making venture. He still owed the city a debt of $33,000 for the balance of the 1933 rental fee. To settle that obligation he offered the city one of his downtown buildings in a prime location. Once the sale went through, he would settle his account and move on to the business of canceling the red ink that penetrated his account ledgers. Bradley had to create a means to shave $150,000 from his expenses. Almost half of that was accomplished by returning to League Park and no longer paying rent. The remaining $75,000 would come from the team payroll.

The first group to receive reductions in pay was the office staff, including the general manager. Billy Evans was asked to accept an incredible 66 percent pay cut. The newspapers believed Evans had a three-year deal that called for $30,000 per year. The agreement ended in November 1933, giving Bradley the opportunity to make the drastic move. Evans knew a cut was coming, but figured on something not quite so severe. Evans proposed to his boss a reduction of 40 percent, which Bradley turned down. Evans had other options, among them getting the chest protector out of storage and returning to umpiring. Still, he had developed a strong working relationship with Bradley and forwarded a counterproposal with a 50 percent decrease. That offer was accepted, but the days of the three-year deals were clearly over. The agreement was announced and Evans told reporters he had no argument with receiving $15,000 for the 1934 campaign. Instead, he preferred to talk about the upcoming season, saying, "I am sure the return to League Park will make the team twenty five percent more efficient because of the effect upon morale. The wide open spaces of the stadium seemed to kill the confidence of our best hitters."

The entire office staff received pay cuts, including the secretaries and the bookkeepers. The scouting staff was trimmed and salaries were reduced. Bradley was not under any illusions that the still-growing unemployment crisis might turn around anytime soon. His baseball club had to accept things as they were. The only feasible way to survive the depression centered on belt-tightening throughout the organization.

The one step remaining to kill the $150,000 of overhead meant the ballplayers were going to suffer. Just about the entire squad had significant cuts on the horizon. A few of the younger guys were slated for slight increases, including Frank Pytlak and Oral Hildebrand. Mel Harder appeared to be the only veteran being considered for a pay raise. Harder produced a fine season in 1933, winning fifteen games with very little support behind him. He posted an ERA of 2.95, better than any starter in the American League. Even Walter Johnson urged Evans to give Harder a better contract. The manager wrote that he did not care if anybody else got a raise, but Harder deserved one. When trade talks commenced in the winter, Evans usually found himself besieged with offers for his pitcher, more so than Averill or Vosmik or, in past years, Ferrell. Harder, through a strong work ethic and determination, had become one of the better pitchers in the league.

By November, Bradley and Evans had determined the contracts for the 1934 season. The mailings were not to go out until January and both men anticipated a long drawn-out battle with players. This scenario was likely to be carried out in all the Major League cities. Initially the owners had downplayed the worsening economy, but after a year or two they realized they needed to take harsh measures to stay in business. The winter meetings of 1933 promised to be to be quite active.

The owners assembled in Chicago to discuss all things base-ball. A considerable number of ideas were tossed about to improve the state of the game. One novel idea was to structure trades in an effort to balance out the teams, meaning that the dominant teams like the Yankees or Cardinals would voluntarily trade some of their best players to the clubs in and around the cellar. This would create a balance of good teams rather than a few dominat-ing the standings each year. Without any lousy teams, attendance should improve for the lowly clubs desperate to survive. A good idea, perhaps, but would New York trade Lou Gehrig to the St. Louis Browns? Probably not.

Another thought was brought forward to increase the num-ber of doubleheaders. Attendance at twin bills usually totaled a higher number of gate receipts. The most innovative plan called for interleague play at the end of the year. September was always a poor attendance month for the clubs not in the pennant race. If games were scheduled between the Giants and the Yankees or the Cubs versus the White Sox, perhaps fans might buy a few more tickets and boost revenue. Rivalries between clubs in the same city could be settled on the baseball field. The one plan easily accepted was that the All-Star Game must continue on a yearly basis.

Baseball Magazine suggested that owners receive a greater share of the World Series receipts. The editors pointed out that Commis-sioner Landis's salary came out of the series money. In addition, the owners of the pennant-winning teams hosted several hundred baseball writers, while hiring additional clerical help and sprucing up the grounds. The players already had a salary and could live with a smaller share of the receipts, or so it was thought.

With all the back-and-forth talk, the meetings still ended with-out any severe changes to the game. In spite of all the concern about money, Connie Mack sent Lefty Grove to Boston for $125,000. Detroit acquired Mickey Cochrane from the Athletics for a mere $100,000. In two years, Mack unloaded five of his best players for the astronomical figure of $305,000. He was doing his utmost to balance the teams even before the suggestion came forward. Ac-cording to *Baseball Magazine*, Red Sox owner Tom Yawkey spent a half million to acquire players. The winter meetings produced food for thought and not much else. The owners moaned about finances, then several broke the bank in spending for players.

Billy Evans spent his time in Chicago trying to find a second baseman. He liked Oscar Melillo, the veteran from St. Louis, and Jackie Hayes of the White Sox. The greedy Browns wanted four players from the Indians, which Evans would not do. Walter Johnson believed Hayes was a decent second baseman but a below-average hitter, and not for Cleveland. Another goal of Evans's was to find a buyer for Wes Ferrell. He had a degree of hope another team might be willing to take a flyer on the damaged goods. At one moment the Yankees were about to offer shortstop Lyn Lary straight up for Wes, but they changed their minds. A disappointed Evans left Chicago without completing any deals.

Back in Cleveland, Evans announced a twelve-game exhibition series with the New York Giants, scheduled for the end of spring training. This change was in contrast to the front-office policy of staying put in New Orleans rather than overexerting the players in additional games and travel. The Giants were moving their training facility from California to Florida and the idea of an exhibition tour came about. Staying away from the West Coast saved New York money, and the twelve-game tour was a chance to defray a good chunk of the spring-training expenses for both teams. Evans now believed playing the World Champion Giants could only make his team sharper for the regular season. A change in the spring training regimen might pay dividends for the season ahead.

With a short lull in activity, Evans devoted time to catching up on his nonstop mail. He estimated receiving one hundred letters a week during the summer months and twenty-five weekly in the off-season. Most of the letters were scribbles from children wanting to be the team batboy. Others were from psychologists looking for work as team advisors. Of course, there were numerous letters telling the general manager how to do his job. The players receiving the largest share of fan mail were Earl Averill and Joe Vosmik. On a fairly regular basis letters would arrive in pink or blue envelopes. Without looking at who they were addressed to, Evans knew they were for Wes Ferrell. The single ladies of Cleveland had a thing for the fine-looking pitcher and had no qualms about letting him know.

When the New Year approached, Evans took a deep breath and mailed out the player contracts. He knew the deep cuts in pay were going to signal a long winter ahead. Several weeks passed without one signed contract returned. Gradually, a number of unsigned agreements filtered into his office. Frank Pytlak wanted a larger raise than the $1,700 offered. Evans shook his head at that one. Though Pytlak hit well for the season, he only played in sixty-nine games due to breaking the same finger three times. Evans worried that his catcher had "putty finger," which meant all you had to do was touch the finger and it would break. A catcher with putty finger on his throwing hand equaled a brief career. Evans hedged his bets by offering Pytlak a small raise. If the injuries turned out to be chronic, then the salary proposal would not affect the budget to any strong degree. He even planned to bring former catcher Steve O'Neill to spring training to show Pytlak how to protect his throwing hand from foul tips. The only issue was getting the stubborn catcher signed and on his way to New Orleans.

Every person who followed baseball in Cleveland and the rest of the United States knew the toughest fight would be with the perennial holdout Wes Ferrell. The contract mailed called for a severe reduction to $5,000. There were incentives included that awarded $500 for every win over ten. If Wes got to sixteen wins the bonus increased to $600. Each win over twenty meant the pitcher received $700–$800. For example, if Ferrell won eighteen games his base salary plus bonus would come to $9,300. That sum broke down to a salary of $5,000, wins eleven to fifteen netting him $2,500, and wins sixteen to eighteen an additional $1,800. Ferrell sent the contract back unsigned, along with postage due: he stuck it to Evans and Bradley for three cents.

Reports came in from North Carolina that Ferrell had no intention of returning to Cleveland. He informed reporters that he wanted a trade, preferably to Boston to join his brother Rick. The elder Ferrell had been traded to the Red Sox early in the 1933 season. Wes said he was prepared to sit out the season and go on the voluntary retired list. For their part, Bradley and Evans were more than ready to let the troublesome pitcher go. Bradley stated that the offer was not open to negotiation. If Ferrell wanted to sit out, so be it. Evans tried unsuccessfully to trade his former ace, but there turned out to be little interest. The short-term experiment in left field had only convinced most of the teams that Ferrell was done as a pitcher. To resolve the impasse, Evans needed to find a trade partner willing to gamble with his money. That limited the field to the Yankees, who always spent a lot, and the Red Sox's Tom Yawkey, who seemed to have a boatload of ready cash. One thing all parties agreed on was that Ferrell had made his last appearance in a Cleveland uniform.

The first regular player to sign a contract was Joe Vosmik, and he waited until February 16 to do so. Pitchers and catchers were due to leave for New Orleans in just two weeks from that date. As it stood, the only players ready to depart were minor-leaguers who did not figure in the team's plans. Earl Averill had not yet responded to his contract offer. Word came from Snohomish that the All-Star had not opened the envelope and had no plans to read it. He knew a significant cut was enclosed, prompting him to toss it aside for at least the time being. Billy Evans was now seen hitting the aspirin bottle on a daily basis.

At the end of February, Evans concentrated on restoration work at League Park. He planned to replace the old field boxes with cement ones and paint all the interior walls and scoreboard. Residents and businesspeople in the 66th and Lexington area were cheered by the news. C. F. McDermott, who owned the Gensert-McDermott Drug Company, spoke for the folks living around the park. He told reporters, "The depression was hard enough on us, but when they deserted League Park they hit our hearts as well as our pocket books. The return will mean 50% business help." Fred Hilliard, when learning the Indians were coming back, rented space on Lexington and opened Hilliard's Wind-Up Cafe. Other people were thrilled they could rent their front lawns again for parking spaces. At least the League Park neighborhood was about to get some genuine relief from the depression.

Several days later, Earl Averill paid a visit to the Indians team offices. He brought with him the unopened contract, which he intended to examine in front of Billy Evans. Sportswriters and photographers dashed to League Park to record the event. With a concerned expression, Averill opened the envelope, removed the contract, and briefly studied it. He smiled, shook his head, and handed the contents to Evans. He told the eager writers that the cut was more than he would accept. To appease the front office, Averill did say he planned to stick around a few days to see if Evans might up the ante. Other players had now caved in and were going to sign by March 11, which represented the opening day of spring training. Cleveland fans still worried whether there might not be enough players to field a team for the regular season. Even with all the salary slashing, though, players, as always, had few options. It was either sign or look for a new job.

A big sigh of relief came when Averill signed his contract. Evans added another $1,000 to the offer and that was enough for an agreement. The Indians made arrangements to fly Averill from Cleveland to New Orleans. The airplane departed Cleveland at 8:00 a.m., scheduled to arrive in Louisiana at 6:00 p.m. Travel time amounted to eleven long hours. There would be time for a few push-ups and calisthenics during the lengthy flight south.

Spring training of 1934 was the first under the direction of manager Johnson. The routine proved to be similar to past years, except for more daily running. The money-saving start date of March 11 gave the players a little more than two weeks of conditioning before the exhibition games. This time the club had no alternative but to play its way into shape. By facing the best team in baseball for two straight weeks, the Indians had the incentive to push themselves to the limit. Swinging against Carl Hubbell and Freddy Fitzsimmons promised to help the hitters sharpen up, while the pitching staff had Bill Terry and Mel Ott to practice their best stuff against.

The Giants-Indians exhibition tour began in New Orleans on March 31. Cleveland jumped out to an early lead and easily took game one, 7–3. From Louisiana the teams traveled to a handful of southern states, including Mississippi, Georgia, Alabama, and Tennessee. The clubs were greeted by large crowds at every stop they made. Rabid fans trailed the players to their hotels and engaged both teams in conversation. The games were well attended, with a great number of cheers and shouts from the grandstand. Revenues were not listed, but, all things considered, the exhibition tour proved to be a success. In something of a surprise, the Indians were pounding the Giants and rolled up a big lead in wins.

On April 11, the tour stopped in Charlotte, North Carolina. A crowd of over 4,500 sat in the stands to see a rare Major League game. Sportswriters scanned the playing field to see if Wes Ferrell might arrive to visit with his friends on the Cleveland squad. He lived only ninety miles away in Guilford. The ball game came and went without a Wes sighting. A few days later, trainer Lefty Weisman received a note from the probably former Indian. Ferrell requested that his gloves and spikes be returned to him as soon as possible. The team learned that Wes had been pitching in several local semi-pro games. Soon, scout Bill Bradley was dispatched to North Carolina to watch Ferrell throw. Billy Evans wanted a better idea of how Wes looked before he resumed trade talks with the two clubs that had interest.

The two squads move northwest to Louisville, Kentucky, for their eleventh game in the exhibition series. Cleveland won again, to stretch their game lead to 8–3. The party traveled further north to Cleveland for a final exhibition game at League Park. The home-town fans were ready for baseball with total attendance at 8,500. They were not disappointed when the Indians edged out their ninth win in twelve games, 5–4. Manager Johnson had to hope the spirited play carried into the regular season. He did have some reasons to be optimistic. Throughout the tour, Hal Trosky had shown flashes of power, hitting several long home runs off the Giants staff. Both Evans and Johnson were confident they had found their first baseman for many years to come.

Two days later the Indians were officially back home to start the American League season. With the temperature a balmy sixty-eight degrees, fans left their topcoats behind and gathered at the park. A good Opening Day crowd of 21,000 was on hand to watch Oral Hildebrand take the mound against the St. Louis Browns. It was not a sellout, but still an excellent number of fans. Among the im-provements at League Park were distance markers placed on the outfield walls. At the end of the left-field line the marker read 375 feet. This contrasted with the towering right-field wall at 290 feet. Those right-handed batters who had tried to adjust their swing at Cleveland Stadium needed to adjust one more time. The distance to left-center field stood at 415, while straightaway center was almost unreachable at 460. To lift the baseball over the right-center-field wall was only 340 feet. Now fans had the opportunity to accurately gauge the flight of the ball and how far it traveled.

Another benefit for fans unable to attend games was the return of live radio broadcasts. Bradley, though still not a radio man, offered broadcasting rights for the sum of $15,000. This change had everything to do with money. The Indians front office realized that having cash in hand was a better option than worrying about how many people were staying home to listen. WHK gladly paid for the play-by-play rights and sent Jack Graney back to the microphone. The station's potential sponsors had increased due to the ending of Prohibition back in December. Baseball broadcasts and beer advertising were a perfectly matched couple that had an unlimited future ahead.

A check before game time showed the Gensert-McDermott Drug Company doing a ton of sales, while the Wind-Up Cafe had customers out the door. The neighborhood bars were doing landmark business now that beer and alcohol were completely legitimate. Ever since the nationwide ban on alcohol was lifted, brewers had been racing to get up and running as quickly as possible. As a result, fans could enjoy Waldorf Lager and Gold Bond Beers sold right at the concession stands inside League Park. The city had numerous brewers, including Carling Black Label, Pilsner's, and Golden Dawn. If after the game one still needed another beer for the road, the choices were plentiful and easy to find. The installation of the numerous breweries around the city opened up jobs for several thousand unemployed workers. It did not end the depression, yet the relief rolls were noticeably lessened.

With numerous saloons to pick from along the way, a large collection of happy fans made their way inside the ballpark. If they glanced upward they would spot a group of people standing on the high roof of the laundry shop on Lexington Avenue. They had a great vantage point but were directly in the line of fire of the home-run hitters. Behind the scoreboard, a gentleman stood on the roof of a three-story home, clinging tightly to the chimney. An ancient tree in left-center field had no less than three men sitting on the branches overlooking the playing field. Hundreds of front lawns had automobiles parked on them. Yes, baseball and all its color had returned to League Park.

To commemorate the homecoming, a reporter from the *Plain Dealer* composed a short poem.

> The tribe is back in the old homestead
> And the fans are feeling high,
> They could see all the way to center field
> Alone, with the naked eye.

The last verse was a direct slap at Cleveland Stadium. Few people had warmed to the facility, citing the huge outfield and the grandstand being too far away from the action. League Park had none of those issues. The fans could carry on conversations with the corner outfielders and not strain their vocal cords.

The Opening Day Cleveland lineup had a number of new faces. Leading off and playing right field was forty-four-year-old Sam Rice. Manager Johnson had leaped at the chance when the twenty-year veteran was released from Washington. Rice had been a teammate of Johnson's starting in 1915 and had remained with the club during the Big Train's years as manager. Throughout his career Rice was a .300 hitter and a fleet outfielder who stole sixty-three bases in 1920. A Navy veteran of World War I, Rice believed he could still play ball, and so did his friend Walter Johnson. Therefore, Dick Porter was forced to take a seat on the bench in favor of the old Washington Senator.

Another new man in the lineup was second baseman Eddie Moore. Another old-timer at thirty-five, Moore served as a stopgap until a permanent replacement could be found at second. Bad News Hale probably had the job, but needed more time to convert from third base. The complete lineup:

> Sam Rice (right field)
> Frank Pytlak (catcher)
> Earl Averill (center field)
> Joe Vosmik (left field)
> Hal Trosky (first base)
> Willie Kamm (third base)
> Eddie Moore (second base)
> Bill Knickerbocker (shortstop)
> Oral Hildebrand (pitcher)

The Indians got on the scoreboard in the bottom of the first inning when Sam Rice doubled and Averill followed with a two-base hit. Of all the players on the Cleveland squad, the happiest to play again at League Park was Earl Averill. No statistics were kept, but at Cleveland Stadium he had probably led the American League in four-hundred-foot fly outs. Time and time again at the lakefront, Averill launched a ball into deep right-center field only to have the outfielder chase it down. The frustration grew, a large part of the reason he had an off year. Now he could redeem himself at the smaller park.

A run in the second inning put Cleveland on top, 2–0. In the bottom of the third with a runner on, Averill blasted a drive to center field. The ball took several bounces, then rebounded off the exit sign, approximately 415 feet from home plate. The fans stood up and hollered while Averill raced around the bases for an inside-the-park home run. In just two at bats he had erased much of the bad feelings from the previous season. The Indians won another opener behind Hildebrand, 5–2.

Opening Day around the Major Leagues turned out to be a success. The attendance for the eight games totaled 186,000. The Senators–Red Sox game at Fenway Park drew 33,000. In the National League, the Phillies at the Giants had 37,000 in the seats. The average attendance equaled a shade over 23,000 per game. Encouraging numbers for the owners, but too early to announce an end to the depression. There were still 153 games left on the schedule.

Seven days later, Cleveland was on the road in St. Louis. The crowd at Sportsman's Park witnessed the coming-out party of Hal Trosky. The twenty-one-year-old destroyed the Browns pitchers with four hits in five at bats. The hitting spree included a pair of two-run homers and a grand total of six RBIs. The Indians first baseman had served notice to the American League that another big bat was joining the likes of Gehrig, Foxx, and Averill. For most of the decade, the bulk of home runs in the junior circuit came from the first-base position. To add to the mix, the Detroit Tigers introduced Hank Greenberg, a long-ball slugger who displayed a tremendous right-handed bat for the rest of the decade.

Through the remaining days of April the Indians bounced up and down, often showing fabulous hitting and not much pitching.

On April 30 the pitching staff allowed an incredible twenty runs to the Chicago White Sox. Pitching hopefuls Denny Galehouse and Thornton "Lefty" Lee gave up seven runs total in two innings of work. A five-RBI effort from Joe Vosmik was wasted. The team needed a much better balance of pitching and hitting before they could announce themselves as contenders. There were high expectations for the pitching of Hildebrand, Harder, new man on the staff Monte Pearson, Clint Brown, and the almost forgotten Willis Hudlin. If the men on the mound righted themselves, the club had a chance to make things interesting.

Throughout May, the Cleveland hitters carried on with their staggering assault. Scores like 12–1 and 18–3 were becoming commonplace. The trio of Averill, Vosmik, and Trosky was slamming home runs at a record-setting pace. The Indians pitchers found a way to get opposing batters out, which translated into a growing number of wins. The front office had to be smiling, with better attendance and a team that appeared to be capable of making noise in the pennant race.

On Sunday, May 20, an overflow crowd of 27,000 saw the Indians outhit the Yankees, 8–5. Two doubles by Averill and two base hits each from Trosky, Hale, and pitcher Monte Pearson were enough to hold off the New Yorkers. Pearson pitched a complete game, despite allowing the five runs and walking a total of seven batters. Lou Gehrig kept things close by hitting a three-run home run in the top of the fifth.

The first holiday doubleheader took place on Memorial Day, May 30. Another full house packed League Park to watch the White Sox and Indians square off. Cleveland dropped the opening game but came back to win the nightcap due to an awe-inspiring performance by Hal Trosky. In the fourth inning he blasted a drive far over the right-field wall. Batting in the bottom of the sixth, Trosky launched another shot even further down Lexington Avenue. He came to the plate in the eighth inning with the sellout crowd on their feet screaming for another one. Hal did not disappoint. He drove a pitch into oblivion, the baseball sailing into a distant parking lot and smashing a windshield on one of the cars. Ed Bang observed that on the same day, fifty years before, Ed Williamson of the Chicago team became the first batter to clout three home runs in a game. Ten years later on May 30, 1894, Boston's Bobby Lowe did one better, belting four home runs in a single game. It seemed that Memorial Day was a time to honor all fallen American soldiers and a day for Major League ballplayers to hit tape-measure home runs.

The 5–4 victory over the White Sox left the Indians in first place, percentage points ahead of New York. It was quite early in the season, but a welcome treat for the Cleveland fans.

To make the environment even more pleasant, Billy Evans successfully traded Wes Ferrell to the Boston Red Sox. Ferrell had been placed on the suspended list dating back to April 27. Major League rules stated that any ballplayer who did not report to his team within ten days after the season opener was automatically placed on the suspension list. To be activated the player needed to petition his league president for reinstatement. A few days prior to being approached by the Red Sox, Evans had turned down an all-cash offer for Wes from the Yankees. Tom Yawkey did the same, but again Evans wanted more than cash. The Boston owner believed Ferrell could still pitch and accordingly sweetened the pot. The trade sent Dick Porter and Ferrell to Boston for left-handed pitcher Bob Weiland and former Indians reserve outfielder Bob Seeds. Tom Yawkey added cash to the deal that writers believed to be in the area of $25,000.

The Indians now boasted of perfect harmony on the club, along with a team on the rise. Although not the best team in baseball, the Indians were becoming one of the most exciting teams to watch. Wherever they played, fans were sure to see a steady barrage of doubles, triples, and home runs. They developed their own murderers' row in Averill, Vosmik, Trosky, and Hale. Every park they appeared in saw baseballs flying in all different directions. Balls in the outfield corners, up the gaps in right- and left-center fields, and far over the home-run barriers.

In a June game at Philadelphia, Cleveland trailed the Athletics 5–3 heading into the top of the sixth inning. With a man aboard, Hal Trosky hit his eleventh home run of the year to tie up the game. The Indians loaded the bases in their half of ninth. Once again Trosky stepped to the plate. In another display of power, the first baseman slammed the ball high over the right-field wall and onto the roof of a nearby home. The grand slam gave Trosky another six-RBI day and made his case for being the top rookie in the American League. The Indians won the ball game, moving them back into third place.

July came around and brought the second annual All-Star Game, this time at the Polo Grounds in New York. The Indians were represented by Earl Averill (his second appearance) and pitcher Mel Harder. The New York fans turned out in great numbers, with attendance equaling a bit over 48,000. Carl Hubbell started the game for the Nationals. The first two batters, Charlie Gehringer and Henry "Heinie" Manush, both reached base. Fans listening on several different radio networks anticipated a big inning for the American League. Babe Ruth came to the plate and hit nothing but air, unable to make contact with Hubbell's pitches. Lou Gehrig batted cleanup, but he too could not get his bat on the ball, making for out number two. That brought up the ever-dangerous Jimmy Foxx. While the spectators howled, Carl Hubbell fanned him as well to strike out the side. The partisan National League fans gave Hubbell quite an ovation as he walked to the dugout. He had faced three of the biggest hitters in baseball and sent them back to the bench without putting the ball in play. Frankie Frisch led off the bottom of the first with a home run to put the Nationals ahead 1–0. Al Simmons started the top of the second by striking out, the fourth in a row by Hubbell. Joe Cronin, the great Washington shortstop, marched to the plate, but he too was a strikeout victim, five in succession by Hubbell. The fans were taken aback by Hubbell's performance, fanning five of the American League's best. Bill Dickey broke the streak by getting a base hit, but the record had been set for a long time to come.

The Nationals extended the lead to 4–0 before Earl Averill entered the game in the top of the fourth. With a runner on, he launched a fastball to the deepest part of right field. According to Earl, the ball traveled 470 feet, the longest smash of his career. It went for a stand-up triple, making the score 4–1. In the next inning the American League rallied to take the lead. Averill batted again, this time hitting a double to knock in two more runs. After the game Averill was asked what his favorite moment was. He said, "The big kick I got was seeing the big kick Mr. Bradley and Mr. Evans got out of it."

Averill had a large part of the 9–7 victory, but he gladly shared the spotlight with Mel Harder. Entering the game in the bottom of the fifth inning, Harder pitched shutout ball for the remaining five innings. The contest had developed into a slugfest until the Indians star entered the game. With a sharp breaking curveball he silenced the big guns of the National League, among them Frisch, Mel Ott, Bill Terry, Chuck Klein, and Harold "Pie" Traynor. Harder tried to downplay his performance, telling the papers he had had a lot of rest and happened to have his good stuff. For his part, Mel did not strike out five batters in a row, but he pitched far better than his American League counterparts, Lefty Gomez and Red Ruffing. Harder pitched on the big stage in front of a huge crowd and thousands of fans tuning in all around the country. Bradley and Evans had a great deal to be proud of.

After the game, Harry Davis, the new mayor of Cleveland, sat down and composed a telegram to Commissioner Landis. Obviously excited by the prospect of hosting an All-Star Game and the benefits it could bring to the city, Davis bid to stage the 1935 game in Cleveland. He wrote, "Cleveland stadium seats 80,000 people. Eighty thousand three hundred and fourteen people attended the game between the Athletics and Cleveland July 31, 1932. We invite you to hold the next all-star game in our city and guarantee first-class condition of playing field." Davis had an advantage in that Landis had attended the 1932 game and knew all about the stadium and the downtown area. In addition, the cities of Chicago and New York had already hosted the game. The city of Cleveland had the inside track to land baseball's second-biggest spectacle.

With the All-Star Game behind them, Averill, Harder, and the rest of the club began to build some momentum. On Sunday, July 15, they swept a doubleheader with Washington by the identical scores of 10–8. The Indians bashed thirty-three hits for the two games, including homers in game one from Vosmik, Trosky, and Averill. The three heavy hitters had eight RBIs between them. In game two it was Bad News Hale's turn to shine. The bases were loaded when Hale stepped to the plate in the bottom of the first. The capacity crowd at League Park had already seen the long ball but wanted more. Hale obliged by sending a pitch over the right-center-field wall for a grand-slam home run. He finished the day with two doubles and six RBIs. All the hitting by both teams stretched the two games to six hours.

The lengthy afternoon caused fans to squirm in their seats. Being mid-July, the thermometer soared to an uncomfortable eighty-eight degrees. The cries for soda pop and lemonade were heard all around League Park. A number of the fans had no extra money for refreshments and searched the pavilions for water. Strangely, none could be found. It seemed odd that all the fountains and water faucets were dry.

Several days later, the *Cleveland Press* received a letter that begged to be printed word for word. A fan at the two games commented on the water situation, writing, "At the doubleheader July 15, approximately 25,000 fans paid good money to see a ball game. Many of the fans could barely afford to pay the sixty cents admission, let alone the ten cents collected at various times during the game for soft drinks. These fans thought they could get by and drink water instead, but when they went to get a drink a park employee turned off the water and said, 'Orders from the management.' Do you think it is possible that the owners also turn off the water in the players' dugouts making them so thirsty they can't play good ball?" Billy Evans did not reply in the paper, lending credence to the fan's letter.

The next three ball games were played at home against the New York Yankees. The doubleheader win against the Senators gave the Indians the impetus to send the Yankees back home as losers. The fans' expectations were quite high going into this series, as wins over the Yankees were always a major accomplishment. Any time the forces of Ruth, Gehrig, Dickey, and Lazzeri could be overcome was a reason to celebrate. Cleveland had a record of forty-two wins versus thirty-seven losses, just a game behind Boston for third place. New York was seven games ahead, but a sweep by Cleveland would reduce the gap to four. They might not catch the Yankees, but they could hurt New York's chances in overtaking the front-running Tigers.

The teams met on Monday for a series of wild, action-packed games that had not been seen in a long while. The opening game had New York's Johnny Allen against Cleveland's seldom-used starter Thornton Lee. Both pitchers were on their game, keeping the heavy bats silent for most of the battle. Going into the bottom of the eighth inning, the Yankees led 3–2. Earl Averill drew a walk, which brought up Hal Trosky. The fans at League Park and the ones listening on WHK sensed this was the moment of truth. Allen delivered and Trosky cranked his eighteenth home run over the right-field wall. The Indians, thanks to another clutch homer by Trosky, had taken the lead, 4–3.

In the ninth inning, Walter Johnson let young relief pitcher Ralph Winegarner try to close out the game. He had retired the Yankees in the eighth inning without any trouble. This may have been the time to bring out one of the trusted starters, like Harder or Hildebrand or possibly Hudlin, to finish off the Yankees. It was common in baseball to use one of your starters to save a close ball game. Pitching one inning with one or two days' rest did not concern most managers or the pitcher involved. Here was a situation where a Harder or a Hildebrand was called for. Nonetheless, Johnson figured his inexperienced relief pitcher could handle the job.

Winegarner started the ninth inning by yielding a double and a walk. Johnson walked to the mound and called on Lloyd Brown to relieve. Brown, a former Red Sox pitcher, had appeared in both games of Sunday's doubleheader. The fans nervously applauded when he struck out Frankie Crosetti for the first out. Try as he might, though, Brown could not find the plate against Tony Lazzeri, loading the bases. Babe Ruth now stood at home, eager to get a pitch he could send over the right-field wall. Brown, probably a touch uneasy, walked the Babe and forced in the tying run. The fans started to boo loudly, angry that Brown was in the game. Lou Gehrig helped the Indians' cause by harmlessly fouling out. One more out was needed, but Brown walked another to give the Yankees the lead, 5–4. Once more Johnson walked from the dugout while the fans vented their anger. In came Bob Weiland, who walked two more batters before Earle Combs ended the disaster by flying out.

Joe McCarthy brought in his All-Star Red Ruffing to face the Indians in the bottom of the ninth. The Yankee hurler set down the Cleveland hitters and the game was lost, 7–4. The end of the contest set off a firestorm rarely seen in Cleveland baseball history. Fans called WHK Radio to voice their complaints about manager Johnson. The three Cleveland newspapers fielded calls from livid fans demanding Johnson's head on a platter. The next morning, petitions were circulated all around Cleveland insisting the manager be immediately fired.

In Johnson's defense, this was a midseason game. It was not late September with the pennant on the line. He evidently believed an inexperienced relief pitcher had the capability to set down the Yankees. Had Winegarner saved the victory the second-guessers would really have had nothing to say about Johnson's strategy. They might have disagreed, but a win is a win. Still, the decision backfired and the Yankees had won. Possibly if it had been the Athletics or Senators, the criticism might not have been so severe. But this was the mighty Yankees! Cleveland fans were all too aware of the many New York pennants through the 1920s. They wanted to see Ruth, Gehrig, and company take a fall. Any win over the Bronx Bombers was a special win, regardless of the standings. Here they had the Yankees on the ropes, but let them escape in a gut-wrenching manner.

Something quite unexpected occurred during all the turmoil. The Cleveland sportswriters blasted Johnson for his late-inning decision, all three newspapers ripping him unmercifully. The *Plain Dealer* ran an editorial criticizing Johnson for lack of leadership. It read in part, "The owners of the Cleveland Indians cannot be oblivious to the fact that Walter Johnson is unpopular with the patrons of baseball and has failed to provide leadership of the kind that makes teams victorious. Cleveland fans admire Walter Johnson as a former great pitcher, as a good sportsman and a gentleman but they are losing confidence in him as a manager." All this after one terrible loss at the hands of the Yankees. There must have been something else bothering the writers about Johnson, yet they alluded to very little other than yesterday's game.

Ed Bang in the *Cleveland News* headed his column with, "Is Walter Johnson on the way out?" Bang maintained that anywhere you went in Cleveland, in restaurants and clubs, on street corners and streetcars, the talk was, fire the manager! Bang wrote, "If the issue were put up to the fans at this moment it is almost a certainty they would vote to have president Alva Bradley's 'personal choice' to lead the Indians step aside and make room for a newcomer." The writer believed Johnson had poorly handled his pitchers in the first game of the recent Washington doubleheader. He said, "In both instances Johnson showed anything but mental alertness and managerial ability. Truth be told he fell far short of what a wide-awake manager should do."

To keep pace with his fellow writers, Stuart Bell of the *Cleveland Press* argued that the patience of everybody following the Indians was exhausted. He asserted that all the Cleveland sportswriters had been fair with Johnson until the Yankees disaster. He called the ninth inning "minor-league pitching." Bell asserted that if Ruth or Gehrig had gone deep on the Indians pitcher, so be it. He emphasized that the walks were "humiliating" and should never have taken place. If that was not enough blame, Bell went on further to announce that most of the Cleveland players did not care for their manager, and that a team that does not believe in their leader will never win. Bell did not call for a new manager, but there was no mistaking his absolute disgust with Walter Johnson.

Alva Bradley read the newspapers with disbelief. His personal choice of managers was under fire from every possible angle. Bradley hurried to come to the aid of his beleaguered manager. After a quick meeting with his partners, Bradley announced that Johnson would remain with the Indians for the rest of the season. Changing managers was out of the question. He said, "When I prevailed upon Johnson to take management of the Indians last year, I gave him a contract extending through the 1934 season. Also I had an understanding with Walter there would be no changing of managers during midseason. I am going to live up to that agreement." Bradley added that Johnson was of good character and was responsible for cleaning up the personnel of the Cleveland team.

What of manager Johnson? His head was probably spinning at the tremendous acrimony sent his way. All throughout his career as a player, he was regarded as a gentleman of high standard. In Larry Ritter's classic book, *The Glory of Their Times*, the ballplayers interviewed had nothing but kind words to say about Johnson. He went out of his way to avoid hitting batters, worried that his streaking fastball might hurt someone. In games where the Senators were far ahead, Johnson at times would slow the ball down and let his opponents swing away. How could this man come under such fire?

The reason lay in Johnson's having switched roles from player to manager. As a player one could be a good soldier, always giving the best for his team. Once you leave the comfort of the diamond for the front office, the relationship has to change. There are managers who made the transition with ease, others who failed to do so. Walter Johnson was in no-man's-land. He had left the playing field behind, but had not yet proven he could manage effectively. He still had time to demonstrate his capability, but nevertheless the count stood at one strike against him.

A few days later Johnson spoke to the media. He owned up to the 7–4 loss and acknowledged he heard the fans quite clearly. Johnson said, "I've been in this business a long time and I'm smart enough to know that you have to take the good with the bad. I must admit that I never thought the time would come when they'd be shouting to roust me right out of the ballpark." Johnson did not hesitate to take shots at the local writers. He believed them to be unreasonable in their comments. The only answer to the current situation was to win ball games and quiet everybody down.

Game two of the series was all Cleveland. The hitters pounded the Yankee pitching staff for thirteen runs and an easy win. In the bottom of the third, Earl Averill came to bat with the bases loaded and two out. He worked the count to three balls and two strikes. As the pitch came, all the runners took off, with Willie Kamm dashing toward the plate. Bill Dickey caught the pitch several inches outside and put the tag on the sliding runner. George Moriarty, the home plate umpire, never moved. He watched the Yankees run toward their dugout with the side apparently out. The Indians bench players raced onto the field yelling that the pitch was ball four and Kamm had automatically scored. The bewildered umpire had to admit he'd lost track of the count and did not realize the pitch was ball four. Moriarty ordered New York back on the field and the inning was resumed.

Oral Hildebrand pitched the first seven innings, allowing five runs and seven walks. After one was out in the eighth, Johnson walked to the mound and signaled for Willis Hudlin to relieve. There were jeers from the fans, still smarting from yesterday's loss. Hudlin finished the game strong, giving reason for some optimism that Johnson had learned his lesson. In spite of this, he was far from being out of the woods.

On July 18, the deciding game of the series took place. This one turned out to be a slugfest of epic proportion. A fine afternoon crowd of 10,000 were in the stands, pleading for the Indians to take the series. Mel Harder started the game against Red Ruffing, but after four innings both pitchers were in the showers. The score was 8–5 going into the sixth inning, then tied at eight one inning later. Moving to the top of the ninth inning, Cleveland enjoyed a three-run lead, 12–9. Despite trailing, the Yankees were by no means finished. A walk and a single put runners on first and third. Earle Combs singled to drive in the first run. Manager Johnson called for Thornton Lee, the fifth Indians pitcher of the day. Tony Lazzeri singled in another run and a sacrifice fly scored Combs with the tying run. Lou Gehrig grounded an easy roller to second, but Sammy Hale fumbled the ball and could not make a play. That brought up Bill Dickey, who tapped a slow ground ball in front of the mound. Lee picked up the ball and threw late to second base to load the bases. Ben Chapman singled to drive in two more runs and the Yankees now led 14–12. The crowd collectively shook their heads, aghast at the five-run rally.

Willie Kamm was the first batter up for the bottom of the ninth. He got the fans on their feet with a double to center field. Frank Pytlak came in to pinch hit and lined the baseball to deep center. Kamm scored, and Pytlak pulled into third with a triple. Reserve outfielder Dutch Holland singled to tie the game at fourteen. Sam Rice bunted, but a quick throw to second retired Holland. The elder Rice still had some spring in his legs, stealing second and racing to third on a ground out. The fans were roaring when Earl Averill came to bat. A second later he delivered, driving the pitch high off the right-field screen. Incredibly, the Indians had come from behind to win the tense struggle, 15–14. Earl Averill was the hero, but all the Cleveland hitters accounted for eighteen hits in the game. The power trio of Averill, Vosmik, and Trosky produced a total of seven hits and eight RBIs. Cleveland won the series two games to one and for a moment the pressure on Walter Johnson ceased.

Earlier in the ball game, Babe Ruth had reached first base. He took a short lead when Lou Gehrig scorched a ground ball right at the stationary Babe. The old legs could not move and the ball smacked Ruth right on the shin. He went down hard and play was stopped. Several of the Yankees carried Babe to the clubhouse, where an ambulance took him to Cleveland Clinic. Doctors examined the shin, which had swelled tremendously. They believed the leg was not broken, but kept Babe overnight to make certain the swelling subsided.

The next day Ruth was moved to a suite at the Hotel Cleveland. Reporters swarmed to the room as if they were visiting a ruling monarch. They sent stories about Babe's breakfast (two lamb chops and tea), all the people stopping by, and what he might be ordering for dinner. The Boston Red Sox were in town and many of the players came by the room to see the wounded warrior. All the attention prompted Ed Bang to write a column suggesting the Indians hire Ruth to manage. He wrote about Babe's great popularity, which might increase attendance and help get the club out of the red. Bang thought the Yankee star was fundamentally sound and could relate to the players considerably better than the current manager. The next day Alva Bradley shot down the talk, calling it "just plain silly." Ruth left Cleveland to rejoin his teammates and the idea faded away, much to the relief of Johnson.

Even though the "fire the manager" talk had slowed down, Johnson could not catch a break. At the end of July he became ill with a fever and cough. Morrison Castle, the Indians team doctor, gave him an exam and diagnosed a case of pleurisy. Apparently Johnson had a viral infection that had spread to his lungs and interfered with his breathing. Fortunately, there was no evidence of pneumonia, which might have sidelined Johnson for the rest of the season. For the next two weeks the Indians manager rested at Lakeside Hospital. He contacted Billy Evans and requested that Willie Kamm take over the ball club. There was no objection, as Kamm was in his twelfth season in the Major Leagues and was regarded as a smart baseball man. At the time the move seemed of little significance, but it would come back to haunt Johnson the following season.

Indians backup catcher Glenn Myatt was in the hospital with Big Barney (another of Johnson's nicknames, which stuck after a teammate got him out of a traffic ticket by convincing the policeman that Johnson was the well-known auto racer, Barney Oldfield). In a game a few days earlier, Myatt had slid home only to fracture his ankle and dislocate his knee. When Johnson's health improved, the two became roommates and talked baseball all day long. Jack Graney and WHK Radio engineers came by with a telephone hookup for a live interview with the two invalids. Cleveland fans were pleased to know that both the manager and catcher still lived and would eventually return to the ball club. However, Myatt's days as an Indian were numbered. Later, fans would wonder if anything happened between the two patients that led to Myatt's release the following spring.

Johnson returned to the ball club in the middle of August. The Indians had just dropped three straight games to the first-place Detroit Tigers. Their record stood at fifty-eight wins against forty-nine losses. They trailed Detroit by thirteen games, effectively eliminating them from the pennant race. In twenty-two games with the Tigers, Cleveland only won six. Had they played Detroit even, or won the majority, a chance for the pennant would have been there, but their weak performance against the Tigers kept them out of contention. They did finish the season on a high note, ending with a record of eighty-five wins and sixty-nine losses. The Tigers easily won the pennant, with New York a distant second and Cleveland in third place ahead of Boston.

Beginning with Hal Trosky, a number of Cleveland players had had outstanding seasons. The rookie first baseman had a remarkable year, batting .330 with 35 home runs and 142 RBIs. His 206 hits placed him third in the American League, behind Lou Gehrig and Charlie Gehringer. He was second in total bases and fourth in slugging percentage. Only Gehrig and Foxx hit more home runs. *Baseball Magazine* called Trosky the best rookie in 1934, even better than Hank Greenberg. Grantland Rice in his syndicated column put Hal on the same level with the game's best power hitters. The Indians had struck gold with the twenty-one-year-old star, who in his first season broke the Indians' home-run record. Before the start of the regular season, Alva Bradley bet Earl Averill that the new first baseman would hit more home runs than the All-Star center fielder. Averill took the bet and had to fork over fifty dollars to the boss. Earl had an excellent season himself, batting .313 along with 31 homers and 113 RBIs. He was fifth in the American League in home runs, fourth in runs scored, and third in doubles.

Joe Vosmik had some injury problems in the course of the season, but batted .341, fifth in the league. Bad News Hale hit .302 and batted in 101 runs. On the pitching side, Mel Harder won twenty games, had an ERA of 2.61, second only to Lefty Gomez, and threw six shutouts, tying Gomez for the lead. His All-Star Game performance gave notice that Harder was now an elite pitcher, one of the best in the game.

The move from Cleveland Stadium back to League Park resulted in a profit for Bradley and his partners. By saving the minimum rental fee of $50,000 and cutting the salaries of front-office personnel and players, they had put the team finances in the black. Attendance for 1934 came to 391,338, an increase of nearly 4,000 fans from 1933. Even though this was cause for a degree of optimism, it did not quite signal a period of unlimited wealth for baseball owners. Still, to earn a profit in the midst of the harsh economic downturn was a major accomplishment. Alva Bradley had to be commended for placing his ball club on a solid footing.

Despite the Indians' newfound stability, the unemployment situation in Cleveland remained critical, as it did throughout the United States. Foreclosures and evictions forced people out of their homes. There were shanty towns all around the lakefront. Hundreds of men with nowhere to go stayed at the Wayfarer's Lodge, where you could get a clean bed and a blanket for the night. Relief agencies continued to be flooded by despairing families on the brink of starvation. The outlook for recovery remained bleak in northeast Ohio. Nevertheless, the Cleveland Baseball Company had found the correct business plan to keep the doors open.

Chapter 10

GOODBYE TO WALTER

In the off-season many of the ballplayers spent their time hunting and fishing. Others might take a trip to Florida to relax on the beach and recharge the batteries. Earl Averill spent his winter months in Japan, playing exhibitions for the American League All-Stars. He had traveled to Chicago in the middle of October to join a group of ballplayers starting a four-month barnstorming tour. The American League All-Stars plus former New York Giant Francis "Lefty" O'Doul, planned a tour of Honolulu and the Far East, including Japan, China, and Manila. Babe Ruth was the leading light of the tour, along with familiar names like Gehrig, Foxx, Gehringer, Bing Miller, and Lefty Gomez. Connie Mack joined the group and two Indians were selected, Averill and pitcher Clint Brown. The squad headed for Vancouver, playing exhibition games along the way. The trip was a great way for the players to see the world and earn additional money. American League president Will Harridge spoke out against these tours, citing the potential for injuries as his main concern. The players believed otherwise. The owners were taking steps to regain profitability, why not the ballplayers?

The Major League owners stayed busy in the winter months. They did not go hunting or fishing, but met in New York to kick around ideas for the 1935 season. The possibility of playing night baseball was discussed at length. Alva Bradley did not favor playing any kind of baseball under lights. He saw night games as a missed opportunity for fans to get out in the sun, relax, and enjoy the fresh air while taking in a game. Night baseball could not offer the same experience. Billy Evans also stated that he was "one hundred percent against baseball under lights." He and Bradley both told reporters that night baseball would be played in Cleveland only over their dead bodies.

National League owners thought differently. They were willing to experiment and see what resulted from scheduling seven games under lights. Cincinnati happily got the assignment to install a lighting system, with the initial night game to be played in May. The Reds had had terrible attendance problems and were the best candidate for the experiment. The price tag for a practical lighting system was $40,000, but the Cincinnati front office had no qualms about investing the money. They were not concerned about the theory that night air was unhealthy, or that players might lose sight of the baseball. The Reds' attendance figures for 1934 amounted to a horrific 206,000, and they were willing to take a chance at anything to boost their revenues.

The owners had no other groundbreaking plans for 1935. It seemed that rising attendance the previous season had quelled their fears about the depression. Rather than play it safe until the economy recovered, most of the owners went about buying and selling players and spending money on stadium improvements. The topic of air travel came up as a means of transporting players from city to city. Passenger flights were now considered routine. Travel time from Cleveland to Detroit was fifty minutes, and Cleveland to Washington took two and a half hours. Airplanes and Major League Baseball were destined to become long-term partners.

Now that Cleveland had shown a profit for 1934, Billy Evans announced that none of the players were going to receive any type of salary cut. A number of the contracts mailed out had raises in them. Hal Trosky saw his salary double, while others received more modest increases. The incentive contract was eliminated in favor of a straight salary. Evans wanted his players in spring training from day one. The feeling in the Cleveland front office and around the American League was that the Indians had the talent to win it all. They had good pitching, a lineup of big-time hitters, and were fair enough in the fielding department. The Tigers could not be expected to have another season of 101 wins, while New York had no prospects ready to replace Babe Ruth.

In another move, Evans hired Steve O'Neill to coach the pitchers. The former Cleveland catching star had been managing Toledo, but he was excited to return to the place where he'd spent his best years. For some reason, Walter Johnson preferred not to have any coaches with him during the season. In 1934, Johnson had coached first base and designated one of his players to handle third. Coaching first was hardly a demanding job. Nevertheless, Johnson stationed himself there rather than in the Indians dugout. He had no choice in the hiring of O'Neill, though. Evans wanted him, and he was coming aboard.

Spring training in New Orleans featured another exhibition tour with the New York Giants. Semipro pitchers were brought to camp to handle batting practice instead of the regular hurlers. The starting pitchers were used carefully, to save their arms for the regular season. O'Neill worked with his staff to correct any flaws he spotted, all with the intention of getting them ready for a championship run. Mel Harder was expected to win twenty games, while Monte Pearson had the potential to do the same. Willis Hudlin had got back on form in 1934, winning fifteen games, and Oral Hildebrand, if he could get out of Johnson's doghouse, might contribute more than the eleven wins he'd managed. The expectations were certainly high.

The 1935 season opener was set for April 16 in St. Louis. Cleveland fans received some great news when WHK revealed they were sending Jack Graney to Sportsman's Park to broadcast live. Through the sponsorship of the Standard Oil Company, Graney would be connected to a special hookup that sent the signal directly back to the radio station. This marked the first broadcast of a Cleveland Indians away game. Standard Oil had the home-season sponsorship, but wanted to give the fans a little bit more than they were used to. Despite several teams still refusing to have their games broadcast, radio had a permanent place in baseball.

Opening Day in St. Louis was freezing cold, just right for football. The Browns took the field with a tiny crowd of twenty-five hundred friends and relatives. Louis "Buck" Newsom drew the pitching assignment for the Browns, Mel Harder for Cleveland. In the bottom of the first, Sam West tripled and player-manager Rogers Hornsby singled for the first run of the game. Newsom threw five scoreless innings before the Indians got on the scoreboard. Rookie shortstop Roy Hughes, filling in for Bill Knickerbocker, reached second base with a double. Joe Vosmik singled to tie the game at one apiece. Neither team was able to score any more runs, sending the game to extra innings. Harder and Newsom were brilliant, dueling each other through the thirteenth frame. In the top of the fourteenth, backup second baseman Lou Berger walked. Glenn Myatt took two balls and a strike before launching the ball to deep left field, and Berger sped around the bases for the go-ahead run. Harder held the Browns scoreless in the bottom of the fourteenth, the Indians winning, 2–1. After giving up a run in the first inning, Cleveland's best pitcher threw thirteen shutout innings while allowing only eight hits. Harder looked to be on his way to the expected twenty-game season.

The broadcast back to Cleveland went smoothly, the signal traveling loud and clear for the fans glued to their radios. WGAR also had men in St. Louis, sending back the play-by-play via teletype. Major League Baseball had ordered any radio station not doing a live broadcast to delay their wire play-by-play for three innings. This rule was put in place to allow the official team station an advantage with listeners. Yet, as they had shown in the past, WGAR did not follow the rules. They were trying to keep up with WHK. When the game went to extra innings, Jack Graney stayed on the air and the regular programming was preempted. Afraid to alienate regular listeners, WGAR cut the baseball broadcast in deference to the wildly popular Amos and Andy.

The Indians got out of the gate quickly, winning nine of their first eleven. They were playing like the team many had picked to win the pennant. Rumors still circulated that the club as a whole did not like Walter Johnson, though results on the field indicated otherwise. In a May 22 column, Ed Bang wrote of the team's 4–1 victory over the Boston Red Sox. Oral Hildebrand had outpitched Lefty Grove for nine innings, while timely hitting helped preserve the win. Bang liked the fact that there was no drama at all between Johnson and Hildebrand, despite their frazzled relationship. He urged that all be forgotten, and that everyone concentrate on winning baseball games and nothing else. Whether or not the players and manager were best friends meant nothing if the team was winning.

The very next day, though, Johnson told reporters that he had dismissed Willie Kamm and Glenn Myatt from the team. There would be no suspensions or fines: they were both banished, without any chance of returning. Johnson informed beat reporter Herman Goldstein of the *Cleveland News*, "If I am going to run this club, I'll run it my way." Johnson believed the two players were criticizing him behind his back, and called them "disturbers." He elaborated, "I was perfectly willing to go along with everybody and thought things were moving along smoothly until I began to get reports on what Myatt and Kamm had been saying. Both of them did a lot of talking to players on other clubs and to some of our own men." The manager claimed Myatt sat on the bench and second-guessed every move Johnson made. For his part, Kamm had been tried and convicted of giving advice to the younger players. The irony here is that in the previous season, when Johnson had the attack of pleurisy, he personally chose Kamm to manage the club. Rather than accepting Kamm's actions, or speaking to him about them, Johnson kicked the twelve-year veteran off the team.

Goldstein believed the appalling news would fail to bring the rest of the squad into Johnson's corner. He claimed that in private most of the team was unfriendly toward their manager, and wrote that, as long as the current manager stayed, trouble would be imminent. He stated of Johnson, "He lacks the knack of keeping his men friendly to him, both socially and as members of the team. With several players it is known only one overt act would be enough to touch off another explosion."

As might be expected, both the terminated players had loads to say. Willie Kamm took the opportunity to fire back at his former manager, saying, "Maybe he's right and I was wrong to do it, though it sounds ridiculous. Sure I've talked a lot to the young players. When I see a kid doing something wrong I try to straighten him out. This is the first I've heard anyone has resented it."

Myatt, who had been the backup catcher since 1923, took the news quite hard. In twelve years with the team he had played for four different managers, including Walter Johnson. There had not been any hint of trouble with the other three bosses. Myatt was informed by Johnson that he had not given his best for the team. If he had shown he was one hundred percent for the team, the release would not have happened. This was the same man who in late July 1934 broke his ankle and dislocated his knee sliding home. If that was not one hundred percent effort, it is hard to imagine what is. Myatt and Johnson had roomed together at Lakeside Hospital for two weeks. The catcher did not return to the Indians until March 1935, which meant that in two months he had drawn the unrelenting wrath of his boss. Myatt said, "I don't know what Johnson means. I've always been in perfect shape, ready to go into a ball game anytime even after long stretches on the bench. I don't know why he did it, unless it was for his own protection. The players consider the whole situation a joke."

Alva Bradley publicly supported his manager. He told the newspapers, "In any business we run, we have only one manager. Walter acted for the good of the club." In addition, he stated that the club had a profit of $100,000 in 1934, for which he gave Johnson part of the credit. From the available record, it appears that neither Bradley nor Evans had any advance notice of what Johnson planned to do. In fact, Bradley mentioned to reporters that he considered Kamm a good fellow, and that when the two could meet he would offer Willie a job in the organization. A fine gesture, indeed, but showing less than complete support of the manager's decision.

What really happened to facilitate Johnson's extreme treatment of Myatt and Kamm? Were they actually the "disturbers" he claimed them to be? A careful examination of the scenario indicates that it was likely a case of Walter Johnson making a last-ditch attempt to get control of his ball club. In two years as manager he had suspended a popular pitcher, made poor choices in a notorious home-game loss against the Yankees, and, according to the writers, alienated most of his players. By firing Myatt and Kamm he attempted to send a clear message to his team: "Play by my rules or don't play at all."

It was no coincidence that both players were in their mid-thirties and near the end of the line as ballplayers. Removing them from the team did no serious damage to the lineup. Johnson picked on the two players that he needed the least. That being said, he did not realize the extent of the backlash the move would create. All three local newspapers ripped him to pieces. It became national news, with writers all around the country taking sides. For a team that had pennant aspirations, his judgment was off-base and ill-timed.

As one might expect, the Cleveland baseball fans went off the deep end over the dismissal of Myatt and Kamm. A chain letter circulated, addressed to Alva Bradley, reading in part, "I, as a loyal supporter of the Indians, don't want Kamm and Myatt released. I deplore the condition prevailing in the present management and ask that steps be taken to make the Indians the winning ball club they ought to be." That was the first of thousands of letters to the papers and the League Park office. There was no count of how many favored Walter Johnson, but the majority of letters printed clearly stated that Johnson should go. He did have support from various fans who believed the players were prima donnas and needed a good, swift kick. Fans did not run the ball club, but Alva Bradley's famous words ring true here. When he sacked Roger Peckinpaugh, he let the public know that the owner hires the manager and the fans fire him. Sooner or later, Bradley had to make a move.

Within days, Glenn Myatt cleared waivers in the American League. Bill Terry of the New York Giants signed Myatt to be a backup for the club. Willie Kamm stayed in Cleveland, demanding his day in court with Bradley and Johnson. He wanted to tell his side of the story and clear his name. Kamm advised curious reporters, "If the players said I interfered with them then okay but I don't think it's true. I want Johnson to tell me who these fellows were that he claimed kicked about me, and I want him to tell it before Mr. Bradley." He called Johnson's remarks a pack of lies and did not want be branded as a "Bolshevik" or as undermining the team. Kamm believed his manager had disliked him from the start and resented when a young ballplayer asked him for advice. In fact, during spring training several of the rookies, including Hughes and Berger, had sought Kamm out for advice. Both had played for New Orleans and the manager there suggested that when they needed help they should talk to Kamm. This caused an outburst from Johnson, who was heard to say, "About seventy-five percent of the players on this team don't seem to know who the manager is."

Though the uproar over the previous year's fiasco with the ninth-inning loss to the Yankees eventually calmed down, this mess would not stop. The Cleveland sportswriters continued to write column after column about Johnson's action. They called for Bradley to meet with his players and find out where they stood. Fans had threatened to boycott games when the team arrived home in early June. The controversy could not have happened at a worse time: the 1935 All-Star Game was scheduled for Cleveland Stadium in a little over five weeks. The last thing the ball club and the city needed was an embarrassing situation on a national stage. Yet the letters came pouring in, demanding that Johnson be fired. Ed Bang claimed the letters were now running nine to one for the manager's ouster.

Alva Bradley arrived in Washington to talk with his manager. In addition to the Myatt-Kamm incident, the Indians were losers of seven of their last eleven road games. For the storm to blow over the team needed to start winning. Bradley advised the *Cleveland News*, "Of course the situation is hot now but you know as well as I do the public is interested in only one thing. If the Indians win, the fans won't care whether they are managed by Walter Johnson or Joe Doakes." Bradley did acknowledge that his office was still receiving many calls about the situation. He claimed they were running about fifty-fifty in regards to his manager. Apparently, Joe Doakes (an old expression equivalent to "John Q. Public") was beginning to be the people's choice

The next day, news broke that Judge Landis had agreed to a hearing with Kamm at his Chicago residence. Landis, resting at home with a head cold, directed Johnson to attend the Friday morning meeting so that he could hear both sides. Bradley announced to the baseball writers that if Commissioner Landis ruled in Kamm's favor he would drop Walter Johnson as manager. Steve O'Neill would manage the club until at least the end of the season. Another strong vote of confidence by the man in charge. This news helped appease the Cleveland fans, who generally believed Bradley was a man of his word. Manager Johnson had to be surprised when he read the papers stating that his job was on the line, pending the hearing's results.

There was no way to tell which way the strong-willed commissioner was leaning. In his fifteen years on the job he had come down hard on ballplayers for various infractions. A number of players were permanently banned from the game, including the eight Black Sox players from the 1919 World Series. At one point he suspended Babe Ruth for barnstorming, then turned around and ruled in favor of Tris Speaker and Ty Cobb in their betting scandal. Willie Kamm had little to lose in the hearing and was actually looking forward to it. He relished the chance to speak to the commissioner in person. Walter Johnson, on the other hand, stood to be fired if the hearing went against him.

The Friday morning meeting allowed both individuals to state their cases. Will Harridge sat in on the hearing but offered no opinion on the matter. After listening to the arguments, Landis issued an odd but carefully worded verdict. He decided in essence that both men were right, but ultimately the manager had the authority to take action. Landis issued the following statement: "In this situation, two honest men found themselves at loggerheads as the result, mainly, of what was said or was alleged to have been said regarding what each of them did or did not do in connection with the ball club. There is no suggestion against the character or repute of either of them. However, as a practical proposition, it falls upon the manager to act in cases where even perfectly honest differences arise. This is so because the responsibility is his and with the responsibility must go the authority."

One could read Commissioner Landis's verdict several different ways. He essentially cleared Willie Kamm of any wrongdoing, terming the whole affair an honest difference of opinion. He noted, as was common knowledge, that the manager had the authority to make decisions concerning his ball club. Still, this was not the crux of the issue. He sidestepped the question of who was in the right by declaring that two honest men simply had a disagreement and the manager had the authority over the player. According to Landis there was no right or wrong here. Both parties could go their separate ways knowing they were honest men. The fact remained, Johnson still had his job but Kamm did not. It would be up to Bradley to sort things out.

After the hearing concluded, both parties came out smiling. Kamm believed he had proven his innocence and voiced no concern about being through as a player with the Indians. In a few days Kamm met with Bradley and agreed to accept a scouting positon with the club. He maintained his regular salary until the season ended. Before leaving town he left a farewell message for his former teammates and fans. Kamm wrote, "Gang, I'd like to be with

No Money, No Beer, No Pennants

you in your drive for the pennant, but the fortunes of war have willed otherwise. You're a great bunch of fellows, a credit to any city, in fact the fans of Cleveland should be, and I believe are justly proud of you. I have no animosity against anyone connected with the Cleveland ball club and while I will not be here in person, remember I'll be with you in spirit."

Johnson believed he had won, with his status as manager still intact. Commissioner Landis had not revoked his authority, allowing Johnson to move forward and get his team back in contention. The real issue now concerned attendance for the June home stand. Fans had threatened to stay away in large numbers. To try and influence the fans, the Cleveland front office took out large advertisements in all three papers. They cobbled together a statement of unity and had all the players sign at the bottom. The ad began with, "This is a story of inside baseball, fast double play from the Indians to Cleveland fandom. We hope it will retire a lot of gossip and rumor that has been going the rounds about our club for the past month. We, the members of the Cleveland Baseball Club, want the fans to know we are not a team split wide open by dissension, arrayed against our manager."

The statement went on to say that everybody has differences of opinion, but that is only normal. An example was given regarding the World Champion St. Louis Cardinals and a fracas involving Dizzy Dean and Joe Medwick. The point being, this type of behavior happens with teams fighting to win the pennant. The text made sure to let the fans know the Indians respected their manager but were not a bunch of yes-men. The proclamation ended with a statement of solidarity: "In conclusion, we, the members of the Cleveland Indians, sincerely hope our showing during the remainder of the season will prove to the Cleveland fans that we are 100 percent loyal to our public, Manager Walter Johnson and President Alva Bradley."

The author of the statement remains anonymous to this date, but the likely writer of the propaganda piece was Billy Evans. He had started out as a newspaper writer, then continued his journalistic pursuits while being an American League umpire. Apparently the front office believed they needed to address the fans directly before the home stand began on June 7. The last thing they wanted was a riot at League Park where fans might storm the field. The statement itself remains quite unusual in the history of Major League Baseball. The fact that the club created the document showed a huge concern for the fate of baseball in Cleveland. There had to be significant alarm that the game with the Browns might have more fans outside the park than inside. A unified front had to be presented.

The Friday afternoon game against St. Louis was a rainout. Perhaps it was good to give the fans another day to think things over. The next afternoon arrived with overcast skies and a temperature hovering around sixty degrees. Attendance was a disappointing 5,000 fans, but other than a round of boos for the manager the game went without incident. Evans hired extra police for the contest and the concessions people had paper cups for soft drinks and lemonade. Outside the grounds the threatened protest line never appeared. Mel Harder pitched a seven-hitter and drove in a run to lead the Indians to a 3–2 win. The club scored single runs in the first, third, and fourth innings to give Harder some room to work. A big sigh of relief came from the front office when the final out was recorded. Now, just maybe, the focus could be on hits and runs rather than who was getting into trouble in the locker room.

With peace seemingly restored, the Indians were now concentrating on moving up in the standings while the city of Cleveland prepared to host the third annual All-Star Game. The mission to bring the event home started back in 1933 when the inaugural game was played in Chicago. According to Ed Bang, the *Cleveland News* sent letters to all the owners plus the American and National League offices. The letters reminded the officials about the tremendous capacity of the stadium, which the paper believed would yield record numbers at the gate. The replies were encouraging, stating that the matter would be taken up at the 1934 winter meetings. Will Harridge assured the *News* their request would get every consideration, while owners such as Clark Griffith, Louis Comiskey, and Thomas Shibe were in complete support. The proposal hit a roadblock when National League owners demanded the game be played in one of their parks. The motion carried and the 1934 game went to the Polo Grounds. All the same, the owners agreed that if there was going to be a 1935 contest, it belonged in Cleveland.

When the city received the official confirmation, it came with a new ruling that free passes, or "Annie Oakleys," were reserved only for members of the media. The usual folks with their hands out would need to stand in line at the box office. The new rule did not keep the non-media people from trying to score a set of free tickets to the All-Star Game. A young woman from St. Louis called one of the Cleveland newspapers and said she had recently entertained a member of the St. Louis Browns. Because the two hit it off, she asked the editor to use his connections and get the player on the American League All-Star roster. In addition, she asked for four tickets near the home dugout so her new best friend on the Browns could see her. Despite her boldness the request was denied.

The demand for tickets came from all parts of the country. Some were polite requests while others were crass and unprofessional. The three newspapers had the authority to comply with or deny any requests from writers affiliated with a newspaper. Columnist John Kieran from the *New York Times* sent a courteous note for tickets and got a positive reply. A small-town sportswriter sent a request for two tickets, explaining that his wife would not let him go without her. He got his tickets. There were pleas from what the papers termed "jerkwater towns" and "two-by-four towns" that got refused due to the ill-mannered tone of the letters. It seemed the local sportswriters were having a marvelous time fielding all the ticket requests.

Soon letters came from the top writers in the United States. Walter Winchell, the country's most popular gossip columnist, asked for a ticket, as did Damon Runyon and Grantland Rice. James Isaminger, sportswriter for the *Philadelphia Inquirer* and president of the Baseball Writers Association of America, was coming and asked for an end seat. Others assured of tickets were Alan Gould, sports editor of the Associated Press, Paul Gallico and Jimmy Powers from the *New York Daily News*, and Arch Ward of the *Chicago Tribune*. The great columnists from New York City, Joe Williams, Dan Daniel, and Tom Meany, wired for tickets.

The news services all planned to attend, including the United Press, the International News Service, and the North American News Alliance, which was represented by John Lardner, the son of Ring. Along with reporters and columnists were the radio networks and film companies. The big three in broadcasting, the National Broadcasting Company, the Columbia Broadcasting System, and the Mutual Radio Network, were setting up microphones for live coverage. Pathé News and Fox Movietone planned to shoot moving pictures of the players and game action.

Newspapermen all across America sent ticket requests. They came from as far away as Aberdeen, South Dakota, St. Johnsbury, Vermont, and Windsor, Ontario. One small paper sent a request saying that their man Joe Glutz would be calling for tickets. Ed Bang answered that if Glutz could not prove he worked for the paper, he should not bother to call.

Alva Bradley rented space in the Hotel Cleveland, where he planned to have the best food and drinks available all day and night for the visiting media. The media room itself, where the reporters would file their stories, had state-of-the-art air conditioning. Western Union planned to install special wires and typewriters for all the writers in attendance. Several hundred of each appeared to be necessary. Mayor Davis decreed that all the media were to receive special badges that would authorize them to maneuver through traffic jams and move them to the head of any line. The city and the ball club spared no expense to ensure a fabulous long weekend for all out-of-town visitors.

The stadium grounds needed a makeover to get the field in playing condition. The League Park crew spent every spare minute planting new sod, grading the ground, and watering the outfield grass. Truckloads of grass seed were spread over the entire outfield to reverse the damage caused by the football and soccer games. Two weeks before the July 8 All-Star Game, the Sokol Gymnastic Club performed somersaults and spins all over the new outfield grass. It had rained earlier and the athletes tore up a number of divots in various locations. An emergency call went to the grounds crew, who hurriedly arrived at the field and made the repairs. Everything was now in place for a first-class event.

The players selected for the game were going to be announced at the end of June. The Indians had an off day on Wednesday the 26th, allowing all the ballplayers to scatter for a day of rest and relaxation. Earl Averill, waiting for his invitation, took his wife and four sons to a farm on the far east side of Cleveland for a picnic and an afternoon of fun. Since he was never home on July 4, Averill brought along a bag of fireworks for an early celebration. He and the boys had a great time throwing the fireworks and watching them explode. Earl lit another one and tossed it high in the air. To everybody's disappointment, it failed to go off. Averill walked to where the dud had landed, picked up the firecracker with his right hand, and it suddenly exploded. He ended up with two lacerated fingers, a cracked bone in his thumb, and powder burns on his face and chest. When the family reached Lakeside Hospital, Dr. Castle, the Indians team physician stitched the fingers together, bandaged the thumb, and gave an estimate of three to six weeks for recovery. This was a terrible blow to the Indians, who lacked any reserves who could adequately fill the center-field position. The injury prevented Averill from appearing in his third straight All-Star Game. The roster spot went to Joe Vosmik, who was enjoying a superb year at the plate and on the field.

Vosmik and Mel Harder were officially named to the All-Star lineup on June 28. They joined an elite group of players, some named for the third straight year. Lou Gehrig topped that list, along with Jimmy Foxx, Joe Cronin, Charlie Gehringer, Lefty Gomez, and Al Simmons. The National League had a number of three-time selections, with Pepper Martin, Frankie Frisch, Paul Waner, Bill Terry, Charles "Gabby" Hartnett, and Wally Berger. Though Vosmik secured his place on the roster due to Averill's injury, he really did deserve a spot. The outfielder was hitting .348, second in the league to the Athletics' Bob Johnson, another All-Star. The day after he received the good news, Vosmik homered and singled in a 6–5 win over the White Sox. He was enjoying his best season to date, with a realistic chance of winning a batting title. Only two points behind the Indians outfielder was Buddy Myer, another first-time All-Star. As the season wore on these two players would make an interesting race for the American League batting crown.

On Sunday, the day before the game, most of the players checked into the Hotel Cleveland. From the moment they set foot in the lobby, zealous fans chased them down for autographs. The ballplayers seemed to enjoy the attention, signing hundreds of autographs at a time. Lefty Gomez believed he signed a total of a thousand baseballs and scorecards in less than a day. A young boy approached Dizzy Dean for an autograph. Diz lifted the boy onto a table so they could be eye to eye while pictures were taken. The pitcher then signed his name with a special flourish.

With all the preparations complete, the gates were opened on Monday morning, July 8, for the third Major League All-Star Game. The weather in Cleveland was at seventy degrees, about ten below normal for that time of year, so the chances of any spectators collapsing from heatstroke were close to zero. In the event the fans needed some liquid refreshments, they had the option to choose from 28,800 bottles of Coca-Cola, 5,200 bottles of Orange Crush, and an identical amount of root beer. For those in need of something stronger, a total of 10,800 bottles of beer were available.

Even though the Indians had abandoned the stadium, city officials allowed them to handle all the concessions. Bob Hamilton, the longtime boss at League Park, got the important assignment to have the food ready. In addition to all the soft drinks and beer, Hamilton brought 12,000 wieners and buns, 8,000 bags of peanuts, and 16,000 slices of ice cream. Added to the menu was an assortment of candy, potato chips, and tobacco. Hamilton based his quantities on the July 31, 1932, opening game at the stadium, where nearly 80,000 fans attended. In addition to food, 50,000 souvenir programs were printed that featured bios of all the players on both rosters.

A number of fans noticed that the price of peanuts, ice cream, and soda pop had been boosted a nickel, to fifteen cents each, and later complained to the Indians front office about the last-minute increase. A spokesperson declared that some of the extra men they hired for concessions raised the prices on their own, and that these unscrupulous men were found out and fired on the spot. The fans asked why, then, did the prices stay at fifteen cents throughout the entire game? The spokesperson failed to answer that question, only stating again that the front office had nothing to do with it.

The American League players arrived on the field first, wearing their home-team white uniforms. Joe Vosmik stepped to the plate to take batting practice amidst cheers from the fans already seated. The Nationals, dressed in their road grays, assembled in the third-base dugout. Soon the camera crews set up on the field, organizing themselves for the newsreels they were about to film. Frankie Frisch was handed a microphone, which he passed to each member of his squad to introduce themselves in front of the cameras. One of the men patrolling the grounds was Indians pitcher Willis Hudlin, who had invested in his own movie camera. He filmed the batters at home plate, probably for his enjoyment and not for study.

There was an uproar when Mr. and Mrs. Babe Ruth walked on the field. Before he had the opportunity to say hello to the players, autograph seekers surrounded him. Soon Babe had his brown sport coat off and was puffing a black cigar while signing everything from baseballs to bags of peanuts. Many of the players greeted the home-run king while cameras were rolling and photographers snapping pictures. Though attending as just a spectator, Ruth got much of the attention from everyone connected to the game. He was still by far the most revered figure in baseball.

Other celebrities attending had no choice but to take a back seat to the ever-popular Ruth. Barney Ross, the world welterweight boxing champ, was in the stands. From the golf world there was the reigning Masters Tournament champ, Gene Sarazen. From Hollywood came comic actor and superfan Joe E. Brown. There were high-ranking officials from the steel, rail, and other industries, descending on the city just to see the ball game.

While the teams practiced, eager fans kept on filing into the stadium. Their numbers eventually reached the paid total of 69,831. This amount broke the two-year game attendance record and remained the highest All-Star Game total for decades to come. The gate receipts equaled $93,000, of which $63,000 went to the Association of Professional Ball Players fund. To accommodate the large crowd, 555 ushers were on duty, with a hundred specially assigned policemen to keep order. The only block of seats left open was the center-field bleachers, the least desirable location to watch the game. Among the crowd was Babe Herman, the big slugger now playing for the Cincinnati Reds. Without any fanfare he had paid his own way to Cleveland and purchased a game ticket, preferring to stay out of the spotlight and sit in the stands as a paid customer.

The game itself turned out to be anticlimactic, with the American League winning 4–1. Joe Vosmik led off the bottom of the first to a tremendous ovation. It had to be a terrific thrill for the homegrown boy and Cleveland Indian left fielder. Try as he might, Vosmik hit a ground ball for out number one. Charlie Gehringer drew a walk from Cardinals pitcher Bill Walker. Lou Gehrig hit into a force play for the second out. Jimmy Foxx got the crowd out of their seats with a home run to left field, and the long shot gave the Americans a 2–0 lead which they never gave up. In the bottom of the fifth, the fans roared again when Vosmik singled to center. Charlie Gehringer stroked a base hit to right field, Vosmik taking third. Lou Gehrig walked to load the bases. Once again Jimmy Foxx was the man of the hour, driving the ball to center field and scoring Vosmik with the fourth and final run.

Lefty Gomez pitched a strong game, lasting six innings and allowing just the single run. Manager Mickey Cochrane pulled Gomez at the top of the seventh in favor of Mel Harder. The Indians ace tossed three shutout innings, giving up only one hit in the 4–1 victory. The performance stretched Harder's amazing streak to eight scoreless innings in two All-Star Game appearances. Both the Cleveland representatives performed admirably in front of a highly partisan crowd. The entire city of Cleveland could take a bow for organizing and hosting one of the biggest spectacles in American sports.

Many of the out-of-towners stayed overnight, lighting up the downtown area until the early morning hours. The lobbies of the Hollenden Hotel and the Cleveland were packed with folks having a few drinks and socializing. For one day and night the lakefront stadium was the catalyst for drawing the elite class to the city. They dined at the restaurants, visited the night clubs, and kept the cab drivers hopping. Money flowed into the city's coffers as well as to the downtown merchants. This was what was envisioned by the men who built the stadium by the lake. No doubt William Hopkins, Daniel Morgan, and Ray Miller walked the streets off Public Square, smiling at the thousands of people having a marvelous time in their city. But then again, it was only one night, dozens more like it were needed to justify their good intentions.

The month of July confirmed that the Indians were anything but contenders. Their win-loss record was an abysmal eight and nineteen. Included in this total were ten losses in eleven games with the Detroit Tigers. Wins over the current American League champs were vital in gaining any ground on the leaders. As the team continued to lose, home attendance dropped significantly. The dwindling numbers caught the eye of Alva Bradley. As much as he supported his manager, gate receipts were always more important. Near the end of the month Bradley issued a vote of confidence for Walter Johnson. He addressed the papers, saying, Johnson was "one of the grandest gentlemen I've ever met. I'd want to see a better man for the job before I'd switch." Regardless of Bradley's support, a crowd only 7,000 attended the ugly 14–6 loss to Detroit on July 28. Usually a Sunday game against a top-flight club meant 15,000 to 20,000 tickets sold. As much as Bradley wanted to look away, action had to be taken.

The team traveled west to Chicago for a three-game series. Gordon Cobbledick wrote a story claiming Johnson's resignation was coming at any minute. Bradley left for Chicago to meet with his careworn manager. The two leaders had a long talk, speaking frankly for several hours. They did not reach any decisions on Johnson's future, but agreed to meet again when the Indians returned home from their series with Detroit.

The Friday game against the Tigers was postponed due to heavy showers and a soaked playing field. The Indians relaxed in their hotel, either sleeping or playing cards. Bruce Campbell, the starting right fielder, joined one of the poker games. Campbell had been acquired in the off-season from the St. Louis Browns. He gave the team another strong hitter, batting .325 going into the Detroit series.

While shuffling the cards, Campbell complained of a pounding headache. He retired to his room and rested in bed for most of the day, but the next morning he felt well enough to dress and ride to the ballpark. A short time later, Campbell mentioned to one of his teammates that he was beginning to feel as if he had caught the flu. Regardless of being ill, he collected three hits before advising Johnson that he needed to go back to the hotel. Trainer Lefty Weisman told Campbell to call the hotel doctor for an examination. When the players returned to the hotel they found Campbell in a deep sleep.

About 4:00 a.m., a feverish Campbell awoke and walked uncertainly around the room. He began to vomit, waking up his roommate, Lloyd Brown. Cold towels were applied to Campbell's forehead but within minutes he started vomiting again. Calls were made and shortly thereafter an ambulance arrived to rush Campbell to Harper Hospital. A quick examination revealed the symptoms of spinal meningitis. Doctors, including a brain specialist, injected the ballplayer with a serum designed to isolate and prevent the meningitis from spreading. The team of doctors believed

Campbell had a fifty-fifty chance of surviving. A call went out to Campbell's mother and brother living in Chicago. They hurried to the train station, arriving in Detroit as soon as possible. Initially, he did not recognize his family, causing the doctors to fear for his life. They believed the next thirty-six hours were critical in determining whether Campbell would live or die.

While the doctors worked around the clock to save Campbell, the Indians returned to Cleveland. They had dropped five out of their last six games to fall below the .500 mark. Alva Bradley called for a meeting at the Hotel Cleveland with Billy Evans, Walter Johnson, and Steve O'Neill. The agenda centered on the pitiful July record and the nonexistent Sunday crowd of July 28. It is not known whether Bradley repeated his "the owner hires the manager and the fans fire him" line. Nonetheless, the handwriting was on the wall and Johnson realized the time to resign had come. Bradley took great care to tell the press the resignation was completely voluntary. Though it may have been, it is unlikely the meeting would have ended with Johnson still the manager. In his two years as field boss, Johnson had suspended one player, dismissed two others from the team, and alienated the Cleveland fan base. Had the Indians been close to a pennant in either year, Johnson might have avoided the Sunday-night meeting. Managers, when all is said and done, are judged on wins and losses. Walter Johnson could not motivate his players any better than Roger Peckinpaugh. As it was, Peck, a popular guy, stayed on the job for five seasons. Johnson, thoroughly disliked, lasted just slightly more than two years.

Johnson remained in Cleveland long enough to answer a few questions. He pointed to injuries, players having disappointing seasons, and circumstances in general. He told reporters, "After several conferences with the Cleveland club, I suggested to them that a change in management might remove a pressure which I think some of the younger ballplayers are working under and their play would improve." Johnson became philosophical, stating that he had been in the game for thirty years and had hoped to remain for more. He thought he would go back to his Maryland farm and concentrate on bringing up his children. Bradley kept him on the payroll as a special scout, but it appeared this was a gesture to justify paying off Johnson's salary.

Several months later, *Baseball Magazine* picked up Johnson's story. Writer F. C. Lane allowed the former manager to speak his mind. In this instance, Johnson chose not to mince words. He reviewed the firing of Willie Kamm and Glenn Myatt, saying, "They were a bad influence upon the ball club. Anyway I let them go and a fresh storm broke out. Kamm took his case to Judge Landis. Why I don't clearly understand. The newspapers made a big issue of it and even had me out of a job." Johnson went on to say claim that he was not overly strict with his players, saying, "I have never fined a player in my life for drinking or for keeping late hours. Some of the players let go were drinkers and friendly with sportswriters." Johnson believed the former Indians players had told tales to the writers who printed their version in the papers. He thought the writers had too much to say about running the club in the past season. Lane added his own remarks supporting the idea that most of Johnson's troubles were due to an unforgiving press. Both men were naive if they thought the piece would get little attention. Johnson must have supposed that nobody in Cleveland read *Baseball Magazine,* or maybe he did not care if they did. This sounded like sour grapes, and whether or not he meant to antagonize Cleveland readers, any goodwill left in Indians town was completely gone.

The new manager of the Cleveland Indians was Steve O'Neill. He did not receive a new contract or an agreement to manage beyond the 1935 season, but did get a boost in salary. Alva Bradley went back to the philosophy he'd announced in 1928, when he and his partners bought the ball club: he intended to stock the front office with Cleveland men. O'Neill, though not born in Cleveland, had spent twelve full seasons with the team. He was one of the many heroes of the 1920 World Championship club. Born and raised in Minooka, Pennsylvania, O'Neill survived years in the coal mines to become an outstanding catcher. He developed into an immovable force behind home plate, inviting fearsome collisions with charging base runners attempting to run him over. As the years progressed, O'Neill learned to become a better-than-average hitter. In the 1920 season he batted .322 with five triples and thirty-nine doubles. He caught nearly every game of the schedule, missing only five games all year. He enjoyed a productive World Series, with seven hits and a batting average of .333.

O'Neill had made Cleveland his permanent home, buying a house in the suburb of Cleveland Heights. He and his wife raised four daughters there, including a set of twins. Even when he was traded to Boston, then New York and St. Louis, he kept his home in Cleveland. Later he managed the Toronto club, then went on to Toledo for a stint there. He had managed current Cleveland players such as Monte Pearson, Bad News Hale, Frank Pytlak, and Hal Trosky when they were playing for the Mud Hens. As a current Indians coach, he knew all the players and what their capabilities were. Under the circumstances, Steve O'Neill was the best fit for managing the Indians.

The new boss took a few moments to address the media. O'Neill said, "I'm going to try to make this ball club more of a fighting club. We are going to be more aggressive. We're going to take chances, gamble. You can't win in baseball by playing safe all the time." O'Neill went on to say he wanted the boys to hustle and hustle some more. He planned no major personnel changes, which probably put his players at ease. They all knew him well and how he liked to handle things. Now they could relax and start playing baseball.

While the boys attempted to win games for their new manager, encouraging news came from Detroit. Bruce Campbell had showed signs of improvement and doctors were optimistic about his survival. They believed the next day or two were crucial, but Campbell was responding to treatment, which gave them reason to hope. His temperature had gone down several degrees, another promising sign. Campbell now recognized his family and appeared to be in a rational state.

One week later, doctors announced that Campbell was officially out of danger. His temperature and pulse had gone down to a normal range. More hospital time was required, but doctors believed his strong physical condition and stamina as a ballplayer had led to his recovery. His future in baseball was in doubt, but his health would be restored above all else. Campbell, once given his discharge, planned to go home to Chicago for a long period of recuperation.

As the baseball season move into late August, the Indians began to display signs of life, albeit a bit too late. On the twenty-fourth they squared off against the Athletics. Willis Hudlin started for Cleveland, matching pitches against an unknown quantity, George

Turbeville. Both hurlers were on their game, throwing one scoreless inning after another. The fans at League Park waited patiently for one of the teams to break through and get on the scoreboard. The Indians threatened several times but were unable to get a run across, and the game went into extra innings. By the top of the fifteenth, Hudlin was still showing no signs of letting up. So far he'd allowed only eight hits and one walk, to Jimmy Foxx, and now he set down Philadelphia one more time. For his part, Turbeville, despite giving up twelve walks, had kept the Indians' big bats silent. In the bottom half of the inning Milt Galatzer led off for Cleveland and managed to draw the astounding thirteenth walk of the day. The crowd became restless, yelling for Earl Averill to send them home. He got a fastball over the plate and drove the pitch beyond the right-field wall to end the long struggle at 2–0. Willis Hudlin had pitched the finest game of his career. In eight of the fifteen innings he retired the side in order. His walk to Foxx was an intentional one, to set up a force play. He recorded six strikeouts in the best-pitched game of the Indians' season.

In September, Cleveland caught fire, going on an eight-game winning streak. On the 18th, Mel Harder won his twentieth game of the season, a 10–0 shutout against the reeling Athletics. Although the season was an overall disappointment, the team was playing inspired ball under Steve O'Neill. Alva Bradley put an end to any speculation by rewarding his new manager with a contract for the 1936 season. There was still some excitement in Joe Vosmik's attempt to win the American League batting title. In the first week of the month Vosmik had an average of .352, ten points ahead of Washington's Buddy Myer. At the midpoint of September he still had the lead, just one point ahead of a surging Jimmy Foxx. Myer stood third, only three points behind the Indians left fielder.

With several days left in the season the race came down to Vosmik and Myer. On the 28th, Vosmik held a six-point lead with an average of .351. On September 30, the end of the season, he still clung to the lead. The Indians had a doubleheader with St. Louis while Myer had a single game with Philadelphia. Vosmik opted out of playing game one, gambling that his margin over Myer was safe. The gamble backfired: the telegraph wire revealed that the Washington star had hit safely four times in five plate appearances. His final average was

.349. To win the title, Vosmik needed a couple of hits. He entered game one as a pinch hitter but could not get a base hit. He played all of game two, with one base hit in three at bats. For the day he went one for four, which dropped his average to .348, just one point behind Myer. It had to be a bitter setback for Vosmik, as he had held the top spot for a large part of the season. Still, he had a tremendous year, leading the American League with 216 hits, 47 doubles, and 20 triples, the best numbers in both leagues. He was third in total bases and a first-time All-Star. The boy picked from the Cleveland sandlots had reached the upper echelon of Major League baseball.

Of the fifty-nine games managed by O'Neill, the Indians won thirty-six, for a percentage of .610. It was quite encouraging that the players had responded in a positive way to their new manager. This marked the first time in two years that peace and quiet reigned in the dugout and locker room. There were no threats of suspension or feuds with any particular player. The apathy and unrest were now in the past.

Cleveland attendance for the 1935 season equaled 397,615, an increase of 6,000 over the previous year. The slight rise was not a reason to celebrate; still, it trended in the right direction. Many of the clubs in both leagues saw an upturn in attendance figures. The Tigers led all teams with slightly over one million in attendance. The New York Giants had a figure of 748,000, tops in the National League. The Cincinnati Reds doubled their attendance by drawing 448,000 fans. A large part of this was due to their experiment of night baseball. Fans took to the evening games with relish, filling the grandstands for the seven trial dates. On the opposite end of the spectrum stood the St. Louis Browns with a miserable 80,922, or less than 2,000 per game.

Alva Bradley softened his position on night baseball but still had little interest in playing after dark. He took the stance that if everybody was going to do it he would join in. Until that time, baseball in Cleveland would be a daytime affair. In addition, Bradley indicated he was ready and willing to spend money to bolster his lineup. Apparently, the club had made a profit for the second straight year. On the opposite side, owners like Connie Mack signaled that another fire sale of ballplayers was coming. Bradley and others were prepared to dip into the war chest and ready their bids.

Before the start of the winter minor-league meetings, the Indians board of directors voted to reduce Billy Evans's salary to $7,500. Oddly, they cited continued losses that required them to take the action. A day later Evans submitted his resignation and with little fanfare the directors accepted it. Alva Bradley prepared a statement for the newspapers. It read, "Two years ago Billy Evans expressed to me a desire to resign as general manager of the Cleveland Baseball Club due to the necessary reduction in salaries but I prevailed upon him to continue. However, this fall, due to curtailment of profit another reduction was necessary. It is with regret that we accept his resignation."

Gordon Cobbledick had a different take on the situation. He maintained that the whole trouble began in May 1935 when Evans refused to endorse Walter Johnson's removal of Willie Kamm. According to the *Plain Dealer* reporter, Evans actually tried to talk Johnson out of making the move. One of the Indians directors accused Evans of being disloyal to his manager. Supposedly Evans responded by saying he was not a yes-man to the front office. Cobbledick's story had Evans submitting his resignation at the time, but Bradley not accepting it. The November salary cut was put in place to help force Evans out the door.

In 1928, when Bradley created the position of general manager, he set the salary at $22,500. Evans was hired and within two years the pay rose to $30,000. In the fall of 1933 Evans accepted a drastic reduction to $12,500 with a bonus clause of $2,500 if the team made money. Now he was asked to take a further slash all the way to $7,500. No wonder he made the decision to find another job.

For eight years Evans had done a capable job despite limited resources. His teams usually finished in the upper division while other clubs floundered. In the beginning he had ample funds to work with, which he used to sign Earl Averill and Dick Porter. With declining attendance and a faltering economy, Evans got quite creative without spending a great deal of money. Over the years he signed Joe Vosmik, Hal Trosky, and Bad News Hale for practically nothing. He orchestrated several excellent trades including those for Bibb Falk and Willie Kamm. While the Yankees and Red Sox spent tremendous sums of money for players, Evans usually kept his signings to $7,500 or less. On the minus side, the Indians had not captured first place during his tenure. That alone was enough reason for Bradley and his partners to make a change.

It did not take an involved job search for the Indians to replace their general manager. Bradley announced the hiring of his chief scout, Cyril "Cy" Slapnicka. The position of GM was abolished in favor of assistant to the president. Any decisions on player trades and signings needed to have the approval of Bradley. Slapnicka was fine with the terms, stating that he did not have enough knowledge yet of Major League players. In his fourteen years as a Cleveland scout he knew everybody in Class D baseball, but he probably would have had difficulty naming the starting lineup for the St. Louis Browns. Slapnicka told reporters that for this year he would defer to Steve O'Neill in evaluating talent. With the winter meeting just a few weeks away, he acted wisely.

Billy Evans agreed to attend the late-November minor-league meetings in Dayton to show Cy Slapnicka around. Despite the meetings concentrating on the farm teams and working agreements, representatives from the American and National Leagues were on hand as usual to talk business. The Yankees proposed a trade of Johnny Allen, Tony Lazzeri, Fred Walker, and Joe Glenn plus $50,000 to Cleveland for Mel Harder and Bad News Hale. Alva Bradley scoffed at the deal, stating that he did not need money but instead was planning to spend it. The trade did not go through, yet the idea of acquiring Allen strongly appealed to Steve O'Neill. During his 1931 season with the Toronto Maple Leafs, player-manager O'Neill had devoted a considerable amount of time to working with Allen. Although approaching his fortieth birthday at the time, he had put on the shin guards and chest protector to catch Allen for most of the season. The strategy paid off, with Johnny winning twenty-one games for the year and being promoted to New York. The Yankees' trade offer intrigued O'Neill to the point of wanting to find a way to bring Johnny Allen to Cleveland.

At the time of the Major League meetings, Alva Bradley sent his new assistant on a clandestine mission to Philadelphia. Slapnicka met briefly with Connie Mack to determine the price tag on home-run machine Jimmy Foxx. For the right amount, Bradley was prepared to write a check to bring Foxx to Cleveland, but the figure turned out to be well beyond the Indians' budget. Foxx would end up being sold to Tom Yawkey and Boston for the astronomical sum of $150,000. The highest amount Bradley had ever paid out was the $50,000 for Earl Averill. It is doubtful he had the resources to match or better what Yawkey agreed to pay. A lineup of Averill, Foxx, and Trosky would have sent Cleveland fans into a frenzy, had Bradley been able to raise the money.

The actual meetings featured owners cutting a number of other deals. In addition to Foxx, Connie Mack sent shortstop Eric McNair and outfielder Doc Cramer to the Red Sox for another $150,000. The Athletics manager just about made payroll by selling only those three players. The Yankees wanted Joe Vosmik and Earl Averill, and later made an offer of $250,000 for the pair. There was no chance the Indians would part with their stars, but the dollar amounts thrown around demonstrated that many of the owners had put aside any worries about the depression and attendance figures.

For several years most of them had followed the plan of retrenchment. Now, with a growing fan base, the owners knew there were enough ticket buyers around to keep the game going. Certainly, unemployment figures were still dismal and government programs were handing out millions in relief. In spite of the tough times, baseball had enough resources to prosper. It would be several more years before the United States would resume economic growth. In spite of the dire circumstances, Major League baseball had managed to stay above the curve. There was no brilliant plan that kept the game afloat, only a series of cost cutting measures that allowed each franchise to stay in the game. By lowering player salaries, cutting back on office staff, and shortening spring training, baseball weathered the storm better than most industries in the United States. A large part of the success was due to the loyal fans who continued to prop up the game. Those who had an extra dollar supported their team. Many could not afford to buy a new car or purchase a cross-country rail ticket, but found a way to save their pennies for a seat in the bleachers. With these folks, and those with an ample bank account, baseball neatly avoided economic ruin.

Chapter 11

A TEENAGE HERO

On December 11, 1935, Steve O'Neill got his Christmas wish early. The Indians traded Monte Pearson to the Yankees for pitcher Johnny Allen. On paper the trade looked like a steal for Cleveland. In four years with New York, Allen had a record of fifty wins against nineteen losses. His first season was his best, winning seventeen and losing only four. Pearson, meanwhile, had slumped to a disappointing eight wins in 1935. The Cleveland front office lost their patience with the young hurler, sending him to New York for an established pitcher in Allen. There was a slight caveat to this deal. For all his talent, Allen came to Cleveland with anger management issues that had to be seen to be believed.

John Thomas Allen was born on September 30, 1905, in Lenoir, North Carolina. He was the first child of Robert and Myra Allen. Lenoir was home to a number of furniture companies, the most famous being Broyhill Furniture. It is the site of the Edgar Allen Poe house—not the famous writer, but a builder and former mayor of the city. No less than five Major League ballplayers came from Lenoir, with Allen being the first.

When Johnny was eight years old his father Robert passed away. His mother tried to take care of the family (there were two other children), but eventually had to send Johnny to an orphanage. He grew up there, working daily on the home's six-hundred-acre farm. Later he would credit all the hard work for his strong upper body and exceptional throwing arm. As a teenager he began to take on the high school course of study. The orphanage had a baseball team, which Allen played and starred on. There were barely enough boys to field a team and they had no manager or coaches. There was no magical success story here. Allen pitched and played other positions but failed to draw any notice from colleges or Major League scouts.

At the age of eighteen he departed the orphanage for Greensboro. He landed an entry job as a clerk at a local hotel. He enjoyed the work, progressing to better hotel jobs in various cities around North Carolina. At no time did he consider a career as a ballplayer. In his early twenties Johnny was doing clerical work for a hotel in Asheville. Several young men approached him there, seeking help for their Sunday school baseball team. He pitched a few games, realizing the unusual speed his right arm could still produce. Others recognized his pitching talent and soon Allen had an offer to play semipro. He rose up the ladder quickly, signing with the Asheville club of the South Atlantic League. A Yankee scout saw him throw and signed him to a contract. Allen was already near his twenty-fourth birthday, but he had a strong desire to see if he could cut it in the American League. He began the 1930 season with Jersey City of the International League. The next season the Yankees advanced him to Toronto, where he became the ace of the staff. Johnny became a brilliant student for manager Steve O'Neill, who cleaned up his delivery and readied him for the move up to New York.

The 1932 season put Johnny Allen on the map as one of the Yankees' top pitchers. His seventeen wins placed him third on the staff led by Lefty Gomez and Red Ruffing. New York won the pennant, then defeated Chicago in four straight games to win the World Series. Allen started game four but failed to get out of the first inning, allowing four runs. The performance was a disappointment to the Yankee faithful and to the front office that expected more from him.

At an early period in his tenure with New York, Allen's menacing temper came to the surface. He excelled at being a bench jockey, yelling insults to opposing teams. Soon he was challenging teammates and umpires to fights under the grandstand. In the locker room he smashed lockers and overturned stoves. On the pitching mound he argued ball and strike calls with the home plate umpire to the point of being ejected from games. He did not care for his manager, Joe McCarthy, engaging in shouting matches with him in the clubhouse. Near the end of the 1935 season, Allen let go with a tirade against his manager. The entire Yankee team watched in silence as the angry pitcher criticized McCarthy for several minutes. The manager walked away, but the wheels were put in motion to get rid of Allen before the next season began.

It is doubtful the Indians were surprised when the Yankees offered Allen in exchange for Monte Pearson. They knew all about the temper tantrums and the awful behavior he had displayed. Despite this, Steve O'Neill believed he could handle Allen and keep his temper in check. Alva Bradley had seen the Allen rage the previous August in a game at League Park. The Yankees were ahead 3–0 in the third inning when Johnny started in on the home plate umpire. After a ball was called, Allen completely lost his cool, throwing his glove high in the air while screaming in the direction of home. He got tossed from the game, and the Indians teed off on the relief pitcher, eventually winning 8–5.

It must have taken some convincing on the part of O'Neill, but Johnny Allen became a member of the Cleveland pitching staff. Talking to reporters, Allen declared that he was elated to come to Cleveland. He showed great respect for his new manager, telling the writers it was O'Neill who had made him a Major League pitcher. He recounted an incident in Toronto when he was on the mound, throwing fastball after fastball at his gray-haired catcher. One of his pitches eluded O'Neill and struck his face mask at a tremendous speed. The ball lodged between the bars of the mask, and it took one of the grounds crewmen several minutes to pry it loose. Allen was surprised when O'Neill, though he was jarred by the pitch, never said a word about it. He looked to his manager as something of a father figure, which he had lacked for most of his life.

With Allen in the fold, Cleveland orchestrated a few minor acquisitions, then prepared for the 1936 season. They picked up catcher Billy Sullivan Jr. from Cincinnati to back up the often injured and ill Frank Pytlak. In addition to the broken finger issues, Pytlak developed problems with his stomach that forced him to leave the team for most of the previous summer. Sullivan, the son of Billy Sullivan of the old Chicago White Sox, was brought on for insurance. He was a solid catcher who could swing the bat effectively.

The Indians entered spring training with the roster fairly well set. A big question mark was the health of outfielder Bruce Campbell. In October 1935 he was hospitalized with a severe cold, and doctors watched him carefully for any signs of the dreaded meningitis returning. Upon his release, Campbell headed for Florida to work out and regain all the strength he had lost since the previous August. He needed to bulk up his diet as the meningitis had caused him to lose a staggering thirty-five pounds. Campbell had won the first battle by simply getting out of his hospital bed and resuming a somewhat normal life. His next fight was to resume his baseball career, in which the odds were against him. He arrived in New Orleans in early March, surprising everyone by topping the scales at 199 pounds, a bit over his regular playing weight. With all eyes on him, he took batting practice and lined the baseball all over the field. The regular season was over a month away, but Campbell appeared to be in midseason shape. He displayed remarkable courage in beating a life-threatening illness and competing for his old job. He told his teammates, yes, he had been sick, but now he was well. There was nothing more to it.

Opening Day at home landed on Tuesday, April 14, 1936. Headlining the festivities was heavyweight boxing contender Joe Louis, who stood on the mound and threw a pitch to popular radio comedian Jack Benny. Mary Livingston, comedienne and wife to Benny, took a wild swing at the pitch, missing by two feet. Everyone enjoyed the entertainment except for Louis, who looked uncomfortable throughout the skit. Jack Graney was behind the microphone once again for WHK and new sponsor General Mills. The radio station held a contest to find the most typical redheaded boy in Cleveland. Over two hundred candidates with flaming red hair reported to the WHK offices. The field was narrowed to forty, and after a close review eleven-year-old Bronson Freeman got the victory. His prize included sitting with Graney for the opening game and all the hot dogs, popcorn, and soda pop he could put away.

A sizable crowd of 18,000 watched the Indians square off against the Detroit Tigers. In the top of the first Hank Greenberg scorched a double down the third-base line, scoring two runs. Tiger pitcher Lynwood "Schoolboy" Rowe held Cleveland to four hits and no runs for a 3–0 victory. Some of the fans were philosophical about the loss, noting that the Indians had won their last five openers in a row. Maybe losing this one could mean they were reversing things and a pennant might be the end result. Other fans just grumbled. Many were upset that the price of a scorecard had doubled to ten cents.

The next day Cleveland got even, scoring eight times in the third inning en route to a 14–7 thrashing of the Tigers. Hal Trosky led the attack with four RBIs, including a three-run homer in the big third inning. The fans jumped to their feet when Bruce Campbell launched a home run in the seventh. If there were any doubts about his physical condition, he answered them with four hits and three RBIs.

On April 23, well after the home opener, Johnny Allen made his debut at League Park. Cleveland scored four runs in the first inning, giving Allen a large lead to work with. He pitched a beautiful game, shutting out the White Sox 6–0. He was in command throughout the nine innings, demonstrating why he won fifty games with New York. The Cleveland fans heartily approved, hoping Allen along with Mel Harder would lead the club to a higher place in the standings. Certainly the two pitchers were capable of doing so.

A week later, Allen was on the mound at Yankee Stadium to pitch against his old ball club. He got through the first three innings, then all hell broke loose. Lou Gehrig came to bat and quickly had two strikes on the count. Allen delivered a high fastball only inches from Gehrig's head. The Yankee dugout exploded with anger, sending some choice language at their former teammate. They continued the taunts, which caused Allen to lose his composure and give up four runs. The Indians lost the game 6–1, and the fireworks were just beginning.

None of the players or managers in the American League would own up to it, but for a good while afterward the opposing team's bench would start screaming "spitball!" whenever Johnny took the mound. Umpires stopped play and examined the baseball, which served to enrage the Cleveland hurler. This tactic went on with St. Louis, where manager Rogers Hornsby instigated things. The Browns manager claimed that not only did Allen use the spitball, but he used licorice as well to doctor the ball. It continued in Detroit, where umpires stopped play fifteen times to examine the ball. They did throw three baseballs out of play but found nothing wrong with the other twelve. The bench jockeying threw Allen off his game. He totally lost his concentration, allowing a five-run outburst in the fourth inning. A moment later Allen charged off the mound and went after Tigers third-base coach Del Baker. He had to be restrained by his teammates or the punches would have been flying. Before leaving the field he challenged Baker to a fight under the grandstand after the game concluded.

Now the Cleveland front office stepped in. A letter was sent to American League president Will Harridge, demanding that the harassment of their pitcher be stopped immediately. The contents of the letter were kept private, but Cy Slapnicka announced to reporters, "We won't sit by and see a fine pitcher and an expensive investment handicapped by tactics that we regard as manifestly unfair." There was talk that Slapnicka threatened to have his players return the favor to every pitcher they faced until Allen was left alone. President Harridge acted quickly to resolve the matter. He instructed all American League umpires to stop checking Allen for throwing spitballs. Since there was no real evidence, Harridge wanted the dispute closed immediately. The teams reluctantly complied and the bench jockeying ceased.

While the Allen controversy dominated the baseball news, Bruce Campbell maintained his excellent play. Near the end of April against St. Louis he homered and made two outstanding defensive plays. In the first one he dove into the right-field stands to snare a fly ball. The second happened late in the game when he leapt against the right field wall to take away a sure double. There was not a Comeback Player of the Year Award yet, but Campbell would have been the runaway choice.

The Indians traveled to Boston, where Campbell became ill with a slight cold. A day later he complained of a severe headache. The club rushed him to St. Elizabeth's Hospital, where once again the diagnosis was spinal meningitis. His doctors had believed the chances of a recurrence were almost nil, but somehow Campbell contracted the illness a second time. The Boston health officials were greatly concerned that the other Indians players might have been infected. Each player on the squad was tested, along with the coaching staff and sportswriters traveling with the team. The Boston Health Department spoke to both teams about canceling games until the results were known. Fortunately, everybody tested got a clean bill of health and the games went on. A very sick Bruce Campbell remained in the Boston hospital for treatment. Once again his life was in the balance and his baseball career hazy at best. Another call went to his mother, who rushed to Boston to again be with her son. Doctors drained more fluid from his spine and injected him with serum. Soon they removed him from the critical list, although a long recovery was projected.

The Indians' performance in May could be termed streaky at best. In the middle of the month they dropped six in a row, then came back to win seven of their next eight. Their record as of May 31 stood at 24–17. Hal Trosky was the bright spot, with forty-one RBIs in just a month and a half. He appeared to be on his way to a record-setting year in both home runs and RBIs. Earl Averill was on pace for another All-Star year, but the other hitters and pitchers were not living up to expectations.

On June 3, the Indians were back in Boston. Johnny Allen started for Cleveland, matching pitches with Wes Ferrell. From the first pitch the two quick-tempered boys from North Carolina began jawing at each other. Cleveland led 2–1 going into the bottom of the seventh, when the Red Sox mounted a big rally, scoring five times before Allen retired the side. The final score was 6–1. Stuart Bell was traveling with the team and sensed there might be a blowup coming. He followed Allen back to the team hotel and up the elevator to Allen's room. The elevator door opened and the losing pitcher erupted by kicking the large cigarette urn in the hallway. The heavy urn overturned, spilling sand and cigarette butts all over. Allen then grabbed either the fire extinguisher or hose and began spraying the general area. A worker perched on a ladder received a shower and nearly fell off. Stories maintain that Allen then went down to the lobby and grabbed several bar stools, flinging them against the walls.

The next morning the hotel presented Allen with a bill for $50 in damages. Steve O'Neill received news of the incident and immediately fined his pitcher $250. O'Neill threatened a suspension if any more disturbances occurred. That seemed to calm Johnny down. For the rest of the season there were no additional fire-extinguisher incidents or broken cigarette urns. Allen directed all his energy to pitching and turned his season around. For the first time in his career, twenty wins were on the horizon.

As the Indians kept on with their road trip, a welcome visitor arrived at League Park. Bruce Campbell walked into the locker room, ready to work himself back into playing condition. The doctors were pleased with his speedy recovery, releasing him from the hospital on May 28. He rested for a short time, then came to the ballpark ready to work. With the team on the road, Campbell tried to find someone to play catch with. He caught sight of a young man wandering about the field with apparently nothing to do. The seventeen-year-old had a glove with him. Bruce Campbell from LaGrange, Illinois, met Bob Feller from Van Meter, Iowa.

Why was a high-school kid from Iowa working out at Cleveland's League Park? Should he not have been home playing amateur ball with his friends from school? The answer is no, because he was Bob Feller, the most heralded pitching prospect in many years. He was a talent so highly regarded that Cy Slapnicka signed him to a contract when Bob was still sixteen, playing for the Farmers Union Insurance club.

Van Meter, Iowa, is a small community located in the southwest part of the state, a farm town in America's heartland with roughly a thousand residents scattered about the hills and valleys. In Bob Feller's time the population was barely four hundred. A grocery store, railroad station, and bank helped make up the downtown area. A single school took care of all the local students.

Robert Feller was born on November 3, 1918, the first child of William and Lena. A second child, Marguerite, would complete the family. The elder Feller had a 350-acre farm with plenty of cows, horses, and chickens roaming about. As a young boy, Bob did his share of chores. He fed the chickens, helped harvest the crops, and carried water from the Raccoon River. The land near the riverbed was too soft to bring up a truck, which meant Bob carried two pails about two hundred yards to get the water. He did this on a regular basis, strengthening his arms as one might lift a pair of serious hand weights. Several years of the hard work transformed Feller into a raw-boned teenager.

William Feller was a no-nonsense individual, devoted to his family and farm. His father developed the homestead in the nineteenth century, leaving it to his son to carry on. That he did, working from early morning to the last rays of daylight. Farming was his prime activity, but there was something else that he had a passion for. He had a keen interest in the game of baseball. As soon as Bob was old enough, the father and son began to play catch.

Baseball became an important part of life on the Feller Farm. Almost every day the two men tossed a ball around and or took batting practice. Still, William had a strict rule which he never deviated from: the farm chores always came first. Bob understood the importance of the rule, at all times giving his best effort to get the work completed. Once the cows were in the barn and the chickens in the coop, out came the gloves and baseballs. At times they had only a few minutes before sunset, but William solved that by stringing up lights for night baseball. When Bob reached his eleventh birthday his father built an outdoor batting cage, using some discarded wood and chicken wire. Bob took his turn at the plate, then would stop to retrieve the balls and start over. When the cold weather set in, William rearranged the barn so they could play catch indoors. Apparently, the horses and chickens were not totally on board with this, but they learned to tolerate the commotion to some extent.

In the spring of 1931, William Feller decided it was time for his son to play organized baseball. Rather than send Bob to Des Moines or another nearby city, he fired up the tractor and leveled a large section of his farmland. With help from his son, he laid out a diamond, built a backstop, raised a small grandstand, and installed a scoreboard at the edge of the outfield. If his Bob was going to be a ballplayer, it would be under William's direction. They named the park Oakview and put together a team, the Oak Views, the following summer. Bob started out as a shortstop, showing a strong throwing arm and driving baseballs all around the outfield. He pitched on occasion, racking up a large amount of strikeouts. Soon he concentrated exclusively on becoming the best pitcher in the area.

When Bob was on the mound, the Oak Views were extremely tough to beat. Large crowds gathered to watch the now fifteen-year-old mow down the hitters. In one particular game Feller struck out a total of twenty-three batters. He had learned how to throw a curveball to go along with his devastating fastball. In the ten games he pitched that summer he rang up 161 strikeouts. Word began to spread around Iowa about the young man from Van Meter.

At the end of the season, William and Bob traveled to St. Louis to watch several games of the 1934 Tigers-Cardinals World Series. They kept a close eye on Dizzy and Paul Dean, Tommy Bridges, Schoolboy Rowe, and others. It had to be clear to Bob he could throw as hard as anybody there. He lacked the years of experience to be thinking about the Major Leagues, but his talent would greatly accelerate the progress. He had some pitching to do for Van Meter High School the next spring, but his days as an amateur were almost behind him.

After an outstanding spring pitching high-school ball, Feller upped the ante by agreeing to join the Farmers Union Insurance team based in Des Moines. The American Legion team offered a higher level of competition. In a game against the Yale, Iowa, team Bob proved he was ready for the challenge by throwing a no-hitter and striking out twenty-two hitters in a 5–0 victory. The Farmers Union team advanced to the state tournament and won a place in the National Amateur Baseball Federation finals in Dayton, Ohio. This was the venue the Fellers had been pursuing since the building of Oakview Park. Sportswriters from outside Iowa would get a close look at the flame-throwing teenager. Representatives from Major League clubs were sure to notice the uncanny skill already possessed by the Iowa farm boy.

In the first round Feller was up against the team from Battle Creek, Michigan. He pitched an outstanding game, allowing only one unearned run. Unfortunately, the Farmers Union club could not manufacture any offense, losing 1–0. From the moment the game ended, though, the Fellers were besieged by scouts. Offers were coming from all directions, but, curiously, William declined every deal. He had good reason for all the polite "no thanks." His son was already property of the Cleveland Indians.

Cy Slapnicka was born and raised in Cedar Rapids, Iowa. Though always on the road scouting for Cleveland, he still kept a close watch on the baseball prospects from his home state. When Hal Trosky began to draw attention, Slapnicka quickly found his way to Norway,

Iowa, to sign the power-hitting first baseman. Several years later the name of Bob Feller made its way through baseball's inner circle. In July 1935, Slapnicka received information on the hot pitching prospect and rode the rails to Van Meter. He arrived at the Feller farm and struck up a conversation with William. They were both Iowa men, plain speaking and no nonsense about them. Slapnicka was a master of many approaches, but in this instance he stuck to his Iowa roots. They understood each other, which put Slapnicka in a favorable position. He made plans to see Bob pitch in Des Moines.

The results were much more than the Cleveland scout expected. He knew a Major League arm when he saw one and this kid definitely had the goods. Later that day, Slapnicka met with the Fellers to talk about a contract. Trust meant everything to William Feller. He believed Slapnicka had his son's best interests at heart and would keep a watchful eye on him. The contract was signed for a bonus of one dollar and a baseball. Bob had instructions to report to the Fargo-Moorhead Twins of the Northern League the following spring. The Class D club, representing the two cities on the North Dakota-Minnesota border, had a working relationship with the Indians. His salary would be roughly sixty dollars a month.

Before Slapnicka arrived in Van Meter, the Des Moines club of the Western League had attempted to sign Feller. This team was at Class A level, an excellent place to start for a young pitcher. As much as they tried, the price was not right, and no contract was forthcoming. About a year later, Des Moines would get back in the picture in a most uncomfortable manner for both the Indians and the Fellers. Being a veteran scout, Slapnicka knew all the Major League rules and how to cleverly get around them. At the time of the Feller signing the baseball laws explicitly stated that no high-school prospect could be signed directly to the American or National League. According to the rules, Feller had to play for a minor-league team before he could advance to the Indians and the Major Leagues. By assigning Feller to Fargo-Moorhead, Slapnicka took the risk that no other organization would notice the sleight-of-hand. Feller had a contract with Cleveland, but the assignment to Fargo-Moorhead seemed to indicate that the young pitcher had a deal with the minor-league team. In truth, the wily Slapnicka had loaned the Cleveland player to Fargo. Only the Indians had the rights to Feller.

When the Fellers signed the Cleveland contract, Bob had just finished his junior year of high school. The contract made him a professional, ineligible for any amateur sports. Yet he played ball all summer with the Farmers Union club and in the winter joined the Van Meter High School basketball team. It is possible that William did not know his son's amateur status was gone, though the signing was done on the extreme quiet side. At least one other Cleveland scout approached William at the National Amateur Tournament, unaware that Bob was already in the house. Slapnicka had special plans for his new signee which were kept from almost everybody in the Cleveland organization.

Bob Feller never played a game for Fargo-Moorhead. He did not attend any spring training nor did he put on a uniform. During the off-season, Bob injured his throwing arm. Slapnicka worried that further damage might be done if Feller was anywhere but Cleveland. Again the scout stepped in and orchestrated a phony sale of Feller to New Orleans, the Indians' longtime farm club. Neither Fargo-Moorhead nor New Orleans had anything to do with the transaction. It was all Slapnicka. This created a paper trail much cleaner than the Indians buying a Class D player directly. Once again, Bob never put on a New Orleans uniform. In June he was sent to Cleveland to report at League Park.

In addition to working out with Bruce Campbell, Feller did not waste his time. His arm had healed, allowing him to throw without any limitations. The club scheduled him to pitch for the Cleveland Rosenblums against a team from nearby Akron. Bob pitched in a twelve-inning game, winning 3–2. It was not the highest level of competition, but it gave Feller an opportunity to take the mound again. He had not thrown in an actual game since the previous fall.

The 1936 All-Star Game was scheduled for July 7 at the home park of the Boston Braves. The day before, the St. Louis Cardinals stopped in Cleveland to play an exhibition game against the Indians. Steve O'Neill decided it was the right time and place to give Feller a chance against Major League talent. The Cardinal hitters knew nothing about the young pitcher and a large crowd was not expected. O'Neill wanted to find out how Feller would handle three innings against the best team in the National League.

Going into the game, Feller had the mindset to just throw as hard as he could. He did not concern himself with curveballs or changeups, only a blazing fastball that paralyzed the St. Louis hitters. O'Neill himself did the catching, trying to make it as easy as possible for Bob to have a successful debut. The Indians manager did not need to worry. In three innings of work, Feller struck out eight batters. He fanned Leo Durocher twice and struck out both Pepper Martin and first baseman Jim "Ripper" Collins. Some of the batters kept their distance from home plate, not wanting to have their careers ended by an errant fastball. The forty-six-year-old O'Neill gave way after two innings, his left hand too sore for any additional catching. Feller was spectacular but not perfect. His delivery was overly slow, allowing two Cardinal base runners to easily steal bases on him.

After the game, local photographers asked Dizzy Dean if he would mind posing with the Indians' brilliant pitcher. Dean issued his classic words, "You better ask the kid if he'll pose with me!" Of course, Dean was joking, but the players and fans alike had witnessed a fastball on par with the best of them. Billy Evans and friend Roger Peckinpaugh watched from the press box, astounded by the talent on the pitching mound. The Indians would be going on the road, but plans were afoot to buy Feller's contract from New Orleans and place him on the Cleveland roster.

In July the Indians had one of their better road trips, winning twelve, losing seven, and tying once. They swept three games from Boston, three more from Philadelphia, and finished the trip with two out of three from Washington. The big hitters were on a roll, bashing doubles and triples in every park. In an 11–4 win over New York, Hal Trosky clubbed two home runs, his 21st and 22nd of the year. Earl Averill hit one over the fences, as did Joe Vosmik. The pitchers turned in creditable performances, with the highlight being Johnny Allen shutting out the Athletics, 7–0. Averill and Trosky both had two RBIs to back Allen.

During the course of the road trip, Cy Slapnicka bought Feller's contract from New Orleans. This move completed the paper trail showing Feller's phantom movements from Fargo-Moorhead to New Orleans to Cleveland. The shenanigans were complete for the time being, although Feller had only ever seen the two cities on a map. Slapnicka must have believed he had engineered a beauty of a trick, but his scheme would unravel in only a few months.

In mid-July, Feller was sent to Philadelphia to join the Indians there. He roomed with coach and former catcher Wally Schang. They sat on the visitor's bench while Schang helped Feller get clued in on the Athletics hitters. He did no pitching until July 19, the last game of the Washington series. The Indians were down 9–2 in the bottom of the eighth inning when Feller got the signal from Steve O'Neill. The catcher that day for Cleveland was Billy Sullivan, who gave Feller the signs and last-minute advice. With the adrenalin flying, Bob retired the side without a hit. At one point he threw a wayward curveball, plunking Red Kress directly in the ribs. He walked another batter, but kept the A's off the scoreboard in the 9–5 loss. Feller had broken the ice: he was now a seventeen-year-old Major League pitcher.

The Indians arrived home and kept up their winning play. On the 24th they crushed Philadelphia, 16–3. Averill had a day to remember with a home run, two triples, and five RBIs. Sammy Hale contributed four hits and crossed the plate four times. With a huge lead, Feller got the opportunity to pitch the last two innings. He was less than sparkling, giving up three hits and a run. He did strike out two batters, but overall he was disappointed with the results. It would get better for him soon.

After dropping two games against the woeful Athletics, Cleveland won the last game of the series, then took four straight from Washington. The club was on fire, having won eighteen of their last twenty-three games. The margin between them and the first-place Yankees shrunk to seven and one-half. With Gehrig and friends coming to town for a three-game series, the Indians had a chance to cut further into the lead. It had been years since the Indians had been in position to control their own destiny. The trumpets were sounded and the Cleveland fans heard the call. The ticket offices began to do a land-office business while the newspapers used page one for the baseball summaries.

Alva Bradley recognized the opportunity to make a killing at the box office. He contacted local officials to move the Sunday, August 2 game to that large facility just off the lake. Actually, he negotiated with the men behind the Great Lakes Exposition, a huge industrial fair that had leased the stadium. The exposition was a grandiose event with modern buildings, upscale cafes, entertainment, and lush gardens covering 135 acres along the lakefront. Because the city had no control over the lease, Bradley worked out a one-day fee arrangement with the exposition. The city, once again, got left out in the cold. The Indians immediately put 58,000 seats on sale. Of that total, 8,000 were box seats and the 50,000 were reserved.

To help boost the crowd, field events were added to take place before the game. Cash prizes were offered to the players for fungo hitting, fastest man to first base, and throwing accuracy. A wheelbarrow race between managers was put in the schedule for some comic relief. For additional guaranteed laughs, the top comedy act in the United States agreed to perform. The three Marx Brothers, Groucho, Chico, and Harpo, were in Cleveland appearing at the Palace Theatre. The boys stood with the best in vaudeville and were current movie stars with a string of hilarious feature films. Rumors circulated that the brothers were bringing along a number of their long-legged chorus girls to enhance their routine.

The series opened on Friday, July 31. It happened to be Ladies Day, with approximately 8,000 female baseball fans cheering for their Indians. The crowd numbered above 20,000, a great start for the weekend. Though two months of baseball still remained, it was essential for Cleveland to win all three. To have a chance to overtake New York, they had to cut the lead to less than five games. Closing up on a four-game lead was doable. Trying to overcome a seven- or eight-game lead was remotely possible. However, the momentum of a great July run would be stopped.

Mel Harder started the afternoon game against veteran Irving "Bump" Hadley. The Yankees got on the scoreboard early, leading 3–0 after three innings. Cleveland answered with two runs in the bottom of the fourth. With the game tightening up, all eyes turned to Harder, who did not seem to have his best stuff. Mel failed to survive the fifth inning, yielding a solo home run to Red Rolfe, then a two-run shot off the bat of Lou Gehrig. Reliever Denny Galehouse replaced Harder, but the damage had been done. New York scored four times to go up 7–2.

Despite the Yankees' commanding lead, the fans stayed in the game, cheering for the Indians to rally. In the seventh inning, manager Joe McCarthy walked to the mound for a conference with Hadley. As he crossed the foul line, a woman in the crowd stood up and fired a hot dog at the startled skipper. This was Ladies Day at its finest. The women took an active role in the game, rather than sitting back passively and following their scorecards. They yelled as loud as their husbands and fathers, completely immersed in the game. The women had found their place in baseball, carving out a role equal to the men.

In the top of the seventh, New York put the game away, scoring four more times. Hal Trosky closed the gap to four with his thirtieth home run, but despite his heroics game one was all Yankees, the final score 11–7. Both teams showed off their power, clouting home runs and extra base hits like no other clubs in the American League. Statistics showed New York batters had combined for 124 homers with Cleveland second at 88. Gehrig was in the top spot with 33, followed closely by Trosky with his 30. Bill Dickey had 18, while an exciting young center fielder named Joe DiMaggio had 16. The Indians countered with Earl Averill at 20 and Sammy Hale at 12. Either team could explode at any moment, as the Yankees did in the first game. It was up to the Cleveland hitters to produce in the last two games or the enthusiasm might end almost before it started.

Game two featured an excellent pitching matchup between Lefty Gomez and Johnny Allen. After five innings the score stood at 2–2. At the top of the sixth, the Yankees scored two more runs off Allen to make it 4–2. Hal Trosky led off the bottom of the eighth with his thirty-first home run, his second in two days. Singles by Roy Weatherly and Bill Knickerbocker put runners on the corners. Allen was to bat, but Steve O'Neill sent in George Uhle to pinch hit. Yes, the same George Uhle who was suspended near the end of the 1928 season and then traded. O'Neill and Uhle were friends from the 1920 team, which led to the pitcher's return as a sometime reliever and pinch hitter. The fans pleaded for a hit and Uhle answered with a single to tie the game at four.

The Yankees went down in the ninth without scoring. Two men were out in the bottom of the ninth when Hal Trosky singled. The Cleveland fans hopped to their feet as Joe Vosmik slashed a hard ground ball past Gehrig. Roy Weatherly was intentionally walked to fill the bases. Frank Pytlak came to the plate and watched three balls land outside of the strike zone. The bottom of the ninth, the score tied, the bases loaded, and the count at 3–0: the fans were beside themselves, screaming for another ball. Yankee pitcher Johnny Murphy coolly threw two quick strikes for a full count. On the next pitch the runners took off as Pytlak launched a high-fly ball to end the inning. A tremendous opportunity to win the game went by the boards. The shouting turned to silence as the Indians trotted out to their positions to begin the extra innings.

New York wasted no time in scoring the go-ahead run. In the top of the tenth, Frankie Crosetti doubled and went to third on Joe DiMaggio's infield hit. Lou Gehrig could not get the ball out of the infield, but his grounder went far enough to score Crosetti. Cleveland could do nothing in the bottom of the tenth and lost game two of the series, 5–4. In just twenty-four hours the Yankees had choked off the pennant fever at League Park. Now the gap was nine and a half games leaving some fans to wonder what the excitement was all about.

Even though the stakes were not as high, Sunday's game at Cleveland Stadium brought a massive crowd of 65,342. The last regular season game at the lakefront had been played on September 24, 1933. It had been almost three years, yet fans turned out in huge numbers. The pregame entertainment started at 1:00 p.m. The most interesting contest was the pitchers from both teams attempting to hit a small target strung over home plate. Each pitcher had five chances. The unexpected winner turned out to be Bob Feller, hitting the target in all five attempts. In his brief time with Cleveland, Feller had displayed some bouts of wildness, so most of the fans watching probably believed him more likely to finish last. Perhaps it was a good omen. Moments later, the Marx Brothers stormed the field with no less than twelve beautiful chorus girls. While the players stood around gawking at the women, Groucho, Harpo, and Chico attacked second baseman Roy Hughes, pulled off his jersey, and sprinted away. The zany antics drew big laughs from the crowd, but not from Hughes.

Oral Hildebrand started the game against former Indian Monte Pearson. All the laughter and lighthearted feelings went away in the bottom of the third. Pearson delivered a high, hard one that caught Frank Pytlak squarely on the face. His jaw was busted in three different places. Doctors immediately took him from the field and rushed him to Lakeside Hospital for treatment. Pytlak, when he could speak, told reporters that he never saw the ball due to the several thousand white shirts in the center-field bleachers. This had been a big issue back in 1932, but somehow was neglected four years later, and it took less than three innings for an ugly accident to happen. At any rate, Pytlak's season was over. He had finally overcome injuries and illness to put together an exceptional year, batting a career high .321. Now a bad pitch and too many white shirts sidelined him again.

The Indians clung to a 2–0 lead going into the seventh inning. Oral Hildebrand had been outstanding up to this point, but faltered as New York tied the game at two apiece. Monte Pearson came to bat in the top of the eighth and Hildebrand knocked him down in retaliation for the head shot to Pytlak. The crowd roared its approval while Pearson dusted himself off and made a gesture in Hildebrand's direction. Play resumed with the Yankees adding two more runs to make the score 4–2.

The Indians refused to lie down and quit. In the bottom of the eighth, Bruce Campbell entered the game as a pinch hitter. He received a tremendous standing ovation from the stands, cheering him for being such a warrior. To survive not one but two attacks of spinal meningitis was enough in itself. If surviving was not enough, Campbell had beat long odds to make it back as a ballplayer. Before the crowd had a chance to sit back down, Campbell belted a drive between the outfielders. He stopped at third, then scored on Sammy Hale's sacrifice fly. An inning later, Joe Vosmik delivered a clutch single to tie the game and send it to extra innings.

Steve O'Neill put in Denny Galehouse to hold the Yankees as long as possible. In his first full season with Cleveland, Galehouse had been used mostly in relief. For seven tough innings he stopped New York without a run, striking out six in the process. Unfortunately, Pat Malone, the longtime Chicago Cub pitcher, did the same. The game reached sixteen innings when darkness began to set in. Umpire Moriarty called the game after four and a half hours.

Remarkably, most of the fans stayed to watch the entire bitter struggle. For the weekend, attendance reached just over the

100,000 mark. Those in the stands witnessed three excellent baseball games, yet the Yankees had pushed Cleveland to nine and one-
half games behind. Any hopes the Indians had for a pennant chase
were gone in a flash. Still, it had been one of the best weekends
in many years. Alva Bradley announced there would be no more
scheduled games at the stadium in 1936. Surely he had to be thinking about future games at the seldom-used facility. His best Sunday
crowd at League Park could be only around 25,000. He more than
doubled that figure by playing one game at the lakefront.

The next afternoon, Cleveland lost to Detroit, 9–4. Bob Feller
pitched the seventh and eighth innings, allowing a run on two
hits. The crowd took notice in the eighth inning when Feller gave
up the run and had men on base with only one out. He did not
panic, striking out Goose Goslin and Al Simmons to end the inning. Manager O'Neill began thinking about giving Feller his first
Major League start. He sought a matchup with a light-hitting team,
preferably at League Park.

On Sunday, August 23, Bob Feller was rewarded with his initial start of his career. It came at home against the seventh-place
St. Louis Browns. O'Neill believed his young pitcher could throw
mostly fastballs and stop the Browns hitters. To hedge his bets,
the manager had Denny Galehouse warming up in the bullpen. If
Feller became unglued in a hurry, a quick pitching change could
be made. It was a sweltering day in Cleveland with the thermometer
climbing above ninety degrees. Feller had no difficulty getting his
right arm loose, primed, and ready to throw his wicked fastball.
Shortstop Lyn Lary came to bat, the first Browns hitter to see the
much talked about right-hander. Feller showed ridiculous speed,
sending Lary back to the bench, a strikeout victim. Two more
Browns went down as Feller struck out the side. The 9,000 fans gave
their pitcher plenty of encouragement, whooping it up as if there
were twice that number.

The Indians offense was tardy in getting started, but Feller
needed little support. The strikeouts were coming at a pace of two
per inning. The St. Louis hitters seemed to be flustered by speed
they had never seen before. Few of them dug in at the plate as
the whistling fastball slammed into the catcher's glove time and
time again. The record for strikeouts in one game in the American

League was sixteen, established in 1908 by Rube Waddell. As the innings flew by, everybody in the park thought about the possibility of history in the making.

In the bottom of the sixth inning, Cleveland scored three runs on a double by Hal Trosky and a Joe Vosmik single. That was more than Feller needed as he continued to rack up the strikeouts. Going into the ninth inning he had a total of fourteen. The Browns refused to give Feller the record by putting the baseball in play for the first two outs. That brought to the plate Lyn Lary, who had been victim number one. Feller still had the fastball humming, and Lary fanned for the third time, to end the game. Cleveland had the victory, 4–1. The American League record survived, but a seventeen-year-old pitcher in his first start threw a complete game with a mind-boggling fifteen strikeouts. Bob Feller had placed himself in the national spotlight. News of his accomplishment spread across the teletype wires to all the American League cities. Team owners wondered where this high-school boy came from. Even more important, they tried to ascertain how the Indians picked him up.

Due to the performance against St. Louis, Feller got an upgrade to the starting rotation. He pitched on the road in a losing effort to Boston, then lasted one brief inning at Yankee Stadium. A September 7 game with the struggling Browns resulted in a 7–1 win. Six days later Feller started at home, against the last-place Athletics. Rain had been falling and the sky was overcast, perfect for a fastball pitcher. In the first inning he walked a batter, but struck out the next three to end the inning. His fastball was blazing and the curveball breaking sharply. The Philadelphia hitters flailed at the baseball, managing only two hits in the entire game. Even though having his good stuff, Feller could not keep the ball over the plate. In the course of the game he walked an amazing nine batters. The base runners ran wild on him, ringing up seven steals. It was all for naught, though, as Feller kept adding to his strikeout total. He fanned three more in the sixth inning to once again threaten the American League record. In the eighth inning he matched Waddell's mark with his sixteenth strikeout. He needed one more to break the American League record and tie Dizzy Dean's Major League record of seventeen. There was one out in the ninth when the A's right fielder, George Puccinelli, walked slowly to the plate.

Feller smelled blood, rearing back for another speed-ball. Before he knew it, the overwhelmed Puccinelli was out on strikes. The Indians won, 5–2, and Feller had tied Dean for the all-time record.

Sportswriters and fans alike were stunned by the news of Feller's unbelievable accomplishment. Still only a high-school student, he had claimed the American League strikeout record and tied the Major League mark. There had been nothing like it in the history of the game. To Feller's credit, he said all the right things and kept his head on straight. That being said, he had to be walking six inches above the ground. Reporters mentioned him in the same company with Walter Johnson, Dizzy Dean, and many more of the all-time greats. The Indians had apparently found their next Cy Young, or at least a Wes Ferrell with a healthy arm.

Feller would have three more starts before the end of the season, losing the first and winning the last two. For his abbreviated year he won five ball games, lost three, and compiled a fine ERA of 3.34. In sixty-two innings he had struck out a remarkable seventy-six batters. Many of the Cleveland pitching records looked sure to fall by the wayside in the years ahead.

When the season ended, Feller left Cleveland for his home in Van Meter. At his arrival, a hero's welcome was waiting for him. There was still a matter of finishing high school and work to be done on the family farm. In typical Feller style he attacked both with his best effort.

Though Feller had drawn most of the headlines, other Cleveland players had brilliant seasons. Hal Trosky led the Major Leagues in RBIs with 162, the most ever by a Cleveland Indian. His record would last for over sixty years. He added forty-two home runs, another Indians record. Trosky was also tops in the American League in total bases, second in slugging average, and third in hits with 216. All-Star center fielder Earl Averill hit a career-best .378, second to Chicago's Luke Appling. He led the Majors in hits with 232 and tied with Joe DiMaggio and Red Rolfe for the most triples with fifteen. Johnny Allen won his twenty games and averaged the most strikeouts per nine innings. His earned run average of .344 was second to Lefty Grove.

The question that comes to mind is, why did Cleveland finish in fifth place with only eighty wins and seventy-four losses? The answer can be found in the pitching staff. Other than Johnny Allen and the late-season heroics of Bob Feller, the remainder of the pitchers fell apart around midseason. Mel Harder had a record of 14–7, but finished the year at 15–15. Arm problems in the second half limited him to only one victory after July. Willis Hudlin had arm issues which kept him to sixty-four innings all season. It did not help matters that Monte Pearson won nineteen games for New York. If Cleveland had been able to acquire Allen without trading Pearson, it would have changed things considerably. That was not the case, though, and Cleveland had to once again revamp for the 1937 season.

While Feller studied his assignments at Van Meter High School, Commissioner Landis was facing a quite difficult situation. Near the end of the season, Lee Keyser, the president of the Des Moines baseball club, filed a complaint against the Cleveland Indians. Keyser believed the Indians and not Fargo-Moorhead had signed Feller to a contract. The allegation accused Cy Slapnicka of violating the Major League rule by directly signing a high-school prospect. Keyser maintained that the assigning of Feller to Fargo-Moorhead and then sending his contract to New Orleans was a sham. Of course, Keyser was completely right, but that did not amount to the entire issue. Sportswriters covering the story reported that other teams in the Major Leagues did exactly what Slapnicka had orchestrated. If the commissioner went by the letter of the law and declared Feller a free agent, a number of other minor-league clubs might follow Des Moines and file grievances. Some writers guessed there could be more than a hundred claims if Landis ruled in favor of Des Moines.

The judge revealed that he had met with the Fellers and Slapnicka to get all the facts together. He would continue to investigate, then render a decision. In spite of the importance of the matter, the commissioner took his time, leaving for an extended fishing trip to mull things over. There was no telling when he might go public with his decision. In the meantime, the parties involved had to sit tight and wait for a verdict.

Alva Bradley told the press he had no worries about Feller's status. He asserted the club had done nothing illegal and would soon be vindicated. He knew that Bill Feller was pleased with his son's treatment by Cleveland, and there was no indication that Bob was angry about Slapnicka's manipulation of his contract. Rather than being miffed and demanding free-agent status, the Fellers said only positive things about the Indians. That attitude made things more difficult for Landis to issue a ruling. If he had had a disgruntled player insisting on action, a ruling in favor of Des Moines would have been that much easier. However, the Fellers were adamant that they wanted to stay with Cleveland regardless of what wrong-doing occurred.

October came and went without a ruling. At the end of November, Landis issued a decision on the status of two Cincinnati players who were "covered up" by the Reds. In essence, the term meant transferring players from one minor-league organization to another to hide the fact that the Reds actually owned the players' contracts. In this manner, Cincinnati could hold onto the players longer without having to bring them up or release them. Once a Major League club held a player's contract, they had a finite amount of time to keep the player in the minor leagues: when the time was up, they had to act. In this case, the Reds hid the fact that they owned the players. Landis frowned on this type of behavior and declared both players free agents.

This case was different from the Feller situation in that the Indians were not covering up. Still, Landis had just indicated he had no problem ruling against a Major League team. This decision had to make Alva Bradley a bit nervous. In spite of what happened, Bradley held to the company line in telling any and all reporters that he still had no concerns about losing his most prized asset. Owners around the American League estimated that as a free agent Feller could easily command $100,000 or better. The Red Sox and Yankees were supposedly prepared to offer that kind of money if the opportunity came along. Still, Judge Landis remained silent.

The winter meeting took place in early December. The owners gathered in Montreal, Canada, to conduct business and negotiate trades. When the meetings ended Landis announced a ruling was imminent. On December 10, 1936, Landis decided in favor of the Cleveland Indians. He acknowledged that the team had indeed violated the rules and ordered Bradley to pay the Des Moines club $7,500. Landis believed a verdict favoring Des Moines would cause chaos in baseball and open the door for multiple similar cases. He stated that Cleveland could have installed Slapnicka as an officer of the Des Moines club. Had they done that the signing would have been considered legal and no action could have been taken. The Indians were guilty of "recommending," as were many of the other clubs in the Major Leagues. They signed a prospect in violation of the rules, then recommended that their farm team add the player to their roster. Later, they recommended that the farm team sell the player to another farm club, and so on until the player was ready for the majors. Then the team would "recommend" the final sale (to itself), in this case the Indians buying Feller from New Orleans.

Judge Landis was wise to this technique, but feared pandemonium would ensue if he granted free-agent status to Bob Feller. Another aspect was that if the judge decided to award Feller to Des Moines, he would be giving them license to sell him to the highest bidder. This sort of thing would only fatten up teams like New York or Boston that had plenty of money to spend. Conceivably, they could gobble up the best talents who'd been made free agents and/or buy players from the aggrieved minor-league teams who still held players under contract. Landis wanted none of that, hence his decision in the Feller case.

Lee Keyser most certainly received a check from the Cleveland Baseball Club in record time. Bradley and his partners were ecstatic that they were able to keep their number-one asset for only $7,500. They could move forward knowing they potentially had the best pitcher in baseball under their control.

The Fellers would ask for a contract of $20,000 for the 1937 season. This was crazy money for a second-year player, yet not a totally unreasonable request. One had to think in terms of the perceived jump in attendance when Bob was on the mound. In the world of Major League baseball, a player of Bob Feller's ability comes along once in a lifetime. He was the anchor, the player who could lead Cleveland to the top of the standings. It would not happen overnight, as circumstances including another horrible World War loomed on the horizon. One thing was for certain, though: in a matter of time Cleveland would return to baseball's summit.

SOURCES

Books

Feller, Bob. *Strikeout Story.* New York: Grosset and Dunlap, 1947.
Johnson, William H., and Shona Frese. *Norway Baseball: Gone But Not Forgotten.* Norway: Iowa Baseball Museum, 2012.
Kavanagh, Jack. *Walter Johnson: A Life.* South Bend, IN: Diamond Communications, 1995.
Kerr, Daniel. *Derelict Paradise: Homelessness and Urban Development in Cleveland, Ohio.* Boston: University of Massachusetts Press, 2011.
Lewis, Franklin. *The Cleveland Indians.* New York: G. P. Putnam's Sons, 1949.
Odenkirk, James E. *Plain Dealing: A Biography of Gordon Cobbledick.* Phoenix, AZ: Spider-Naps, 1990.
Reichler, Joseph L., ed. *The Baseball Encyclopedia.* New York: Macmillan, 1979.
Ritter, Lawrence. *The Glory of Their Times: The Story of the Early Days of Baseball Told by the Men Who Played It.* New York: Macmillan, 1966.
Rose, William Ganson. *Cleveland: The Making of a City.* Cleveland, OH: World Publishing Company, 1950.
Sickles, John. *Bob Feller: Ace of the Greatest Generation.* Washington, DC: Brassey's, 2004.

Periodicals

Baseball Magazine (1927–36)
Cleveland News (1927–36)

Cleveland Plain Dealer (1927–36)
Cleveland Press (1927–36)
The Sporting News (1928–29)

Libraries and Archives

Chardon, Ohio, Municipal Center, Recreation Department (Mel Harder
    scrapbooks)
Cleveland Public Library
Cleveland Heights–University Heights Public Library
Clerk of Courts, County of Cuyahoga
Iowa Baseball Museum of Norway
Edward H. Nabb Research Center
National Baseball Hall of Fame Library, Cooperstown, New York (player
    files, Alva Bradley and Billy Evans files)
Snohomish Public Library, Snohomish, Washington
Society for American Baseball Research
Syracuse University Archives
University School Library (Alva Bradley file)
Western Reserve Historical Society (Daniel Morgan papers)

Personal Communications

Family of Earl Averill
Family of Mel Harder
Family of Roger Peckinpaugh
Family of Hal Trosky

Internet Sites

http://www.baseball-almanac.com

INDEX

Johnson hiring, 188–90; Johnson-Kamm-Myatt controversy, 228–34; radio broadcast debut, 40–41; Cy Slapnicka–Bob Feller American League hearing, 271–73

Cleveland Municipal Stadium, 1, 70, 113, 153–54, 161

Cleveland Naps, 3, 18–19, 64, 137, 161

Cleveland News, 45, 47, 75, 93, 126, 149, 154–55, 158, 169–70, 190, 197–98, 217, 228, 231, 234, 275

Cleveland Plain Dealer, 9–11, 30–31, 39, 47, 67, 76, 91, 93, 132, 166, 174, 185, 209, 217, 247, 276

Cleveland Press, 47, 62, 69, 93, 99, 113, 190, 215, 218, 276

Cleveland Public Library, 67, 276

Cleveland Railway Company, 156

Cleveland Rosenblums, 261

Cleveland School Board, 46

Cleveland Spiders, 1, 18, 161

Cleveland Stock Exchange, 45

Cleveland Trust Company, 157

Cleveland Umpires Association, 48

Cobb, Ty, 8, 17, 57, 127, 154, 180, 232

Cobbledick, Gordon, 39–40, 58, 64, 84, 241, 247, 275

Coca-Cola, 37, 163, 238

Cochrane, Mickey, 2, 4, 22, 91, 163, 165, 186, 202, 240

Cohen, Andy, 33–34

Collins, Eddie, 18

Collins, Harry "Rip, 21

Collins, Jim "Ripper," 262

Collinwood (Cleveland school), 174

Collinwoods (semipro baseball team), 18

Columbia Broadcasting System, 62, 235

Combs, Earle, 216, 220

Comeback Player of the Year Award, 255

Comiskey, Charles, 54

Comiskey, Louis, 234

Comiskey Park, 54, 187, 192–93

Common Pleas Court, 70

Connolly, Tommy, 144

Cornell University, 14, 16

Cotton State League, 178

Coveleski, Stan, 5

Cramer, Doc, 249

Cronin, Joe, 187, 213, 237

Crosetti, Frankie, 216, 266

Cuyahoga County Bar Association, 155

Daniel, Dan, 194, 235

Davis, Dick, 156

Davis, Harry, 214

Dean, Jay Hanna "Dizzy," 233, 237, 259, 262, 269–70

Dean, Paul, 259

Delahanty, Frank, 64

Delahanty, Jimmy, 64

Dellen, Frank Van, 134

Democratic National Convention, 147

Dempsey, Jack, 88

Detroit Tigers, 6, 8, 44, 63–65, 76, 87, 89, 127, 129–30, 137, 143, 165, 181, 215, 226, 241, 246, 254–55, 259

Dickey, Bill, 192, 213, 219–20, 265

DiMaggio, Joe, 265–66, 270

Doakes, Joe, 231

Dow Jones Industrial Average, 79

Doyle, James, 76

Dreyfuss, Barney, 33, 119

Druid Hill Grammar School, 82

Dugan, Joe, 21

Dunn, Edith, 6–12

Dunn, Jack, 48–49

Dunn, James C., 1, 5–6, 9, 13, 15, 56

Durocher, Leo, 262

Dykes, Jimmy, 150–52, 175

Earhart, Amelia, 45

Earnshaw, George, 49, 77, 120, 167

East Douglas, 65

East High School, 18

East Senate League, 18

East Tech High Schoo,l 123

Edwards, Henry, 9, 11, 19, 39

El Dorado, AR, 178–79

Elgin National Watches, 88

Erasmus High School, 32

Erie, Lake, 2, 24, 93, 161, 183

Erie Canal, 45

Erie Sailors, 180

Euclid Avenue, 13, 39, 157, 160

Evans, Billy, 16–17, 22, 24–26, 32, 36, 40–41, 44, 46, 48–50, 53, 58–60, 62, 66, 69, 80, 88–89, 101, 119, 122, 124–26, 129, 132–33, 138, 153–54, 158, 160, 163, 172, 176, 178, 181, 188–89, 192, 194–95, 197, 200, 203, 205, 207, 212, 215, 221, 225, 233, 242, 247–48, 262, 276

Falk, August "Bibb," 59–60, 75–76, 86–87, 89, 91, 120, 132, 247